Edited by Christopher Molander

Human Resource Management

D1437841

Chartwell-Bratt

British Library Cataloguing in Publication Data
Human Resource Management
  1. Personnel management
  I. Molander, Christopher
  658.3

ISBN 0-86238-230-0

© The Authors and Chartwell-Bratt Ltd, 1989

Chartwell-Bratt (Publishing and Training) Ltd
ISBN 0-86238-230-0

Printed in Sweden,
Studentlitteratur, Lund
ISBN 91-44-45752-9

1 2 3 4 5 6 7 8 9 10 | 1993 92 91 90 89

Contents

Foreword

It gives me great pleasure, both as an Industrialist and as the Chancellor of the University, to have this opportunity of writing a foreword to Christopher Molander's book on the Management of Human Resources.

Firstly, the book is very much in the stream of everything we at the University set out to do. It is a team effort, all the contributors having connections with the University's Management Centre.

It is above everything practical and pragmatic. I found in the book little that I have not experienced or expected, and that should be looked upon as a compliment rather than as a criticism. What is needed is the certainty of the practicality and applicability of ideas, rather than stimulus to new and untried areas of advice. The book explains, codifies and illuminates the processes we as managers and personnel practitioners follow and that alone causes one to think about, reflect upon and understand more deeply the significance and contribution of so much that we undertake.

Our University is built on the twin pillars of practical applicability of the subjects we teach, and the more abstrues one of 'adding value' by combining every skill we can to make the whole greater than the sum of the parts.

The second point I wish to make is a more general one. Interest in the arts and skills of different areas of business life tend to wax and wane in a cyclical fashion. Now it is the period of the Accountant, now the marketing man. From time to time the skills of the production man or the personnel specialist are most in fashion. I suspect for many reasons the day of the professionally equipped personnel man may be about to dawn again. So many fundamental changes are occurring in our society that Industry is inevitably faced with a massive period of adjustment to external change.

The demographic decline in young people entering our ranks entails much more competition for the available talent. The development of a vicious spiral of decline in our educational system with fewer and fewer students seeking to study technical subjects again leads to more competition in recruiting, and retaining scarce skills. International and national mobility of management is intensifying. Major changes are occurring in Trade Union structure, behaviour and expectations. Further changes seem likely in industrial relations law and so on. And on one can fail to be aware of the different aspirations, expectations and ambitions of today's young men and women.

All this ferment of change is impacting on business organisation and is going to force major reappraisals of the ways in which we relate to, manage, motivate and reward people. To look at things anew and adapt to the future one requires a profound understanding of one's craft and its practice.

That is the reason I can commend this book, not only to personnel practitioners but also to the line managers who are, after all, the actual customers and on whom the responsibility for personnel relations so clearly lies.

Sir John Harvey-Jones
Chancellor
University of Bradford

The Editor

Christopher Molander is responsible for the teaching of Human Resource Management at the University of Bradford Management Centre. He was previously Plant Personnel Manager at the Ford Motor Company and Personal Assistant to the Director of Personnel, the Littlewoods Organisation. His research and consultancy interests in Britain and Europe are the introduction of management development systems in large scale public and private sector organisations. He is author of *Management Development – Key Concepts for Managers and Trainers*.

The Contributors

Mark Hall is Senior Research Fellow in the Industrial Relations Research Unit, University of Warwick. Previously he worked for the Trades Union Congress, becoming Assistant Secretary in the Organisation and Industrial Relations Department. He was also Lecturer in Industrial Relations at the University of Bradford Management Centre.

Ian McGivering is Reader in Organisational Behaviour at the University of Bradford Management Centre. He has co-authored the books *Management in Britain* and *Coal and Conflict*. His consultancy work is mainly in the areas of Organisation Development and Team Building.

Angela Mulvie. Following personnel management experience in manufacturing industry and the health service, she began a career in management education, specialising in the personnel area. She is currently employed as Lecturer in Human Resources Management at the University of Stirling. She has worked as part time Lecturer at the University of Bradford Management Centre.

Alistair Ostell is Lecturer in Occupational Psychology at the University of Bradford Management Centre. His research and consultancy activities are in the areas of the development of managerial skills; the analysis and management of employee performance problems and psychological health. His main publications are in the field of stress and coping.

Andrew Pendleton is Lecturer in Industrial Relations at the University of Bradford Management Centre. He has also taught at the Universities of Bath, Kent and Shanghai. His main research interest is the management of human resources in the public sector.

Gerry Randell is Professor of Organisational Behaviour at the University of Bradford Management Centre. Previously he was Lecturer in Occupational Psychology at Birkbeck College in the University of London. He is joint author of *Staff Appraisal – a First Step to Effective Leadership*.

David Taylor is Lecturer in Applied Experimental Psychology at the University of Bradford Management Centre. He has teaching, research and consultancy experience in several areas of applied psychology. He is author of *Performance Reviews: A Handbook for Tutors* and co-author of *Improving Leadership Performance* and *Developing Interpersonal Skills through Tutored Practice*.

Sarah Vickerstaff is Lecturer in Industrial Relations at the University of Kent, specialising in Human Resource Management. Current research and consultancy interests include the provision of training opportunities in the Kent economy; appraisal systems and Strategic Human Resource Management.

Peter Wright is Lecturer in Occupational Psychology at the University of Bradford Management Centre. He is joint author of *Improving Leadership Performance* and *Developing Interpersonal Skills through Tutored Practice*. He has conducted interpersonal skills training for a wide variety of British and European companies.

Introduction

Students of Personnel Management will hardly fail to be aware of current discussions surrounding the need for change in the commonly accepted notion of the role. Whilst as yet comparatively few firms in the UK have seriously confronted the need for change, some organisations, notably the larger multinationals, have reappraised the personnel function. This reappraisal has often been signalled by the retitling of Personnel Management as Human Resource Management.

In these cases, there is hopefully more than simply a change in name. Many Personnel Departments are seen not to be offering the kind of service which line managers require – where and when they want it. In particular some line managers complain that personnel policies are not closely enough linked to corporate planning – both to its development and its day to day application. Others have argued that the relationship of personnel specialist and line manager is not close enough, leading to the development of policies 'out of gear' with the operating needs of managers. Yet others have pointed to the changing environment in which Personnel Management operates and have suggested for example that whilst traditional Industrial Relations issues remain, more innovative attempts should be made to win the cooperation of the labour force – at all levels. The combative and procedural approach to IR should not, it is argued, blind personnel people to the need for additional methods of winning the hearts and minds of employees.

In the Editor's view, the changes in the role of the Personnel or Human Resource Department constitute another stage in the evolution of the profession, and as such the more alarming cataclysmic views of the future of personnel administration are both without cause and overstated. Rarely has such attention been paid to Personnel Management and never have the opportunities for development been greater. A cursory reading of the quality Sunday press will reveal the increasing number of vacancies for personnel staff at the highest levels.

The various contributors to this book are either on the Staff of the University of Bradford Management Centre, or are connected with it. The University is widely recognised as a centre of excellence for the development of managers at the undergraduate, graduate and post experience level. Human Resource Management is taught at all these levels, and a major purpose in the production of this book was the felt need to provide one coherent text which would cover the syllabus of a number of different courses. Inevitably therefore, the choice of topics covered and the method of treatment of them reflects individual teaching purposes. Each contributor however has experience not only of teaching in an academic context, but also of consultancy – working alongside managers and supporting them as they attempt to resolve 'real live' problems.

The choice of topics covered in this book necessarily involves the making of choices and it might be argued that there are omissions in the range of issues covered. The final product does however represent a sustained attempt to address the changes taking place in the profession of Personnel Management and to deal with those issues which have special relevance to the general themes of Human Resource Management. Each chapter has a direct relevance to HRM as it is currently defined. The whole, we believe, is a comprehensive, authoritative and 'up to date' practical guide to HRM.

Even so, in order to keep the book to manageable proportions, each topic has been covered as succinctly as possible. No pretence at an exhaustive coverage is made. Key issues are highlighted and trends in current thinking are explored. The reader wishing to take further particular issues should refer to the suggested further reading at the end of each chapter.

In addition to these recommendations for further reading, attached to each chapter are a number of typical examination questions. These should act as a check to readers that they have internalised the chapter content and also serve to alert examinees to the kind of question likely to be sprung upon them by the various examining bodies.

It is expected that this book will be useful to students of HRM; professionals already in the field who wish to keep abreast of modern developments and line managers who are anxious to come to grips with the most effective methods of managing people at work.

Christopher Molander
University of Bradford

Summer, 1989

Chapter 1

Personnel Management – From 'Welfare' to 'Human Resource Management'

Christopher Molander

Introduction

This chapter begins with a brief historical review of Personnel Management and of the impact the past has had on recent thinking about the function. A second section will look at the major activities which normally go under the title of Personnel Management. Later sections will examine the relationship between the personnel department and other sections of the organisation. There follows a discussion on recent developments in thinking about the personnel management role – particularly with regard to the emergence of Human Resource Management.

Origins

Any work organisation, however small, must pay some attention to personnel administration. At the very least, employees must be hired, and their work allocated. They will require payment, and eventually arrangements will be necessary for their leaving the organisation – voluntarily or involuntarily. In this minimal sense, Personnel Management has existed since people organised themselves to achieve a task.

For our purposes, we need go no further back than the entrepreneurial activities of the Industrial Revolution. The move from the countryside into the towns to service the rapid growth of small firms was well advanced by the early nineteenth century. Industrial and urban development obliged a significant proportion of society to live out their lives in appalling social and economic conditions. Wages were low, conditions poor and the entrepreneurs for the most part operated with a managerial style which can only be considered as harsh, even feudal. Workers were often beaten; wages reduced for trivial 'misdemeanours' such as singing, and employees were frequently obliged to spend their earnings in the company shop. Many of the entrepreneurs were stimulated by non-conformist religious beliefs which sought through the 'puritan ethic' to reinforce the view that hard work and discipline were virtues and that the entrepreneurs by providing the same would win not only rewards in this world but also in the next. Hard working employees, it was argued, could also share in these rewards. Only apathy and ill-will could prevent the arrival of the Kingdom of Heaven on earth.

Conditions were demonstrably so appalling that in 1833, the Government intervened with the passing of the Factories Act and the setting up of a Factories Inspectorate. Originally the Act applied only to the textile industry and dealt with the working conditions of children. Later amendments in 1867 and 1878 expanded the regulations to encompass other industries. Even so, a standard working week of 60 hours and a minimum employment age of 12 were still in force as late as 1918.

By means of a mixture of christian conscience and enlightened self interest, some employers responded to the growing disquiet about working conditions. In 1896 the first full time industrial welfare worker was employed at Rowntree's of York. The role of 'Social Secretary' was very limited. She and those that followed her had no role to play directly in the workplace but were expected to act as the 'Workers' Friend'. They helped employees to manage their budget better; to lead a healthier life and to develop useful and moral out of work activities. Even in this limited capacity, they generally earned the distrust of both management and the emerging Trade Unions. The former resented their intrusion into the workplace; the latter perceived them as a management device for controlling employees.

From this middle class welfare origin was later to come the 'Welfare Workers Association' and eventually, in 1946, the Institute of Personnel Management. These early beginnings have had a profound impact on the development of Personnel Management. In some people's minds, the function is still seen as largely welfare oriented. The Personnel Manager should be a 'Good Fairy', or at least the impartial 'even handed middle man'.

The First World War and After

The outbreak of the war brought with it the need to increase production –

particularly munitions. The influx of women into the factories with no experience of working outside the home; the general state of health of many employees, and the continuing poor conditions in which many employees were obliged to work led to increased government intervention.

In 1915, the 'Health of Munitions Workers Committee' was set up to look at the effect of working conditions on output and health. Although the Committee produced much useful work which had an impact on the munitions factories, it was disregarded elsewhere.

In 1916, the Ministry of Munitions set up the Industrial Welfare department under Seebohm Rowntree to encourage the introduction of welfare practices in factories. In the same year, welfare services became obligatory in munitions factories. By the end of the war about 1,300 welfare officers had been appointed, by no means all of them women.

During the war, on the Industrial Relations front, there were many bitter wrangles, despite the introduction of compulsory arbitration. These mainly concerned the dilution of skilled trades by the employment of unskilled women to do craftsmen's work. The growth of unions and their activities during the war introduced a new dimension to Personnel Management – a specialist interest which could take its place alongside the welfare role.

The war was followed by severe economic depression. Many of the welfare workers lost their jobs and many of the advances in Personnel Management seemed to be lost. But all was not gloom. In 1918, the Industrial Welfare Society (now the Royal Industrial Society) was established together with the Industrial Fatigue Board and in 1921, the National Institute of Industrial Psychology, which carried out research into ergonomics and the psychological problems of work – boredom, fatigue, monotony and so on.

After the war it became clear that the State would have to intervene more effectively in the work place and in particular, establish a dialogue with the Trade Unions. Various forms of joint consultation were proposed. Most of these have long since disappeared. But from this time stemmed the belief in government circles that a more or less recognisable policy about Industrial Relations would be expected of any government.

In the inter war years, Employment Management took its place alongside welfare. Labour Managers appeared in large factories, especially in engineering. These people were often taken from the ranks of timekeeper or clerical worker in the factory office. Employers had responded to the growth in Union activity by forming themselves into Federations which attempted to fix national wage rates and to set up procedures for handling Trade Union disputes. Specialists were often needed to keep the necessary records; handle negotiations at local level and liaise with the Employers' Federation. This phase too has had lasting effects on Personnel Management in Britain. The view that the personnel administrator is almost exclusively concerned with Industrial Relations and with meeting government requirements still has a strong hold in some people's minds.

The Second World War – 1960's

The economic decline of the inter war years and the increased demand for production during the Second World War led to the need to relearn many of the lessons which appeared to have been forgotten.

During the War little attention was paid to the physical and mental wellbeing of employees. Absenteeism and sickness increased alarmingly. Ernest Bevin as Minister of Labour introduced new disputes and dismissal procedures; established a minimum wage and extended the power of factory inspectors. A Factory and Welfare Department was set up with the Ministry of Labour to seek to improve the health, safety and welfare of people at work.

This led to an increased demand for personnel staff. By the end of the war, little short of 6,000 personnel and welfare workers were employed. The combined forces of research and government measures had established the importance of the personnel function.

The war was followed by a period of economic boom. This climate was more conducive to a scientific management, influenced by the work of writers such as Taylor[1] and later by the research findings filtering across the Atlantic from the United States (eg. the 'Hawthorne Experiments' at the Western Electric Company).[2]

But the boom, together with changing technology and social attitudes led to increased problems for management. Highly centralised Union negotiation tended to be replaced by 'Shop Floor Bargaining'. The number and power of Shop Stewards increased and eventually the power of the Employers' Federations was relinquished in favour of a greater degree of autonomy for managers within their own factory. This led to an increased demand within the factory for specialists to cope with Industrial Relations. Larger companies began to develop their own policies in line with company strategy. In the 1960's there was rapid growth in productivity bargaining such as the 'Fawley Agreement'.

4

The 1960's

By the mid 1960's all types of work organisation, including hospitals and Local Authorities were employing personnel staff, and Personnel Management was well established as an occupation in its own right.

Recruitment, work study, payment systems, and IR procedures were being introduced. It could be said, however, that this 'establishment control' phase was reactive in nature. Most of the personnel activities were concerned with maintaining the 'status quo'; of servicing the needs of line managers for staff, and handling such issues as stoppages on a 'firefighting' basis.

Little activity was taking place on the training front. Few employees received anything but the most basic training, apart from apprentices – and even then girls were excluded. The government intervened in 1964 with the passing of the Industrial Training Act which by means of both positive and negative inducements pressurised most organisations into providing training opportunities and encouraged the recruitment of training specialists within the personnel department.

There was little concern during this period with such issues as the impact of the organisation on the environment – or indeed the impact of the environment on the organisation. Longer term company wide personnel strategy leading to organisation change and development was an emerging concern of only the largest and most economically stable firms.

This concern with the 'status quo' was taken up in the Donovan Report of 1968 – a report to the government on the state of Trade Union and Employer relations.[3] The report pointed to the failure of Personnel Management either to cope with the economic changes taking place or to develop efficient IR policies. In many cases the disagreements which so often led to unofficial union action were said to be the result of management not giving the personnel function sufficient priority.

The 1970's and 1980's

Many organisations – particularly the small in scale – still operated on a basis of a welfare orientation to personnel administration. Others, larger in scale, and including some of the highly bureaucratic such as Local Authorities still defined the personnel role in terms of establishment control – with a heavy emphasis on work study, job evaluation and routine IR procedures. The latter was particularly important in the '70's. New employment law and a highly active IR climate called for the legal expert and the skilled negotiator.

The '80's saw a new recognition that whilst the day to day reactive elements in the personnel function must remain – recruitment, payment, discipline and so on; a more proactive role was possible, based on the impressive body of sociological and psychological research.

There was indeed a significant body of behavioural science knowledge which could be usefully applied to the work organisation by the professionally competent personnel administrator. Even with regard to such routine areas as recruitment and training, more effective selection procedures were being introduced and more relevant and imaginative training methods employed. It was however in the analytical area that Personnel Management was thought to be able to develop most fruitfully. The role of 'organisation consultant' presupposed representation at the top of the organisation. This ambition was rarely achieved however. What tended to emerge in the most 'advanced' companies was an elite which prided itself on its professionalism, and distanced itself from the day to day concerns of management. Many innovations – particularly in the field of Management Development were not always understood or seen as relevant.

Inevitably resistance developed. The '80's saw the emergence of a number of iconoclastic management 'gurus' who claimed that the personnel function should be reviewed and dramatically reduced.[4] In the writer's view, this was an overreaction, albeit understandable. There were significant advances in the '80's, particularly with regard to thinking about Organisational Development. What was clear however was the need for Personnel Managers to integrate their activities much more closely with the changing needs of line managers, and to ensure that their priorities stemmed not so much from a theoretical base, but from the more pragmatic demands of corporate strategy. This in turn would require closer involvement with line management in the development of this strategy, and also a greater regard to the view that if personnel policy was to be implemented successfully, it would have to be done through the line and not directly from the personnel department. What was not by any means a novel view that the personnel professional must be represented right at the top of the organisation began to assume a new urgency.

Into the '90's

Few will be unaware of the rapid socio-economic changes of recent years. Whether the personnel function remains credible in the 1990's will depend largely on its capacity to respond by developing appropriate organisational systems and structures which reflect these changes. Below follows a list of some of the more important pressures for change.

- The declining labour force ('the demographic time bomb') has already led to shortages of skilled labour. At the same time, there is in many organisations a middle management 'bulge' much of which is unlikely to progress, but which is made up of those who have many years of service ahead of them before retirement.

- Work patterns are changing. Post retirement; part-time and short term working will become more common. More women are returning to work. Outworking will become more prevalent. All this will mean a decreasing number of core workers – both managers and non-managers, who will require intensive training and nurturing. Peripheral workers will pose a problem of motivation.

- The EEC single market in 1992 whilst increasing opportunities, will also pose potential threats to established markets.

- Employer attitudes of 'collectivism' are giving way to 'individualism'. Encouraged by government emphasis on individual initiative, companies are already beginning to look for secondary decentralised systems for worker representation which are less negotiation based.

- This individualism is linked to the search for commitment and the winning of the 'hearts and minds' of employees at all levels.

- Increased pressure is being put on managers by technological advance – particularly information systems. Decisions can be made much faster.

- Pressure for retraining at all levels will increase, just as state support is decreasing. Individuals too will be expected to retrain and generally take responsibility for their own salvation.

- Management systems such as 'cost centres' and 'internal markets' will become the norm. This will accelerate the search for new management structures and more effective Management Development. Increasing emphasis will be placed on linking more closely performance and reward. Innovative rewards systems as well as more task related performance review systems will be called for.

- All these specific changes will not be looked at in isolation. Corporate and strategic planning will be given more emphasis and there will be closer scrutiny of all staff functions, the performance of which will be assessed on the same financial basis as any other activity.

In sum, the organisations which will survive in the 1990's will be much more concerned with flexibility; competence and motivation. We may expect Human Resource Departments to become more actively involved in strategic planning; and then to respond to the outcomes by developing appropriate systems and structures. Closer links with line managers in the corporate planning process will undoubtedly mean the closer involvement of line managers in the carrying out of personnel policy – from top to bottom of the organisation.

The Arena of Personnel Management

In 1980, the I.P.M. (Institute of Personnel Management) produced a 'Code of Industrial Practice in Personnel Management'. It begins with a definition: 'Personnel Management is that part of management concerned with people at work and with their relationships within an enterprise. It aims to bring together and develop into an effective organisation the men and women who make up an enterprise and, having regard for the well-being of the individual and of working groups, to enable them to make their best contribution to its success'.

The main concern of Personnel Management is jointly to develop with line management procedures and systems on behalf of all levels of management for their approval and use. These procedures and systems normally cover some or all of the following areas:

Corporate Strategy. Understanding and contributing to the development of purposes and objectives of the organisation. The giving of specialist advice as to the impact of strategy on the demand for labour and vice versa.

Organisation Design and Development. The development of an organisational structure which effectively achieves organisational goals and encourages the integration and co-operation of organisational units. Attempts to improve the organisation's ability to respond to change.

Manpower Planning. The production and maintenance of data detailing the demand and supply of labour and its costs over a period of time. (Any imbalance then becomes clear, and its correction the subject of the manpower plan).

Recruitment, Selection, Induction and 'Exiting'. The process of filling vacancies in line with the manpower plan, and of introducing new employees into the organisation. The development of systems to identify overmanning, and of effective redundancy arrangements.

Training and Development. Formal and informal methods of instruction and development to improve employee performance and develop potential. The evaluation of training and development techniques, and the monitoring of cost effectiveness.

Performance Review. The development and monitoring of performance review systems and the linking of these to policy regarding rewards.

Wage and Salary Administration. The development of appropriate systems of payment for all employees and the linking of these to performance. The search for new and effective methods of rewarding individual effort. The production of wage and salary budgets. Job evaluation and the resolution of wage and salary disputes alongside the relevant line managers.

Industrial Relations. Development of procedural agreements relating to Management/Union relations. Ongoing review of systems of Union representation. Bargaining and disciplinary procedures. The development and evaluation of non Union systems of representation.

Health and Safety. Development and application of safety regulations. Accident reports. The inspection of work processes with a view to improving the physical working environment.

Welfare. Personal support for individual employees (e.g. Counselling). The provision of recreational and social facilities.

The necessarily brief descriptions can only suggest the kinds of activities which come under the various headings above. All of them require the active support of line management in their implementation. The reader will realise that they fall into two broad categories.

Maintenance. Activities which must go on to some extent in every organisation, large or small, and without which they would grind to a halt. In themselves, however, although they may involve a search for new methods (e.g. selection), they maintain the 'status quo'. They are largely reactive in nature. For example, vacancies occur, and the organisation responds by attempting to fill them. Redundancies may be seen by management as necessary, and procedures are invoked to reduce the size of the labour force.

Development. Activities which are proactive and are undertaken with a view to determine longer term goals. Organisation design and development activities are based on the recognition of the need for change in the way work is organised and in the type and quality of working relations, so that the organisation is best fitted to recognise and exploit opportunities. They are more than simply adjustments to events. They involve the application of behavioural science knowledge to help an organisation assume responsibility for its future by examining alternatives to currently accepted methods of getting work done.

Typical activities under these headings might include re-designing the organisation structure on a divisional basis to take account of increased size and consequent control problems. Another example would be the introduction of autonomous work groups with a view to improving motivation levels by increasing the level of individual responsibility. A further example might be the review of reward systems in order to motivate employees to achieve goals more effectively. Finally, the careful introduction of quality circles, as part of corporate strategy, will serve as another example.

Which of the ten areas outlined above are more important for any particular organisation depends on a number of factors, including size, stage of development and technology. Very small firms, particularly at the growth stage, will manage these functions in different ways and will allot them different priorities. Such firms are unlikely to have a specialised personnel function at all. The owner or managing director will handle these issues himself often on the basis of intuition.

In the large scale technologically sophisticated organisation, however, the personnel issues will in themselves be so time consuming and complex as to merit the activities of a group of specialists unencumbered with day to day technical problems. It should be remembered, however, that the closer the personnel specialists are to line management, and the more the latter are involved in the development of policy and its implementation, the more likely is the personnel function to be seen as relevant and effective.

The Responsibility for Human Resource Management

This leads us on to a closer look at the issue of responsibility for Personnel Management, or Human Resource Management as it is beginning to be called. It should not be left with a few generalised comments such as those with which we concluded the last section.

Personnel Management, the effective management of human resources, can sensibly be seen as a central management activity – the getting of effective results with people. Every manager, from the Managing Director downwards, can only achieve results with the assistance of others. Often managers have so many technical responsibilities that they see themselves as having little time for personnel matters. Managers are frequently assessed on the basis of achieving tangible results of a short term nature which further encourages them to put aside 'until they have time' personnel issues such as training, motivating and rewarding subordinates. It is a shortsighted strategy. Ultimately, all managers are responsible for the performance of those who work for them. It is in their own interest to see that employees are sufficiently capable and well enough motivated to help them achieve results. The word 'management' implies the control and co-ordination of others. If we accept this basic assertion, then clearly every manager should take a major responsibility for the recruitment, development and motivation of staff at all levels.

The notion of Personnel Management as a 'staff function' is more complex. The terms 'line' and 'staff' require some discussion.

Line managers are said to be those with overall responsibility and authority for the performance of their department. Staff managers are specialists providing line managers with a service and advice. So, a marketing and a production manager are said to be line managers. The company accountant, legal officer and personnel administrator are examples of staff management.

It is, however, also argued that staff managers have line managerial responsibility for those whom they manage within the staff department. Authority for activities and accountability for results will stem from senior management in the same way as they do for any manager. It is doubtful whether the distinction between 'line' and 'staff' as commonly defined has much meaning.[5]

For our purposes, it will be more appropriate to look upon specialist managers as not being directly responsible for any specific element in the output or distribution of goods or services in which the organisation engages. They are rather managers who have a contract with the organisation to provide a specialised service for others engaged directly or indirectly in the production and distribution process. The service to be provided by the Human Resources Department will normally be defined, and achievement targets set. As with any other department, these will often be the subject of negotiation, and competent specialists will feel free to argue the case for change and development of their role.

An important difference between the specialist and the non-specialist manager is in the area of authority. The former is expected to have specialist expertise but not the formal authority to ensure that any advice given is implemented by the line manager. Even this distinction is frequently blurred. In many organisations, especially in the United States, the personnel executive does have the authority to insist that line managers implement what are in effect instructions. With the development of HRM, it is likely that the U.S. experience will become more common in Britain. In any organisation, when a senior manager gives 'advice' to another with less status, it is often interpreted as an instruction – wisely in most cases.

Although there are areas where instructions from the Personnel Manager are appropriate – for example in ensuring that Industrial Relations law is implemented, or when a particular manager is out of line in not following a widely accepted practice, experience suggests that the use of direct authority by the personnel specialist can cause problems. In particular, the confusion of the policing role with that of specialist may often undermine the advisory role. Managers directly involved in the work process should be encouraged to take responsibility for their subordinates. The role of the personnel specialist is to provide a service based on technical applied behavioural science knowledge. It is appropriate to make this service available – even on occasion to draw the attention of senior management to cases where the service is ignored. It is not appropriate for managers to abandon their necessary concern for Human Resource Management to the specialist.

The role of the specialist is one of developing policies and suggesting organisational strategies in line with overall company goals. In addition he or she should be free to respond to requests for help from line managers whose skills may not fit them to resolve personnel related issues without support. The day to day implementation of personnel policy and strategy should rest with the non-specialist manager.

The role of the specialist Human Resource Manager has led to endless conflict and frustration. Senior line managers often resent 'advice' from specialists, especially in an area where many managers believe themselves to be already expert. Where there is a defensive reaction from the personnel specialist of a retreat into 'jargon' the problem is made more acute. The behavioural science base of the personnel specialist is not unknown to arouse great waves of apathy if not hostility.

A lot therefore depends on the style and approach of personnel specialists. Given that they do not have authority over managers other than those who work for them directly, then they must earn the commitment of other managers to listen and implement suggestions. This requires highly developed

12

interpersonal skills as well as specialist knowledge. This has proved difficult for many personnel people, especially older professionals who were trained in the days of 'labour management' as referred to in an earlier section, when their role was mainly a more limited and direct one of implementing government legislation on behalf of the organisation.

The device of wrenching direct control for aspects of personnel administration from line managers leaves little time for wider policy consideration as well as mistakenly assuming a role better left to the managers responsible for their section of the labour force.

There is another not unknown method of seeking to improve status. Some personnel people have taken every opportunity to increase their workload, providing a golden opportunity for their managerial colleagues to offload trivial matters for which they have neither the time nor interest. This strategy is sometimes referred to as the 'corporate trashcan' approach and has led management writers such as Drucker to query whether personnel administration was not 'bankrupt'.[6]

Neither should personnel specialists see themselves as the organisation's 'watchdog'. It is difficult to play a more demanding and useful role once the Personnel Department has gained a reputation as being skilled solely in spotting overmanning or handling disciplinary procedures for example.

Many large scale organisations seek to overcome the problem of the specialist's role in relation to general managers by 'placing' personnel administrators in the various operating divisions. Here they are subject to the authority of the managers concerned in a direct way as would be any other manager. By this means much of the aggravation can be avoided and the credibility of the personnel officer or manager is likely to be higher. This relationship is often combined with a 'dotted line' relationship with a senior manager in the central personnel department. Corporate personnel policies can then be implemented and issues which might have organisation wide implications can be reviewed centrally. This system is not without its difficulties, but at least specialists so placed should have a much closer understanding of the needs of the group they service. The dotted line relationship can prove useful as a possible source of advice and if necessary a means through which pressure can be brought to bear on a general manager by the contact of a senior personnel specialist with the manager's own boss.

At best, the relationship of specialist and general manager will remain problematical. Much depends on the technical and influencing skills of the personnel administrators. However it is done they will need to 'sell' themselves and their services on a value for money basis. The work of the personnel department is as susceptible to cost benefit analysis as that of any other department.

It is essential that the head of the personnel group should be represented on the Board or Executive Committee and should be responsible to the Managing Director or Chief Executive. The personnel chief can then make important contributions to the corporate planning process. He or she can thus also ensure that personnel policies are developed in line with the organisation's objectives and policies.

The Role of the Personnel Department

Policies and systems which are recommended by the Personnel Department should be sensitive to organisational requirements and circumstances. It is important that the stage of development of the organisation; the pressures it experiences in the environment in which it operates; the kind of technology it uses and the types of employee engaged are all taken into account in the development of personnel policies and departmental relationships with managers. The credibility of the personnel management function depends on matching the service offered to the needs of the users.

There are two myths which are still common about the nature of Personnel Management. Both stem from its historical roots.

Personnel administration is *not* a particularly relevant career for those who reckon they are 'good with people'. It is hoped that all managers perceive the need for good human relationships at work. These skills are not the prerogative of personnel people. The view that they are cannot be demonstrated in practice. This should not be a matter for concern. Through the development of sound policies, the Personnel Department has an important role to play in developing systems of relationships; managerial and technical skills and sound operating procedures which will help the organisation achieve its goals. Only in the smallest companies is the combination of personnel administration and welfare of any value.

A second myth which still has currency is that of the personnel administrator as 'man in the middle' – poised somewhere between management and workforce – with the task of seeing that justice is even handedly dispensed. It is important to recognise that personnel administrators are managers employed by other managers to represent the managerial point of view and to help them achieve managerial objectives. Where the pursuit of these may lead to ham-fisted managerial activity which may prevent the achievement of objectives, Personnel Managers have a duty to point this out, and to suggest more appropriate alternatives. This is not the same thing as arguing they act as a buffer between management and other levels of employee. Such a role has never existed in practice and it is hard to imagine how it might be adopted. The myth has its roots once again in the welfare oriented history of the personnel function. The early 'Social Secretaries' come to mind as do the later welfare officers often unwillingly taken on by firms under government pressure after the Second World War.

We have noted that all managers should be concerned about human resources. It should not be left to Personnel Managers. The role of the Personnel Department is to help management do this part of the job better and to provide services which it is more convenient to group together under a functional head – because line managers may lack the expertise and the time, or because a common, organisation wide procedure is important.

This is not to say that the Personnel Manager does the work for the general manager. There is a distinction worth making between policy and day to day activity. On the basis of expertise, for example, the Personnel Manager should research into the appropriate methods of selecting staff, taking into account developments in selection technique. A policy as to the selection methods for the various grades of staff should be devised, and help provided in framing advertisements and shortlisting candidates. But the formal responsibility for selection must remain with the manager who will be responsible for the new employee.

Again, it makes sense for there to be a coherent disciplinary policy to ensure the law is complied with and that there is similarity of procedure across departments. The invoking of the procedure and its implementation should rest with the relevant operations manager.

This distinction between policy and implementation is important. It underlines the proposition made earlier that Human Resource Management is a responsibility of every manager.

Both of these examples relate to the day to day activities of the Personnel Department. Success criteria can be developed and the performance of the Personnel department measured against them – vacancies filled successfully; labour costs saved and so on.

Whether a more powerful approach to the function in the U.K. can be developed depends greatly on the ability of the personnel professionals at the highest level to 'read' their organisation and the environment and identify priorities for the individual firm or group of companies.

This leads us on into a review of current trends in Human Resource Management.

Personnel Management and Human Resource Management

Whilst teaching students on various personnel management programmes, the writer has become aware with increasing unease, of a general feeling that Personnel Management is undergoing a revolution and will change radically; or worse – will all but disappear.

Such forecasts seem unrealistic and an over-reaction to a change of emphasis, which marks the end of one phase in the constant development of the function and the beginning of another. What will the current shift in emphasis involve?

Integration

Current economic pressures have ensured that the drive for efficiency in the 1980's has gathered momentum. Particularly the larger, more sensitive organisations are re-evaluating the contribution to economic stability of every department. The drive for close integration and with it tighter centralised control of objectives is part of the same process.

There appears a regrowth of interest in the view that only those organisations which have a clear sense of purpose and a commitment to ensuring that every department and individual shares the same basic organisational objective will survive. There is no reason to suppose that the personnel function will escape this scrutiny.

The title 'Human Resource Management' is held by companies such as IBM to reflect the pressure for greater integration of personnel activities. The effective mobilisation of human resource effort will be crucial to organisation survival, and since all managers manage the 'human resource' then HRM will become increasingly a shared concern for both personnel professional and line manager. In practice, this means that central personnel specialists may well be fewer in number (but not necessarily less powerful). They will be expected to place greater emphasis on ensuring that personnel policies reflect organisational priorities. The responsibility for execution of policy will shift to line managers to a greater degree than at present.

In themselves these propositions are nothing new. As long ago as 1912, Edward Cadbury observed that personnel activities:

'... must not be regarded as something outside the general organisation of the factory but as a vital part of factory organisation and it should be shared by all as far as possible, including directors, HODs, foremen and forewomen and should not be left to those who are specially set apart for this work'.[7]

Students of the slightly more recent literature will recall the oft quoted maxim of Pigors and Myers that 'All management is personnel management'.[8]

It can hardly be said that the notion of integration is a new concept. Its importance has become clearer, however, and in need of restatement to counteract the trend for Personnel Management to become increasingly isolated from mainstream management as the body of social scientific knowledge on which it is based has become more impressive.

Pragmatism

This leads us on to a second aspect of HRM. The 1990's are likely to see a shift from professionalism for its own sake to a more pragmatic approach in which personnel policies will reflect the immediate needs of the organisation – or more exactly the needs of managers. Those readers who are familiar with the IPM will have noted over recent years a perceptible change in the structure of membership examinations, which are now being re-designed to reflect a flight from behavioural science based professionalism. Further changes in this direction are being mooted at the time of writing. It is to be hoped, however, that a professional knowledge base is not entirely abandoned.

In those companies which embrace the practice of HRM, we may expect to see a greater movement of managers in and out of personnel administration and a decline in the practice of the 1970's and 80's for personnel managers to develop their own discrete professional career progression. HR managers will be expected both to make a greater input to corporate and strategic planning and also to develop personnel policies which reflect this planning closely. A consequence of this closer relationship to line management will be more demonstrable evidence that Human Resource Management is an integral part of management and for the most part exists to meet its needs. Once again this is not a novel position. Many senior personnel specialists have argued over the years that the personnel function is part of management and its survival depends on the extent to which managerial needs are met, as against any other sector of the work organisation.

Dualism

Organisational attitudes to the field of Industrial Relations is an area most likely to be affected by HRM. It would be erroneous to suggest that the traditional field of IR is fast diminishing and that the Trade Unions are likely to disappear. So far as one can see, the Unions will still exercise a powerful influence in the field of IR. There is little evidence that collective bargaining will become anything other than the norm, for example. Nor is it likely that the traditional domains of TU influence at national level will disappear. It may very well be that the tactics of the TUC will change to reflect a closer connection with European trade unionism and a closer knowledge of EEC and ILO legislation. It is unwise to interpret these changes as a loss of power, however, or to predict the demise of collective bargaining.

Current practice suggests the emergence of what might be called 'dualism', in which traditional bargaining arrangements will remain in place alongise newer systems of representation which will not necessarily be linked to Trade Unions and which will cover areas wider than that of traditional bargaining. There is evidence of increased concern with the needs to improve communications – by such methods as quality circles for example; and to explore more flexible payment systems both more closely linked to individual performance and at the same time giving the individual greater choice in how his or her reward package is made up.

Having said this, the observer of current trends in HRM will have noticed a rekindling of interest in a unitary approach to the organisation, which is based on the assumption that managers and non-managers share many common interests which outnumber those areas in which they differ; and that therefore although it may not be wise to replace the traditional pluralistic bargaining systems, there is a case for supplementing them with other systems of representation and communication which do not reflect what is said to be an outworn combative approach to IR. The return to a unitary approach may be more realistic than it was in the first half of this century. This time, however, it may reflect both a more determined attempt by management to manage and a managerial recognition that power has swung in its favour. In any event, the 'man in the middle' approach to Personnel Management has no place in this scenario!

A core element in the strategy of organisations which have embraced HRM

18

as a personnel strategy is the winning of 'the hearts and minds' of employees. No field as much as IR will be affected by the implementation of this strategy. The search is on to develop systems to increase the loyalty of the individual by looking for more imaginative ways in which to involve the workforce in decision making and for methods of reward far removed from traditional dependence on incremental progression up well defined salary scales. Many British managers are looking at the Japanese experience with regard to motivation, though no doubt they will wish to be selective as to the elements they attempt to transpose from one national culture to another.

Conclusion

In this chapter we have examined briefly the developmental stages of personnel administration from 'welfare' to 'Human Resource Management'; and have attempted to outline what should be the areas of concern for the personnel specialist. With regard to the latter, it has been argued that the personnel function will retain credibility only in so far as it changes its priorities to fit the changing needs of line management, which in turn closely reflects changing socio-economic conditions.

In a survey of just under four hundred Chief Personnel Executives in the U.K., Heidrick and Struggles[9] list the items which were considered by the respondents to be key areas of concern in the coming years:

● Identification of Future Top Management

● Organisational Responsiveness to New Technology

● Employee Participation and Motivation

● Reduction of Labour Costs

These issues require a proactive analytical and developmental approach to the use of manpower in the work organisation. The areas of concern for the Human Resource Manager will remain what many think they always were and which we have spelt out in an earlier section of this chapter. Current interest in HRM may reflect however a shift in emphasis both with regard to the making of policy and to the means by which policy is implemented: *process*.

Increasingly we may expect policy to be implemented by line managers, whilst the development of policy will remain the concern of the personnel specialist working closely with those line managers whose role includes the development of corporate strategy. As Guest remarks: 'If HRM is to be taken serously, Personnel Managers must give it away'.[10] We may also expect a diminution in size, but not in power, of central personnel groups, which will go hand in hand with the placement of many more personnel people into the line management structure – reporting to, and being paid from the budget of line managers. It is far too early in the course of the current phase of Personnel Management to predict exactly how it will develop – or indeed, whether it will develop significantly at all. Recent research suggests that only something like eighteen percent of British companies have shown any real interest in HRM to date.[11] In some cases it is likely that the change in title of the personnel function wil amount to no more than, as Armstrong suggests, 'old wine in new bottles'.[12] Even where there is a genuine attempt to introduce HRM, such effort should not in the writer's view be seen as revolutionary, but as evolutionary: another stage in the history of Personnel Management.

What does appear to be clear is that the power of the personnel function will further diminish if personnel specialists do not strive to ensure that personnel policy is integrated more closely with organisation wide strategic planning, thus adjusting to the current needs of line management: the effective deployment; training and motivation of scarce and expensive human resources.

References

1   F W Taylor, *Scientific Management*, Harper and Row, New York, 1911.

2   F J Roethlisberger and W J Dickson, *Management and the Worker*, Harvard University Press, Cambridge Mass., 1939.

3   *Royal Commission on Trade Unions and Employers Associations*, Cmnd. 3623, HMSO, London 1968.

4   T J Peters and R H Waterman, *In Search of Excellence*, Harper and Row, New York, 1987.

5   G G Fisch, *Line Staff is Obsolete*, Harvard Business Review, Volume 39, September 1961, pp. 67-79.

6   P F Drucker, *The Practice of Management*, Pan Books, London, 1968.

7   E Cadbury, *Experiments in Industrial Organisation*, Longmans, London, 1912.

8   P Pigors and C A Myers, *Personnel Administration: A Point of View and a Method*, McGraw Hill, New York, 1947, (1st Ed.).

9   Heidrick and Struggles, *Chief Personnel Executives in the United Kingdom*, Heidrick and Struggles, Publishers, 1981.

10 D Guest, *Personnel and HRM: Can You Tell the Difference?*, Personnel Management, January 1989.

11 P Marginson et al., *Beyond the Workplace: Managing Industrial Relations in the Multi-Establishment Enterprise*, Blackwell, Oxford, 1988.

12 M Armstrong, *Human Resource Management: A Case of the Emperor's New Clothes?*, Personnel Management, August, 1987.

Suggested Reading

Although old, still good for a historical perspective:

A Crichton, *Personnel Management in Perspective*, Batsford, London, 1962.

Two articles relating to HRM:

J W Hunt, *The Shifting Focus of the Personnel Function*, Personnel Management, February 1984.

D E Guest, *Human Resource Management and Industrial Relations*, Journal of Management Studies, September 1987.

Questions

1   'All management is Personnel Management'. How far do you agree with this view?

2   'The shift towards HRM from Personnel Management is an evolutionary rather than a revolutionary progression'. Give reasons why you agree or disagree with this view.

3   'If HRM is to be taken seriously, Personnel Managers must give it away'. What do you think is meant by this statement?

Chapter 2

Human Resource Planning

Sarah Vickerstaff

Introduction

In the last twenty-five years Human Resource Planning or Manpower Planning has had a number of prophets. It has consistently failed, however, to attract many followers. Managers often remain unconvinced of the claimed benefits of human resource planning. This chapter will argue that all organisations can benefit from planning their human resource flows. It will link human resource planning to current trends in personnel management and in particular, will argue that personnel planning is an essential part of the Human Resources Management perspective which is increasingly dominating theory and practice in the management of people. The centrality of planning activities for a strategic, proactive approach to the task of managing people will be demonstrated.

The chapter is divided into three main sections. The first will define human resource planning and provide arguments for the importance of planning activities. The second section will look at why many organisations have remained unconvinced of the benefits of planning their human resources and suggest how organisations of all sizes, and in whichever sectors, can improve their performance through human resource planning. The final section will look at the techniques of manpower planning and give the reader a basic introduction to available methods.

What is Human Resource Planning?

Managers are often sceptical of the value of devoting resources to planning a future which appears, by definition, to be unpredictable. Concentration on the long range forecasting aspects of human resource planning has tended to make it appear an unrealistic proposition for the 'average' organisation.

Many of these criticisms arise from a false view of what human resource planning is all about. If it is thought to be about producing a once and for all accurate prediction of the long term situation and a corresponding blueprint for personnel policy action in the next 5 to 10 years then disappointment will result. Human resource planning has both less and more to offer than this kind of futurology.

The attempt to plan for future labour/staff needs is likely to be the first aim or activity most of us associate with personnel planning systems. This is often expressed as the attempt by an organisation to ensure that it has the right people at the right time with the right skills. This is the first objective, an attempt to forecast likely future demand for labour/staff and identify the gap between this and expected future supply of labour. In order to be able to do this the organisation must have some analysis of the expected future demand for its product or services, a picture of its current workforce and some understanding of the labour markets from which it recruits. However, forecasting demand and supply for future needs does not exhaust the objectives of human resource planning.

A second objective is to analyse and improve upon the utilisation of existing resources. The focus here is less upon the future and more on what the organisation is doing now, for example, developing measures of labour utilisation, work loads, productivity and understanding the current stock of skills and talents within the organisation. Human resource planning systems in this respect map and analyse contemporary stocks and flows of people within the organisation. But even with this second element we do not have an exhaustive definition of the objectives of the personnel planning activity. A third aim is to integrate and coordinate personnel policy responses to ensure that existing and future labour needs are met.

The Human Resource Management perspective suggests that the people in an organisation should be seen as valuable resources. Capitalising on the investment in people requires the planning and integration of human resource policies, involving the development of explicit employment strategies. Policies in different areas interact and can be mutually reinforcing of objectives or, if unplanned and uncoordinated, can constitute a set of policies producing inconsistent outcomes. For example the adequacy of a training policy cannot be assessed solely in terms of its immediate objectives i.e. the upgrading of skills, but should also be reviewed in respect of the extent to which it reinforces or frustrates other policy responses for example, recruitment and retention, career and succession planning, longer term skill requirements, labour utilisation targets and so on. Here human resource planning is serving to audit and review existing policies.

These different objectives give us a three-fold definition of the aims of human resource planning:

1   to meet future labour/staff needs,
2   to utilise existing human resources more effectively,
3   to integrate and monitor human resource policies.

Defining human resource planning in this way shows us that it is not simply about trying to forecast the future but also about what the organisation is doing today. Thus, we see that personnel planning has a vital role in contributing to the diagnosis of the need for change. Personnel planning is an information gathering and analysis system to assist management in making decisions. Increasingly organisations are concerned with the effectiveness of their personnel policies. Human resource specialists are being evaluated in terms of their contribution to corporate goals. The information and analysis in the human resource planning process should make personnel policy better informed and better targeted, improving its contribution to corporate success. Good personnel planning systems also provide the means for the human dimension to be satisfactorily coordinated with the planning of other resources in the organisation, giving personnel specialists the opportunity for a more developed role in business planning generally.

Many companies are willing to admit that the people they employ are a vital factor in the success or failure of the business; rather less take this point to its logical outcome and concede the need to plan for their human resources as thoroughly and effectively as any other aspect of the business. A Human Resource Management approach to the task of managing people is based upon the premise that people are a vital ingredient in the performance equation and one that can, and must, be proactively planned and managed, for effective utilisation. As Peter Wickens, Director of Personnel at Nissan (UK) has said:

> . . . it is essential that we look at the 'people' part of our businesses
> in the same way as we look at investment or product – and that is
> strategically.[1]

What this means, practically, is that decisions about for example recruitment, training and compensation should not be left to the last minute. Policy towards people should not be formed as a reaction to already concluded business decisions, but, like the finance or marketing function in an organisation, the personnel function should be seen as part of the bottom line, that is, a key aspect of profitability, growth and organisational success.

Every market or corporate strategy has human resource implications; the introduction of new product lines may require extra staff, new skills, promotions and transfers all of which have varying lead times and associated costs. Failure on any of these dimensions, or significant delays, may well jeopardise the plan for getting the new products into the market place. In short, efficient and effective utilisation of human resources requires planning. If personnel specialists are to play a key role in corporate decision taking circles human resource planning systems are an indispensable item in their tool kits.

This view of human resource planning is more sophisticated than a traditional picture of manpower planning as being essentially about attempts to forecast future demand for labour/staff. It provides us with a particular picture of what good Human Resource Management looks like. It suggests that good personnel policies cannot be developed on the basis of poor information and analysis, and cannot be derived entirely in reaction to other business objectives and in response to changes in the environment. The value of human resource planning is that it raises the quality of decisions made as knowledge and understanding of the organisation's current position and possible future directions improve.

Why Organisations Should Plan Their Human Resource Flows

Companies often first realise the need for better human resource planning at the point at which a major new development in operations is on the horizon or, at the point where past failure to plan has led to chronic problems, for example an inadequate supply of certain skilled workers, low morale, high turnover and career blockages. It has been much less typical for companies to realise the benefits of human resource planning in advance of a particular crisis.

The most familiar criticism of human resource planning is that it is difficult to predict future demand for labour in a volatile market. Furthermore, it is often asserted that people are inherently unpredictable and may leave at any time for any number of reasons and therefore attempts to monitor labour wastage, especially in sectors with traditionally high turnover, are doomed to failure and are a waste of time and effort. It is also sometimes felt that the language of manpower planning depersonalises the management of people and creates the false impression that employees and staff can be practically manipulated as easily as the statistics that represent them.

It is indeed true that human resource planning, like the planning of any other resources, is not a panacea. The act of planning itself does not ensure success as all planning is only as good as the information upon which it is based, and people are potentially less predictable than other kinds of resources. Human resource planning cannot pretend to be an exact science, nor should it aspire to providing optimal solutions. It is important to remember that personnel policies are always, in some measure, subject to negotiation, that is between trade unions and management, between an individual employee and his/her supervisor or between managers in different departments. As arguments against planning however, these points amount to an endorsement of the sentiment that 'ignorance is bliss'. It is surely in the face of uncertainty that information gathering, analysis and improved understanding are likely to be most valuable.

An example may help to dispel the 'ignorance is bliss' myth. It has been recognised for some time by demographers, and publicised by government agencies such as the Training Commission, that the number of young people in the age range 16-24 in the British labour market will decline by one-fifth – a projected fall of some 1.2 million between 1987 and 1995. The effects of this decline will vary from region to region but will obviously first effect those sectors which have traditionally recruited school leavers.

A postal survey of employers conducted by the Training Commission and the National Economic Development Office in the Spring of 1988 revealed that only one in seven employers were well informed about these trends and that organisations in sectors such as Hotel and Catering and the Distributive Industry, which are typically dependent upon a relatively abundant supply of cheap youth labour, were the least well informed, with a quarter of respondents in these sectors actually believing the number of school leavers was going to increase![2]

Clearly organisations in parts of the country where the labour market is going to tighten up should be developing strategies for dealing with expected recruitment difficulties. Companies that are late in realising this will lag behind those organisations who have already started to modify recruitment policies to attract alternative sources of labour and those who have modified reward and training packages to improve their recruitment chances and their retention profiles. The major supermarket retailer Sainsbury has considerably modified human resource policies to take account of these labour market shortages. In the South East of England, where the reduction in the number of school leavers is particularly significant the company has introduced a Retail Training Scheme which gives new entrants one year's training on full pay and has increased the pay levels of 16 and 17 year olds by up to 40% in some areas.

These changes in policy serve to enhance the attractiveness of Sainsbury in the youth labour market but they are also important for longer term staff needs. Traditionally a large majority of Sainsbury store managers have joined the company as school leavers and worked their way up to managerial positions. In improving its recruitment capability now, Sainsbury is also trying to have an impact upon retention and ensure future supplies of home grown managers. For organisations in the retail sector, and elsewhere, who have failed to plan ahead ignorance of labour market trends is likely, at least, to be very costly and at worst disastrous.

Not all changes in the labour market or product markets are as easy to predict as the above example; what the case does show is that some understanding of trends in the environment is better than no knowledge or false assumptions. Routine scanning of the labour markets in which an organisation operates should at least ensure that predictable changes are not missed. The value of knowledge to the companies in the example above is the flexibility it gives them to make choices between different policy options, and to cost the implications of different responses to the changes.

The time horizon and planning cycle for successful human resource policies is often over the long term, but traditionally the personnel function has not been a party to long range corporate decision making, and has been in the position of having to react to business plans already decided. The effect is to starve corporate planners of useful, if not vital, information about the human resource impact of different projected developments, such as the lead times and costs of recruitment or training drives needed to fulfil various objectives. It is difficult to contest the usefulness of good data about productivity, skills and labour availability when considering different product development strategies.

However, the problem is often much deeper than the absence of Personnel Managers from corporate decision taking circles. Many organisations engage in very little systematic planning of anything, but tend to lurch along from one short term horizon to another. Clearly, a company that does little business planning is unlikely to have sophisticated human resource planning systems. This point is borne out by an IPM survey of human resource planning practices in which 58% of the respondents identified the 'low priority of planning compared with immediate management concerns' as a major difficulty in attempting to implement planning systems.[3]

Even if the future is uncertain, the definition of human resource planning advocated here points to the fact that it is not only about forecasting future events but also about current labour utilisation and the effectiveness of existing policies. The external environment may indeed be difficult to predict and even more difficult to control but there is not the same excuse for poor understanding and control of the internal environment of the organisation. By monitoring current stocks and flows in the organisation, management is in a position to diagnose existing and potential problems for example promotion blockages; insufficient talent rising for management succession; particular retention problems and training needs. Here the advantage of planning activities is knowing the start position. In the IPM survey mentioned above, over 50% of the respondents mentioned the following as key benefits of systematic human resource planning: improved identification of training needs; more appropriate staffing levels and improved management development. Just under 50% mentioned savings in unit labour costs and increases in employee productivity.[3]

Human resource planning is not an all or nothing activity; it has utility at different levels of sophistication and at different points in the organisation. There is a tendency in the personnel management texts to concentrate upon the grand strategic planning issues – where will the company be in 7 years time? How are we going to get there? What skills and resources will we need? This is certainly one function of planning but there are also more mundane, if no less important, advantages from routine planning activites. For example, human resource planning activities can be concentrated at the level in the organisation at which decisions are made. To achieve good decision making, managers at various levels need the information relevant to their areas of concern and they also need to feed information in to more centralised information recording systems. At the level of a particular section for example the maintenance of good up to date information on work loads, labour utilisation and turnover can facilitate the scheduling of work and provide a ready means for assessing the impact of predicted peaks and troughs in work levels. This might result in the ability to better match supply and demand and avoid expensive overtime, production delays or the need for hurried recruitment drives. This routine information can also be fed into more complicated long range modelling and planning and help enrich discussion and consideration of future improvements.

If it is realised that human resource planning has benefits at an operational level then we can perhaps overcome some of the scepticism and distrust of complicated techniques that lie behind much managerial resistance to human resource planning. As will be seen in the following discussion of methods, there are a range of planning and forecasting techniques which require substantial mathematical and statistical expertise, which is likely to be outside the range of skills available in most small and medium sized companies. Unwillingness or inability to use these does not invalidate the potential of human resource planning, however.

Different organisations will have different requirements from a human resource planning system depending upon their size, their product or service market, the labour market(s) they operate in, the skill profile of their workforce and the pace of change that they face. Not all companies will want or need to forecast promotion flows for the next 7-10 years. Smaller companies may have more particular problems like skill shortages and persistent turnover. Human resource planning has something to offer for the resolution of all these issues. A good understanding of the current position should give any organisation a better base from which to respond to changes and developments.

The approach to human resource planning will also be affected by organisational structure and culture. Personnel policies are one of the prime ways in which these can be maintained or modified and therefore we would expect human resource planning activities to reflect the organisation's style and philosophy. For example in a large relatively stable bureaucracy such as the army or the police force the human resource flow pattern is characterised by an internal labour market with restricted ports of entry from the external labour market, and strict budgetary controls over manning levels. Here we would expect a preoccupation with age profiles, promotion patterns, career and succession planning issues. In one of the big six accounting firms where individual success is based to a large degree upon competition with peers and individual professional performance, we might expect greater attention to attracting high calibre recruits in the first place, followed up by training and retention strategies to develop and keep the 'right' resources in the firm. Here the environment is very dynamic and the strategies market led. The demands upon the human resource planning systems will be different in each case but are nevertheless important to the successful execution of corporate policies in both.

Good human resource planning systems may also have a beneficial impact upon the employee relations climate. Well worked out promotion and career planning policies will be attractive to individual employees who want future advancement possibilities; planning policies will be critical for companies that seek to offer job security through the operation of internal labour markets; forward planning can reduce the impact of a downturn in activity or a restructuring policy and thereby minimise the conflict and distrust frequently generated in such situations by enabling the shedding of labour without compulsory redundancies.

A human resource management perspective suggests that one of the primary goals of people management activity is the development of employee commitment to the firm; the development of consistent and fair personnel policies likely to develop such commitment will be dependent upon the good planning and integration of policies that is a feature of human resource planning.

The specific advantages to be gained by organisations from formalising their human resource planning procedures will obviously vary from one company to the next. The balance between strategic long range planning and more day to day operational concerns and between quantitative and qualitative techniques will depend upon the organisation's size, markets and management style. What should be clear is that planning activities are of relevance to all companies because a lack of understanding and knowledge about current employee stocks and future possible trends is bad management, for which there is really no justifiable cause.

Human Resource Planning Methods

As many of the preceding remarks indicate human resource planning is neither a one-off activity nor a single strategy but requires a cycle of information gathering and analysis. Following the three-fold definition of human resource planning used here we can conceptualise the planning process schematically as shown in Figure 2.1.

The benefit of this framework is that it communicates that the human resource planning process is a continuous activity. It also links together long term and short term planning and, importantly, it indicates that the planning activity can start at any point of the cyclical process. For example, review of current recruitment policies may indicate that the prevailing strategy is failing to produce the right numbers of the right kinds of applicant. The cycle would then suggest several possibilities including further analysis of current stocks to see whether internal sources of supply could meet the demand; reanalysis of demand to see whether better utilisation of existing resources could reduce the demand; or continued scanning of the environment for alternative sources of supply.

A more typical example would be that the company intends to expand existing capacity and wants to forecast likely demand for labour given certain budgetary, time and technological constraints. The demand forecast reveals a human resources gap which supply analysis proves can be met by internal transfers and the labour savings expected from the introduction of new production processes. This is then converted into a number of policy options in terms of retraining, reassignment etc. This framework for human resource planning also puts emphasis on the first vital step of any personnel planning system, that is, the analysis of current stocks, flows and utilisation.

30

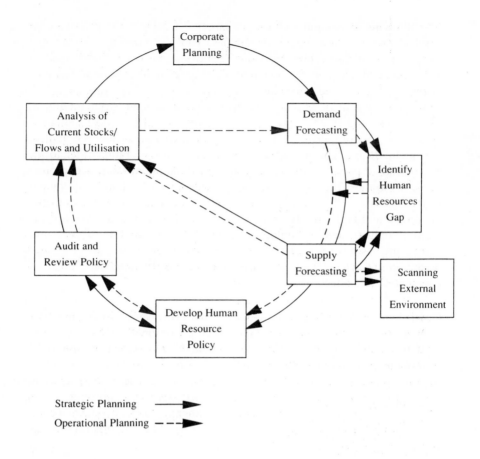

Strategic Planning ——————▶
Operational Planning — — —▶

Figure 2.1: A Framework for Human Resource Planning

The following discussion and use of examples is designed to give the non-specialist a sense of available techniques. Those wanting a more detailed discussion of methods should consult the books suggested as further reading at the end of this chapter. The inevitable starting point for any human resource planning system is the information base about its existing work force. The systematic analysis of existing resources revolves around two main dimensions: stocks and flows analysis. Stocks refers to existing staff, numbers, ages, skills, performance, work load measurement and productivity indices which should be kept and updated on a routine basis. Flows refer to the movements of people within and in and out of the organisation e.g. promotions, demotions, transfers, turnover, absenteeism, dismissal, retirements, maternity leave and so on. This information should also be kept as a matter of routine and be regularly updated. In a small organisation this will not require sophisticated technology, although the availability of personnel management software packages for microcomputers means even a small organisation can have their basic personnel records computerised, subject of course to Data Protection Act provisions.

Good, regularly updated, stocks and flows data is the basic building block for subsequent human resource planning. At an operational level stocks information can assist in the scheduling of work and can provide the opportunity to monitor productivity and work loads. It can also provide the basis for monitoring the progress of equal opportunity policies. These activities assist line managers to feed into wider policy discussions and contribute to the diagnosis of the need for change. Bids for further personnel by line managers or departmental heads may also be strengthened if their arguments are supported by good analysis and data.

Basic information sources are also important for longer term, strategic planning. Stock flow analysis provides the opportunity to investigate wastage patterns, identify career structure problems and future recruitment and training needs. The maintenance of good data on wastage patterns has significant benefits, allowing the organisation to diagnose particular turnover problems and propose new policies. Turnover can be a costly problem. Continuous recruitment costs; loss of training investment, poor morale amongst remaining staff; delayed production and unnecessarily high manning levels readily come to mind. Management needs to be able to try and predict and plan for outflows if the effects of wastage are to be, at least, minimised and at best, controlled.

Wastage is made up of a number of different elements: voluntary resignation, redundancy, retirement, dismissal, death or incapacity. The first is usually the most significant because it is the most difficult to control. There are a number of different ways of measuring and monitoring turnover; the simplest index of labour wastage is a separation rate as follows:

$$\frac{\text{nos of employees leaving in a period}}{\text{average number of employees in a period}} \quad \times \quad 100$$

However, this is too crude to be of enormous use in many situations. It does not differentiate between those who left voluntarily and those who had other reasons, nor does it distinguish between different grades or groups of employees, so that it may in fact mask significant problems in a particular department by producing a reasonable average rate. With regard to the latter problem it is possible to produce indices for each department or section or grade of employee. With regard to the former problem an organisation may want to calculate for voluntary resignations separately. Even with these refinements the separation rate does not give us any clue as to whether it is new recruits or old established employees who are leaving which would point to different likely causes for voluntary separation. To find out who is leaving we can use a stability index as follows:

$$\frac{\text{nos of employees with one year's service or more now}}{\text{number employed one year ago}} \quad \times \quad 100$$

If data is available on a time series basis it is obviously possible to compare these rates over varying time periods to monitor trends in wastage.

One can also gain more information about who is leaving by plotting the survivor function on a graph, that is the number of survivors as a function of length of service, as shown in Figure 2.2.

The value of this is to improve the understanding of the patterns of wastage. It is also possible to plot graphs showing the relationship between wastage and variables such as age. In addition to such indices it is often useful to try to get qualitative data on wastage, for example, through exit interviews and automatically keep records of reasons for leaving. This will never be a perfect source of information but can usefully supplement statistical techniques. The more information that managers have on the reasons for, and likely magnitude of, voluntary wastage, the better they can understand the problem and target their response. This is important for both short term utilisation and longer term supply forecasting.

The next major type of flow within the organisation is likely to be promotion. One of the simplest models of flows allows us to map the typical promotion routes through the organisation and, on the basis of current stocks and wast-

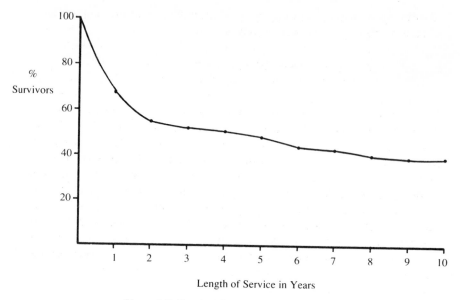

Figure 2.2: Survival Rate as a Function of Length of Stay

age assumptions, identify possible career blockage points or future promotion shortages, offering the opportunity for managers to consider the implications of different remedial policies by playing the model under different assumptions. The model is known as a Markov model as indicated opposite.

On the basis of current stocks at each level and expected wastage from each stage, we could work out the effects of different promotion rates for staff distribution across the different levels. We could also model any other assumptions we wished to test, for example the possibility of a reduction in wastage levels at the top of the profession coupled with a freeze on promotions. This model is appropriate in a situation where promotions are determined on a regular basis, for example so many in a particular year. It is less useful for the more typical situation in private business where promotions only occur when vacancies are created above, i.e. through wastage, transfer or promotion higher up. For this we need what is called a renewal model. One model which combines analysis of stocks by age and grade with wastage data and promotion flows is the Kent Model which has been used in the civil service.[4]

These modelling activities are most useful for large organisations which need to forecast stocks and flows of very large numbers of employees over 5-10 years. However, the principles used here are of relevance to simpler prob-

34

lems. In a small organisation simulations of individual promotion paths, rather than the modelling of statistical aggregates, can provide useful pictures of the current and future situation. In small organisations, or for particular sections of larger ones, replacement charts can be constructed which show the possible candidates for particular promotions and their current promotion potential. Information of various sorts can be included in these charts, for

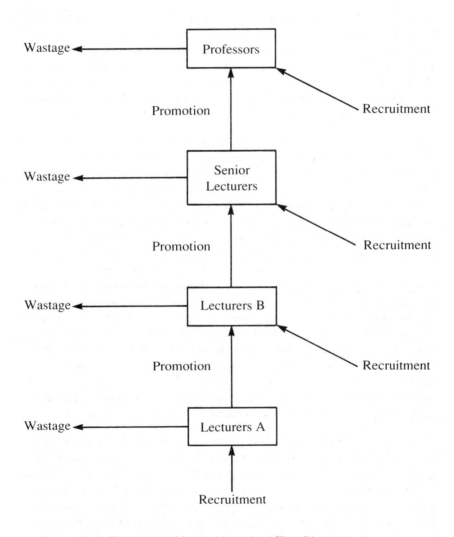

Figure 2.3: A Markov Model Stock/Flow Diagram

example, age, promotion potential, need for extra training, current performance assessment and so on.

These modelling activities at whatever level of sophistication they are performed give managers the opportunity to diagnose in advance short term gaps and long term problems in age distributions and act as early warning systems. The significance of all these kinds of analyses are also related to the next part of our model of the human resource implications of corporate and business plans.

Corporate plans and stock analysis provide the basic data for assessing and forecasting future needs. Demand for staff is obviously derived from expected future demand for product or services combined with imbalances in current stock. The ability to forecast future demand will depend firstly on the effectiveness of the business planning processes and secondly on the quality of stocks data. There are a number of methods for calculating labour demand. Demand forecasts should be seen as guides not blueprints.

A relatively simple method for assessing demand for human resources is ratio trend analysis which seeks to calculate a ratio between activity levels and staff numbers. This can be expressed as the number of people required for a certain activity level or the number of work hours for given levels of output. For example, for every 25 students a school should have one teacher; therefore if the number of students is increased by 100, 4 extra members of the teaching staff will be required. The need for support staff as a function of teaching staff levels can then be derived. The problem with this is that it assumes a number of things that may be false, for example that all subjects require the same teacher/student ratio; that productivity cannot be improved by changing methods such as the introduction of open learning or distance learning; that all employees work as efficiently and effectively as each other; that current staffing levels are adequate in terms of desired performance levels, or that there are no possible economies of scale. We would therefore need to build into such an analysis managerial understanding of the effort bargain, the nature of the work and the scope for changes. However, despite these shortcomings we could still use this basic method as a means for calculating the staffing implications of a desired increase in productivity of say 10%.

Time series methods of calculating demand for human resources have the basic problem, indicated in the above example. The process of rolling forward past trends may simply continue past poor productivity. One way of avoiding reliance on data from the past in this way is to use a standard such as cost and work back from a projected level of labour cost, to work out the numbers oand kinds of human resources available for that level of expenditure. This is likely to be a much less mechanistic process and may encourage more inventive

36

consideration of alternative labour utilisation strategies. The demand for people can be assessed as a ratio of output, sales, clients, patients and crimes for example. Analyses of this sort can become extremely complex; the vital factor to remember is that demand is generally a dynamic process and that there are always a variety of ways of meeting a given level of demand.

Other methods for determining the demand for labour are work study techniques. These involve measuring the work activity to calculate how long particular tasks take. This can then be translated into the number of hours of work required for a specified level of production. Work measurement can be done by direct observation and measurement; by activity sampling; and through work diary techniques. All of these methods share the problem that they can be time consuming and therefore costly to do. There is also the problem that non routine jobs may be difficult to measure. Once again managerial judgement is an important source of information, as is the job knowledge of supervisors and the employees themselves.

The next stage in our framework for human resource planning is the forecasting of labour supply in terms of short term or long term predicted demand. Routine supply analysis of internal stocks and flows tells the organisation the likely position under prevailing assumptions for given levels of demand; but to provide a realistic forecast of future internal supply of labour we must build into this analysis the effects of possible changes in utilisation – for example changes in patterns of hours worked or shifts. It is in this way that some of the more mechanistic tendencies of trend analysis can be mitigated and the importance of managerial ability and judgement is reinforced.

Apart from internal labour supply, organisations also have the option, or the necessity, of buying in new staff and employees from the external market. Another critical feature of forecasting future supply of labour is therefore understanding the availability of human resources in external markets. Scanning of the external environment involves the monitoring of trends in the labour markets in which the organisation operates. Reviewing sources of supply in national and local labour markets for different categories of staff; monitoring schools and colleges for their output in particular subject areas serve as examples. In addition to these labour market features there are likely to be laws and proposed legislation that effects the supply of labour. Some of this information will be available from government agencies such as the Department of Employment and the Training Agency, or from employers and trade associations. Other information, especially of a local nature, is more likely to be informally available in the business community.

Many of the manpower planning texts characterise the next stage of the planning process as the reconciliation of demand and supply forecasts to reveal the gap between what is predicted as available and what is predicted as necessary, thus indicating whether on existing planning assumptions there is a need to recruit, retrain, transfer or dismiss. Reconciliation is perhaps an unfortunate word as it implies that a perfect balancing of demand and supply may be possible, contradicting the view of human resource planning provided here, as a necessarily dynamic and continuous process. The identification of a predicted gap between supply and demand is better seen as the information upon which managers consider different policy options. At the policy planning stage managerial judgement is critical and where time allows there should be scope for scenario building, that is the suggestion of various alternative policy responses to the identified problems and the talking through of the benefits and defects of different solutions with further analysis and modelling if appropriate.

The policy development stage is unlikely to actually involve the production of a manpower plan as such, in the sense of a single document. It is more likely to involve a series of interlocking strategies in different areas. The important point here is that policies should be properly communicated to those that need to know – line managers responsible for recruitment or perhaps employees who may be eligible for retraining or promotion. Other key issues at the policy development stage are the lead times for particular policies, for example the time it takes to recruit skilled engineers, or to train semi-skilled operatives; and any possible organisational constraints, such as employee resistance to policy changes.

Another important point for policy development or modification is setting in place the means for reviewing the policy outcomes. This might take the form of producing targets for recruitment or training or labour costs, instituting an annual review to assess progress or whatever is appropriate in the particular circumstances. The human resource planning framework builds in policy audit and review as a necessary and vital part of the process; not only should organisations as a matter of course assess policy to see if it is effective and efficient but in this process the continual search for improved utilisation and coordination is often initiated.

It may seem from the foregoing discussion of methods and techniques that human resource planning is indeed as complicated and time consuming as many managers have always feared. It will require an investment of time in the first instance for those organisations who have not in the past kept good personnel records or done much forecasting. It simply remains in this chapter, by way of a conclusion, to reinforce our earlier argument as to why it is indeed worth investing in the planning of human resources.

Conclusion

Hitherto, the most sophisticated human resource planning practices have occurred, not surprisingly, in large organisations such as the civil service. Many small and medium sized organisations have believed that the techniques are too complicated or too costly for their use. As we have argued throughout this chapter human resource planning is not only about the attempt to forecast future demand for labour but also about current utilisation and the coordination of personnel policies.

For the organisation that is new to systematic planning of its human resources the way into better practice is likely to be by tackling particular problems such as skill shortages or turnover problems in the first instance, rather than through the overnight conversion to a fully blown planning system. For those organisations that feel they operate in too volatile a market to forecast future demand for labour at all meaningfully, the model of human resource planning used here suggests that there will still be gains to be made from looking at current utilisation and understanding the medium and long term implications of current stocks and flows positions. It is difficult to imagine the organisation that could not improve upon current practice in some measure.

The success of the prophets of human resource planning will not be in the widespread use of particular planning and forecasting techniques but in the extent of conversion to the philosophy of people management that human resource planning implies. Recognising the need to plan for, and coordinate policy towards, the people in the organisation concerns much more than modelling techniques or statistical analysis. It signals acceptance of the perspective that Human Resources Management increasingly suggests, namely, that the employees of an organisation are a vital resource and one that must be managed strategically. Guest has recently characterised Human Resource Management, as compared to more traditional approaches to personnel management, by its emphasis upon four particular policy goals: strategic integration, commitment, flexibility and quality.[5] It can be seen how human resource planning has a vital role to play in all four goals.

Strategic integration refers to the need for personnel policy to be properly and productively integrated into wider strategic planning to ensure that the human resource is managed effectively in terms of corporate goals. The data collection and analysis implied by human resource planning provides the means for the people element to be integrated into wider planning discussions. The possible effects of personnel planning on employee commitment have already been mentioned above, clearly commitment is never generated by bad or poor management. Human resource planning should improve the quality of managerial decision taking and if the processes and outcomes of planning are properly communicated, it should have beneficial effects upon employee relations in the long term.

Flexibility refers to the desire on management's part to be able to respond effectively and proactively to changing markets and environments. The bedrock on which flexibility is built is information; the better the understanding management has of its current position, and the better its intelligence on environmental developments the greater the scope for considered choice of response. Flexibility in terms of labour utilisation is also founded on well integrated and coordinated personnel policies that facilitate internal mobility.

Quality, of course, will be an outcome of improvements in utilisation, and the increased efficiency and effectiveness that sound human resource planning can bring. The quality of managerial decisions should improve with better data on, and analysis of, the human resource. Regular audit and review of personnel policies will provide the critical element needed to constantly assess current practice and the possibilities for improvement.

References

1   P Wickens, *The Road to Nissan*, 1987, Macmillan Press, p. 182.

2   See *Young People and the Labour Market*, NEDO/TC, July 1988.

3   *Follow up to the IPM Statement on Human Resource Planning. Initial Analysis of Survey Results*, IPM 1988.

4   For further information about the Kent model and other available systems see Edwards, 1983.

5   D Guest, *Personnel and HRM: Can You Tell the Difference?* in Personnel Management, January 1989.

Suggested Reading

J Bramham, *Practical Manpower Planning*, 1982, IPM. This is an easy to read introduction to all aspects of manpower planning, giving a non-specialist account of available techniques and their main advantages and disadvantages.

J Edwards, et al (eds), *Manpower Planning*, 1983, John Wiley & Sons. This is an interesting collection of articles giving both quantitative and behavioural approaches to manpower planning.

J Fyfe, *Putting the People Back into Manpower Planning Equations*, in Personnel Management, October, 1987. A short article that makes the important plea that we should all remember that manpower is not an exact science.

Questions

1   Why do you think so many organisations have remained sceptical of the benefits of human resource planning?

2   How would you convince a manager of a small engineering firm that human resource planning was of relevance to them?

3   How would you set about assessing demand and supply for labour in your organisation over the next five years?

Chapter 3

Personnel Selection

Alistair Ostell

Introduction

Recruitment, selection and placement are the activities concerned with finding suitable people to fill job vacancies within organisations. Since one of the most important factors which determines the success of an organisation is the quality of the people it employs it is obviously crucial to establish effective ways of conducting these activities. In many organisations and particularly small ones such activities are often conducted in a 'blinkered' manner just concentrating upon finding an appropriate person to fill an existing vacancy. However, if an organisation is to obtain and utilise effectively, on a *long-term basis*, the employees it requires its approach to personnel selection needs to be guided by a more general strategy for the management of human resources within the organisation as a whole.[1]

Studies of personnel specialists reveal that they usually have a major role in conducting selection activities. It is thus necessary for them both to understand the conceptual basis of selection and to be able to design and implement appropriate selection procedures within their organisation. This chapter describes the phases and activities of a comprehensive procedure and discusses the criteria by which such a procedure can be evaluated. First, however, some of the reasons why personnel selection should be viewed as one aspect of a broader human resource management policy will be considered.

Human Resource Management and Personnel Selection

The need for effective selection and placement procedures arises from the simple facts that people differ and so do jobs. People vary considerably not only in their physical characteristics such as size, weight and strength but also in such psychological characteristics as intelligence, motivation, skills, temperament and goals. Because jobs also vary in terms of the attributes people must possess in order to do them, it is therefore important to find someone whose attributes match as closely as possible those necessary for a given job if it is to be performed well. It is important, however, to view this process in terms of the broader human resource needs of the organisation over the longer term.

The Changing Nature of Organisations and Their Environments

In order to achieve corporate objectives, organisations may have to expand or contract, to diversify or rationalise products (or services) and to modify or replace existing technologies for new ones. All such changes have implications for an organisations's workforce in terms of employee numbers, their levels of education, skills, mobility and so forth.

It is also a fact that organisations exist within a social-political-economic environment which can have a strong impact upon the ways they operate. Changes in employment legislation and industrial relations promoted by the current government have led to the erosion of restrictive practices and to a requirement for many employees both to acquire more skills and to be more adaptable in their use. The same requirements for 'multi-skilling' and flexibility in employees has also arisen in the past decade as organisations have attempted to match the economic competitiveness of their rivals, particularly from overseas.[2]

These facts mean that from a management of human resources perspective, organisations obviously need to identify the numbers and kinds of employees that will be necessary to achieve short and longer term corporate objectives and to determine when these employees will be required. In establishing these facts it is important to take into account the influence of the environmental forces already mentioned and projected changes in them, together with factors such as employee turnover and promotion rates and the availability of relevant people in the labour market (see Chapter 2). These data as a whole should provide the focus and direction for selection procedures.

Selection as a Two-Way Process

For the sake of convenience we tend to describe the selection process from an organisational point of view thus ignoring the fact that individuals are also choosing between organisations and jobs thus making selection a *two-way process*.[3]

This fact has two important implications from a human resource management perspective. First, it highlights the need for organisations to market job vacancies in a manner which will attract the best candidates, especially when there is a limited supply of qualified people. Second, it emphasises the need to offer job applicants who will occupy important positions a 'rewarding' role in terms of job satisfaction, remuneration and genuine career prospects. The marketing of jobs in an attractive manner can create problems for selectors, however, because applicants who want particular jobs will often 'manage' information about themselves to create the most favourable impression possible. Certain facts will be omitted, others will be exaggerated or even invented. Thus selectors need to collect pertinent information and to make discriminating judgements about job candidates. It is not always easy to see beneath the facade of competence and enthusiasm which an applicant may present but it is essential to do so if the organisation is not to end up with employees whose performance is mediocre.

The Costs of Poor Selection

The selection process is the point of access to an organisation and, as such, it is a crucial aspect of Human Resource Management which, if not treated seriously, can prove costly to the organisation. When an *unsuitable* candidate is appointed to a job the organisation not only incurs the immediate direct cost of poor performance but various indirect costs as well. For example, the employee may need further training, or the motivation of this person's colleagues might suffer if they have to undertake increased work loads. Conflict between employees and increased absenteeism can ensue and eventually an unsuitable candidate might have to be transferred or even dismissed with all the additional costs of finding a replacement. The following description of a selection procedure concentrates mainly upon conceptual and procedural issues but it assumes that the whole selection process is guided by the human resource management policies and strategies of the organisation.

A Comprehensive Selection Procedure

The typical definition of selection – finding the right person to fill the right job – emphasises the aim or objective of this activity but does not give any indication of the processes by which it is achieved. Yet without an understanding of the essential tasks entailed it is not possible to develop flexible selection procedures. Instead people will tend either to trivialise the importance of certain activities or to adhere slavishly and blindly to unnecessary practices, often with mediocre results, when more simple and efficient procedures might be available.

The crucial tasks in personnel selection are to accurately *predict* the future job performance of applicants on the basis of matching information about them (e.g. past work record, education, personal characteristics, etc.) against the known requirements for particular jobs and then to *decide* which applicants are most suitable for these jobs. Thus selection is a probabilistic process and errors are always likely as there often is not sufficient information about applicants for making sure predictions and the decisions of selectors are frequently subject to bias. In order to minimise errors when matching applicants with job vacancies two things are required: an accurate and detailed model of the kind of person(s) being sought, known as a person specification, and pertinent, reliable information about applicants, collected through such means as application forms, references and interviews. If these are not available to selectors there is little chance that a selection procedure will be effective, no matter how complicated or sophisticated it might appear to be.

There are two common approaches to matching people and jobs, similar in many ways but with quite different emphases. *Selection* adopts a job-centred approach: it starts by defining the essential activities of a job, from this the requirements (experience, personal characteristics, etc.) a person must have are then determined and people are selected according to how closely they match these requirements. *Placement* utilises a person-centred approach to filling job vacancies. It involves hiring people on the basis of their 'general suitability' for joining the organisation rather than for a specific job. New employees typically undergo a period of training during which time the most appropriate job is identified for each one in the light of his or her particular attributes. This approach is frequently used when selecting school leavers or graduates who have little if any previous job experience.

A third approach to matching people and jobs is used when there are relatively few, if any, qualified people available to fill the vacancies. In this case people (who are considered to be suitable candidates for the jobs) are first *trained* to do the job. Those who are successful in training then form the pool from which people will be selected as required. Two notable examples of this approach are the selection of astronauts by NASA and the identification of deep-sea divers for oil exploration work in the North Sea.

PHASES	**ACTIVITIES**

DEVELOPING A PERSON SPECIFICATION

Job analysis: conduct a systematic analysis of a job to identify the specific tasks it entails and how they should be performed.

Job description: write a full and accurate statement of what a job entails using a job analysis, indicating the activities/responsibilities of any incumbent and expected standards of performance.

Person specification: using the job description, develop a statement of the 'requirements' (e.g. education, experience, personal characteristics) any applicant must possess in order to do the job to the expected standards.

RECRUITMENT

Advertise the job in an attractive manner through the appropriate media providing sufficient information to attract suitable applicants and to deter unsuitable ones.

Application form: design a form to be completed by applicants which will provide the essential biographical and other data needed to determine their suitability, distribute copies to applicants with additional information about the job.

SCREENING

Use the 'topping and tailing' method to eliminate from further consideration applicants who lack appropriate qualifications, or who are too highly qualified, based upon data from application forms and perhaps references, psychological tests etc. The screening process may be extended over several stages, eliminating further applicants at each stage. Draw up a short list.

Test applicants using valid and reliable psychological tests known to predict 'requirements' in the person specification. (These tests may be used to aid initial screening).

References: obtain 'structured' references from referees on the suitability of applicants for the job. (Could be obtained for initial screening or after the interview).

SELECTION

Interview applicants on short-list to: check and clarify information already collected; obtain additional information from face-to-face encounter; answer questions; influence applicants (possibly) by persuading them of their suitability or otherwise for the job.

Decide which applicant(s), if any, is (are) suitable by matching information obtained from the application form, tests etc., with the requirements of the person specification, looking in particular for evidence of both the *capacity* and *willingness* to work to the required standards. The 'objective' information (e.g. educational qualifications, past work record) should be given the greatest weight when making the decision.

INDUCTION AND TRAINING

Induction: arrange an appropriate welcome and familiarisation with the organisation for all new employees.

Training: the systematic management of the work activities of new employees, when necessary, so that the information, attitudes, technical skills and other essential behaviours needed to perform their jobs effectively are acquired.

Figure 3.1: Phases and Activities in a Comprehensive Selection Procedure

46

For the sake of simplicity the following discussion will concentrate upon selection rather than placement although many activities are common to both approaches. The usual phases included in a comprehensive procedure are listed in Figure 3.1 together with the main activities associated with each phase. The exact position of certain activities (e.g. psychological testing) in the overall procedure can vary, as indicated by the broken lines (- - - -) and the number and scope of phases in a selection procedure will differ according to the type and level of job involved. The most thorough procedures go beyond making initial selection decisions and are also concerned with sub-sequent training (see Chapter 7) and even later appraisals of job performance (see Chapter 9). Information gained from these later phases can then be used to evaluate the success of selection decisions. Similarly, information from any phase can be used to evaluate the activities involved in the previous phase and to guide decision making in subsequent phases. For instance, information gained during the selection phase can be used to evaluate the recruitment and screening phases and also to guide the development of induction and training programmes. The sequence of phases (➤) and the interchange of information about phases (⟶) are identified by arrows in Figure 3.1. The selection of most employees is a joint activity undertaken by represen-tatives of line management and Personnel. Some indication is given below of their respective roles during each phase of a selection procedure although their exact roles will vary from one organisation to another.

The Conceptual Phase: Developing a Person Specification

A crucial part of any selection procedure is the initial conceptual phase of determining the nature of a particular job, the kind of person most suitable for it and how that person can be recognised. This work is frequently skimped, perhaps because the information seems too 'obvious', but failure to do it adequately may mean that the remaining phases are pointless no matter how carefully conducted. The activities entailed in this conceptual phase are detailed below.[4] They may appear easy to do; in practice, however, they can be quite difficult. It is for this reason that they are usually made the respon-sibility of someone in the Personnel Department who has had specific training in this field. The advantages of training are normally offset, however, by ignorance of what the job entails. Such information is best supplied by a successful incumbent of the job or by his or her supervisor. Thus if the con-ceptual phase is to be performed adequately it normally requires close coop-eration between Personnel and line management in order to end up with a useful person specification for a job.

Job analysis is any systematic procedure designed to provide information about the specific tasks involved in doing a particular job and how these tasks should be performed. There are many ways this information can be obtained. For example, employees can be observed doing the job, or they might be interviewed and asked to describe what the job entails. Sometimes employees are required to keep a diary so that the range and frequency of the different things they do can be identified.

A number of standardised techniques of job analysis exist which can in theory be used to describe most jobs. These tend to be useful only for lower level jobs, however, and less formalised approaches are generally necessary to capture the significant aspects of many managerial jobs. A reason for this is because managers' jobs are less determined by specific technical skills and require people to possess various interpersonal skills as well. Whereas there is normally one correct or ideal way for performing a technical activity, interpersonal activities such as motivating subordinates, conducting interviews and running meetings can be performed in a variety of ways with similar success. Thus to analyse many managerial jobs methods of identifying the *more successful ways of performing* tasks, particularly interpersonal ones, are required. A technique which lends itself to this approach is the *Critical Incident* technique which can, in fact, be used for analysing any kind of job. The aim is to identify specific behaviours that are particularly important (i.e. critical) to the successful performance of a job, rather than to simply identify the tasks involved. The merits of this approach are that it tends to ignore the more trivial details of jobs and, by concentrating upon 'behaviours' rather than tasks, it provides a better idea of the kind of person best suited to the job. In practice, a sound strategy for conducting a job analysis would be to employ a variety of approaches and to collect information from a number of sources in order to obtain a comprehensive picture of that job.

Job Description and Standards of Job Performance

Once a job analysis has been completed it should be written up in the form of a job description which is a full, accurate and precise statement of what performance entails for a particular job. The job description should define the overall purpose of the job and list the specific activities required of any incumbent. As it is often less easy to list the specific activities of a managerial job than one on the shop floor, descriptions of the former frequently emphasise the *responsibilities* instead of the activities of the incumbent.

It is also important to identify the *standards of performance* expected of a person for each activity listed in a job description as standards might vary depending upon the importance of a particular activity to that job. For instance, while a technical draughtsman will be expected to achieve very high standards for drawings, less will normally be expected in terms of interpersonal and administrative skills; whereas in the case of his manager the reverse might be true. These standards are the *criteria* which provide the focus for predictions and selectors have to decide whether an applicant will meet these standards if appointed to the job.

Person Specification

A person specification is a statement of the 'requirements' (e.g. experience, education, skills, personal characteristics) a person needs to possess if he or she is to achieve the standards set for the activities/responsibilities listed in the job description. Inferring what these requirements should be from a job description is by no means an easy task for some jobs. Once again this process tends to be easier for lower level jobs where technical skills are paramount than for managerial jobs where interpersonal skills are also important. Thus it is easier to determine the requirements for a lathe operator than to say what they should be for a marketing manager.

A number of writers have suggested ways of structuring the items in a person specification under set headings. Two well known approaches, the seven-point plan of Alec Rodger and the five-point plan of J. Munro Fraser are summarised in Table 3.[5] Such plans should be viewed as useful tools for directing thinking and not as rigid frameworks. It is important to guard against the assumption that there is one 'ideal type' of candidate suitable for a job, whose requirements can be detailed exhaustively, when this stereotype has not been and perhaps cannot be validated. It is usually true that a range of candidates would prove suitable for a job as long as each possesses certain critical requirements and does not possess other important but unacceptable characteristics.

A problem of approaches similar to those above is that they do not indicate the *relative importance* of the different requirements. Thus an alternative way of organising a person specification is to group the requirements into essentials, desirables, undesirables or disqualifiers. *Essentials* represent critical requirements a person must possess and there are usually few of these; *desirables* refer to experiences, attainments, personal characteristics, etc. known to *aid* learning or job performance; *undesirables* include experiences or attributes known to cause difficulty to other people on the job (e.g. someone

The Seven-Point Plan (A. RODGER)	The Five-Fold Grading System (J. MUNRO FRASER)
1. **Physical make-up:** health, physique, appearance, bearing and speech	1. **Impact upon others:** physical make-up, appearance, speech and manner
2. **Attainments:** education, training, qualifications, experience	2. **Acquired qualifications:** general education, vocational training, work experience, qualifications
3. **General intelligence:** fundamental intellectual capacity	
	3. **Innate abilities:** general intelligence, natural quickness of comprehension and aptitude for learning
4. **Special aptitudes:** mechanical, manual dexterity, facility in the use of words or figures, talent for drawing, music	
	4. **Motivation:** the kinds of goals set by an individual, his consistency and determination in following them up, his success in achieving them
5. **Interests:** intellectual, practical-constructional, physically-active, social, artistic	
6. **Disposition:** acceptability, influence over others, steadiness, dependability, self-reliance	5. **Adjustment:** emotional stability, ability to stand up to stress and ability to get on with people
7. **Circumstances:** domestic circumstances, age, mobility	

Table 3: Two Plans for Organising the Items in a Person Specification

who smokes) but must not be illegal (e.g. racial characteristics); *disqualifiers* represent experiences or attributes known to be directly related to failure at a job (e.g. certain medical conditions). Of course it is possible to combine both approaches as illustrated in Figure 3.2. This specification is a summary of one produced for the secretary to the chairman of a medical products company which has dealings with overseas clients.

Note: the terms 'job specification' and 'person specification' are inter-changeable. The former is possibly used more frequently than the latter but is, to my mind, misleading as it implies requirements of a job rather than of the person doing that job.

Predictors

A question which has to be answered at this early stage is how selectors will recognise suitable candidates for particular jobs. If the person specification requires someone who can work in difficult circumstances (e.g. long and unpredictable hours), ways of identifying such a person must be established. What is required are sources of information, known as *predictors*, which will indicate whether an applicant possesses the requirements detailed in the person specification. Bearing in mind the tendency of applicants to 'manage' the information they present about themselves it is necessary to look for predictors which will provide reliable evidence of whether an applicant both can (i.e. has the *ability* to) and will (i.e. be *motivated* to) do the job to the required standards.

A well recognised principle in selection is that 'past performance predicts future performance', thus predictors should be used which provide evidence of what a person has done and achieved in previous jobs. In the case of school leavers and graduates with little or no previous job experience, it is important to examine their educational and social experience for evidence of the ability (or potential) and motivation necessary for a job. The traditional predictors used in selection procedures are references, application forms/biographical data, interviews, psychological tests and samples of work performance. All, or most, of these predictors are used routinely within many selection pro-cedures. Each should only be used, however, if it provides specific, reliable information regarding the suitability of an applicant for the job. The final activity of the conceptual phase is to determine which predictors will be employed in the screening and selection phases.

PERSON SPECIFICATION		

Job Title:	SECRETARY TO CHAIRMAN	Job. Des. No.

Requirements: (Disqualifier = Dis; Essential = E; Desirable = D; Undesirable = Un) ⟶

PHYSICAL: health, physique, appearance	good physical health, no recurring illnesses pleasant, neat appearance strong regional accent smoker	E E Un Dis
EDUCATION/ QUALIFICATIONS educational and vocational attainments; general abilities; skills and intelligence	shorthand: 80 w.p.m. minimum typing: RSA II minimum at least 'O' level English or equivalent medical shorthand	E E E D
SPECIFIC APTITUDES/ SKILLS verbal, numerical, clerical, mechanical, conceptual, ability to learn/develop	able to produce high quality work when meeting tight deadlines reliable, accurate memory knowledge of medical terminology capable of developing appropriate filing systems good word processing skills	E D D E D
EXPERIENCE: duration, range etc.	wide experience of office practices minimum five years office experience experience of operating as a P.A. experience of dealing with overseas customers etc.	E D D D
ADJUSTMENT/ SOCIAL SKILLS: emotional stability; personal and interpersonal qualities/skills	shows initiative and self reliance able to deal with a wide range of people in a tactful and sensitive manner able to manage 'crises' without becoming disturbed does not require a high level of social contact with other employees	E E D D
MOTIVATION: kind of motivation required for job; nature of rewards it offers	places importance on achieving high standards of accuracy and presentation has a commitment to high ethical standards satisfied to work within this role without looking for career advancement	 E E D
CIRCUMSTANCES: age, mobility, location, domestic factors	possesses driving licence and willing to use own car during office hours when necessary able to work normal office hours without interference of domestic commitments probably in the age range 35-50	 E E D

Figure 3.2: Example of a Person Specification Form

Recruitment Phase

Recruitment is the process of attracting suitable candidates to apply for the jobs available. It involves deciding upon the most appropriate sources of candidates to approach and the best ways of approaching them.

Sources

The main sources of applicants for jobs fall into two categories, those internal to the organisation including employees looking for 'sideways' appointments as well as those aiming for promotion, and sources external to the organisation. The latter category includes government employment agencies (Job Centres, Professional Executive Register) and private agencies such as secretarial bureaux, schools, colleges and universities, groups contacted by direct advertising such as through trade magazines and journals, and finally private contacts.

The advantage of using internal sources for appointments are obvious as an internal applicant is generally well known to the organisation and the costs of advertising, recruitment and training are much reduced. The disadvantages of internal appointments include the failure to inject 'new blood' into the organisation and the possibility of causing friction between existing staff, several of whom may be applicants for the same job. The merits and de-merits of external appointments tend to be the reverse of those for internal appointments.

Attracting Applicants

The primary means of drawing the attention of candidates to jobs and persuading them to apply is through well prepared advertisements placed in local or national newspapers and trade and professional journals. Determining the content, layout and presentation of advertisements is a skilled job which organisations may sub-contract to a professional agency rather than run the risk of producing copy which either does not attract applicants to read it or fails to stimulate them to make enquiries about the job(s).

When individuals follow-up advertisements and enquire about jobs their interest needs to be maintained and even increased. This can be achieved in several ways. The usual method is to send out additional details about the job and perhaps an attractive brochure describing the organisation, together with an application form. Some organisations also provide a contact person within

53

the organisation who can talk to enquirers in a knowledgeable way about the job.

The processes of recruitment and screening are sometimes best undertaken by external agencies. When an organisation has a small Personnel Department and/or lacks any individuals with real expertise in selection methods and/or is heavily overworked it can be cost-effective to employ recruitment consultants, particularly if they specialise in certain sectors of the labour market (e.g. computing, finance, electronics). Certain consultants, known as 'head hunters', may also be employed by organisations when there is only a limited number of suitable people for a specific job (usually a very senior appointment). These people are probably already well established in another organisation and it will require direct and discreet contact with them to establish their possible interest in a new appointment.

The time, effort and costs entailed in the recruitment phase of a selection procedure will vary, as with all other phases, according to the number, level and type of vacancies which have to be filled. Most activities in this and indeed the screening phase will be undertaken by personnel specialists who will probably want to consult line management about the best sources for obtaining applications and for information regarding trade or professional journals.

Screening Phase

Many people who apply for jobs are simply not suitable and the numbers of applicants frequently exceeds the vacancies available so that it is necessary for selectors to 'screen' all applications. *Screening* is the process by which candidates are eliminated from further consideration because they do not possess the essential requirements for the job, or because they possess certain disqualifiers. Thus the purpose of screening can be described as *eliminating failure*.

The predictor used most frequently in screening is the application form but references, scores on psychological tests and a preliminary interview might also be used. (See Figure 3.1). It is often possible to screen out the majority of applicants simply by checking whether they fulfil the basic age and educational/technical requirements for a job, or achieve a particular score on a psychological test. Other applicants will be eliminated after more careful inspection of their application forms, perhaps because their prior job experience is inadequate or unsuitable. For more senior appointments the screening phase will often be divided into several sub-phases spread over a period of time (returning the application form, completing a psychological test, attending an initial interview). Different applicants will be rejected at each sub-phase if they fail to meet the relevant criteria.

A form of screening, often forgotten, yet which is important for all jobs and even mandatory for some is *health screening*. The purpose of such screening is to ensure that employees are fit to do particular jobs and that the jobs will not adversely affect their health. It is also to preclude people from certain jobs where their health problems could, for example, be hazardous to the manufacturing process (e.g. in the food or medical products industries). Screening is often restricted to problems of physical health although it is of more prognostic value to also assess psychological health.[6]

The end product of a screening process should be short-list of candidates *all* of whom appear to be reasonably suitable for the job and who will proceed to the selection phase.

Selection Phase

Selection was described earlier as a process of predicting the future job performance of applicants on the basis of *matching* information about them with the requirements in a person specification, requirements which are believed to be related to successful performance of the job. Thus, whereas screening can be defined as the process of *eliminating failure*, matching might be described as *identifying success*. That is, the qualifications of those applicants who are not eliminated during screening are matched with the requirements of the person specification in order to find the 'best fit', as this person is the one who is likely to be most successful at the job. Screening and matching are not just different ways of describing the same activity, however, because the attributes of a person which might predict failure at a job are not necessarily useful for predicting success. For example, high anxiety-proneness and low intelligence will be good predictors of failure for many jobs, but low anxiety-proneness and high intelligence will not necessarily predict success. This is because there is not a linear relationship between scores for these attributes and success or failure at a job. Thus screening and matching are complementary processes in a selection procedure.

Of all the devices available to selectors the interview is the primary and often the sole predictor used (in conjunction with an application form) during the selection phase.[7] As it involves the only face-to-face encounter between applicants and selectors it is probably best used after data from all other predictors have been collected so that they will be available for checking and further exploration during the interview. Therefore the value of several other predictors will be considered first.

Application Forms and Biodata

Application forms can be particularly vaulable sources of information to selectors for two reasons. First, they (should) document an applicant's prior record in terms of educational qualifications, work history and other experience which is relevant to the job in question and as 'past performance tends to predict future performance' these data are very pertinent to decision making in the screening and selection phases. Second, because of its standardised format, an application form provides *comparable* data for all applicants thus simplifying the decision making process. Applicants who submit a *curriculum vitae* (C.V.) should also be encouraged to complete an application form as they might omit from the C.V. (knowlingly or otherwise) certain information which is important for predictive and comparative purposes.

The potential value of an application form can be lost, however, if it is poorly designed. Forms which look unattractive, are complicated, difficult to complete and unnecessarily intrusive about an applicant's personal life can deter individuals who would be suitable for the job from applying. A well designed form can encourage people to apply by providing a clear and sensible format to help them structure their answers. It should collect information which is relevant for predictive and comparative purposes and, as far as possible, avoid questions which will prove offensive to applicants.

A problem selectors often experience with application forms is knowing how to assess the sheer volume of data they contain. At the initial screening stage it is important to check whether candidates meet the essential, objective requirements for the job as detailed in the person specification (e.g. educational qualifications, technical skills). The majority of candidates can usually be rejected after such a check. Next, it is useful to examine a candidate's prior record for *discontinuities, trends* and *explanations*. Discontinuities refer to unexplained gaps in a candidate's educational or job history, often indicated by dates which are not perfectly consecutive, and which might need to be explored during an interview. Trends are particularly important to identify; for example, do frequent job changes represent career progression or simply career change, is there evidence of early achievement in a job followed by steady decline, or vice versa? Any consistency in trends should be a good predictor of future behaviour. A well designed application form will ask applicants to outine why they changed jobs or how their prior experience is relevant to the job for which they are applying. Explanations given can often provide useful insights into a candidate's beliefs and goals.

The use of biographical facts (biodata) about job applicants (e.g. age, qualifications) which have demonstrable validity in predicting work performance for particular jobs has grown recently.[8] The importance of such predictors, if valid ones can be found, is that they considerably simplify the decision making process. When used alone, however, biodata have limitations: they are probably only suitable for relatively low level jobs, certain vaild predictors (e.g. sex/marital status) are not legally acceptable and many biographical items only retain their predictive validity for short periods of time.

References

It is probably most useful to take up references prior to interviewing applicants as the references can then be considered at the interview stage. Unfortunately, this is not always possible as some applicants are reluctant to let their employers know that they are applying for another job. Thus an organisation might take up references only after interviews have been conducted, in effect to confirm or refute tentative selection decisions. To avoid such problems as breach of confidentiality it is important to obtain the permission of candidates to take up references at a specified point in time.

References are one of the most controversial sources of data about applicants and are seen by some as little more than worthless pieces of paper. This is because references tend to convey 'selected opinions' of referees rather than wide ranging factual data about applicants. In part this problem originates with the selectors who often fail to provide adequate guidance to referees concerning the information required. A referee who is the current or past employer of an applicant is, potentially, one of the most valuable sources of information about that applicant. He or she can be properly 'exploited' by being asked to complete a structured reference – essentially a series of questions – which requests primarily factual information about the applicant's performance, successes and problems, and future potential. It is useful to collect at least two references in case there are conflicts of data and opinion. References are sometimes very revealing through the information they omit, therefore it is often useful to follow up references with a telephone call to a referee who will almost certainly provide more detailed and accurate information verbally than in written form.

Psychological tests and inventories are standardised instruments designed to measure individual differences in some aspect of human knowledge, attitudes, interests, personality traits or skills. They can take the form of written, verbal or perofrmance tasks and be completed under time restrictions or without consideration for time. The best known of these instruments are probably intelligence tests and personality inventories. The use of the words 'test' and 'inventory' is not arbitrary: a psychological test is one for which individual questions have right or wrong answers, whereas answers to the items of an inventory simply reflect differences in individual preferences, habits and beliefs and there are no right or wrong answers.

There are literally thousands of tests and inventories and it is easy for an untrained person to be rather gullible about their value. Many of these instruments are acutally of little use because they do not possess the characteristics of a 'worthwhile' test or inventory. A worthwhile psychological test or inventory should be both a *valid* and *reliable* instrument. The former term is difficult to define but, technically speaking, it is a measure of the strength of relationship between a test/inventory score and whatever that score purports to assess (determined using statistical tests of correlation, the stronger the correlation the more valid is the test). In other words, validity is concerned with *how well* a test measures what it purports to measure. In a selection context it is the *predictive validity* of an instrument which is particularly important. When a test has high predictive validity differences in test scores can be used to accurately predict differences in the *future* job behaviour of applicants. Reliability refers to the consistency of the results obtained from testing (again assessed using measures of correlation). A test is reliable when individuals obtain similar scores upon repeated completion of the same test over a period of time, or for equivalent versions of a test.

For a test or inventory to be of use it is also essential that normative data exist which indicate the average score achieved by individuals from a specific group (males, females, graduates, engineers, doctors etc.) and some measure of the distribution of scores for each group. For example, the standard deviation is a well-known statistic which is easy to calculate and from which it is possible to determine the range of scores within which 67%, 95% or 99.9% of a specific group fall. The significance of a person's score can only be assessed in the light of such data which will relate the performance of that individual to the performance of others. Finally, it is also crucial that whatever a test or inventory measures, it is *relevant* to predicting the future job performance of an applicant. It is a waste of time and money to collect information if it does not have predictive value for selection purposes.

Broadly speaking, psychological measurement devices fall into three categories: achievement tests, ability and aptitude tests and personality and interest inventories. Research to date has demonstrated that tests tend to have moderate to good predictive validities whereas inventories tend to have low predictive validities when used in a selection context.[9]

Achievement Tests. These tests assess a person's level of achievement in some specific area. They might be concerned primarily with assessing knowledge (e.g. university examination) or skills (e.g. driving) or both. Educational and professional examinations and tests to assess the results of industrial and occupational training fall into this category. The results of such tests are frequently used as predictors in selection procedures.

Ability and Aptitude Tests. Tests of aptitude are concerned with assessing whether a person has the capacity (potential) to acquire particular skills. In order to determine aptitude individuals are usually given tests of fundamental abilities which are believed to be essential prerequisites of the capacity to acquire skills. As these so-called fundamental abilities are themselves partly products of prior learning, the distinctions between achievement and aptitude tests and between ability and capacity are at times more apparent than real.

Tests of general intelligence are the most well known tests of mental ability, but tests of more specific abilities such as verbal and numerical skills, perceptual abilities (tests of vision and hearing) and psychomotor skills (eye-hand coordination) also exist. Most of these tests are relatively easy to administer and personnel specialists can be trained to use them in a relatively short period of time. They can be useful predictors, particularly when a job applicant lacks a prior work history.

Personality and Interest Inventories. These instruments hold a particular fascination for some individuals who feel that through such inventories they will learn 'deep' things about themselves or others. Generally, the view is inaccurate and derives from a misapprehension about the nature of personality inventories. Two points are important to remember about inventories. First, inventories tend to be 'transparent' in that it is often easy to infer the purpose of a question thus making it possible for people to distort their answers in order to create more favourable images of themselves than are actually true. Few people, for example, will honestly admit how prone to anxiety they are in social situations. Second, inventories tend to have low predictive validities in a selection context, a fact which partly reflects the transparency of these instruments and partly demonstrates that personality traits, such as 'dominance' and 'extroversion' are less important in determining job performance than are specific abilities such as problem-solving skills.

Although psychological tests and inventories may not be particularly useful as selection devices for many jobs, they can be valuable screening devices identifying candidates who fail to meet certain criteria which are considered 'essential' in the person specification, or who possess 'disqualifiers'. Reputable tests and inventories are normally available only from a limited number of sources (e.g. National Foundation for Educational Research) and to appropriately qualified and trained users.

Work Samples

The foregoing predictors do not sample directly actual behaviours which will be required for successful job performance, instead they provide 'signs' of what a person can do.[10] Thus correspondence between the predictor (e.g. psychological test) and the criterion (job behaviour) is limited. A work sample is a specimen of some aspect of an applicant's work behaviour which is relevant to the job for which he or she is applying so that the correspondence between predictor and criterion is close and its predictive validity is usually higher than that for a 'sign'.

A work sample can be obtained in two ways. The first is to utilise existing samples of an applicant's work. For instance, academics might provide copies of recent publications and graphic artists or photographers could supply their current portfolios. As long as such samples are pertinent to the job for which a person is applying they can be immensely valuable predictors. One important limitation of an *existing* work sample, however, is that it is not always clear who produced it. It is necessary to clarify, for example, whether an academic actually made a substantive contribution to an article or simply 'polished' the original manuscript supplied by an assistant. Another limitation of (almost any) work samples is that they indicate what a person can do (i.e. *ability*) but not what the person will do (i.e. *motivation*) if appointed to the job.

The second form of work sample is one an applicant is required to produce during the selection process. For instance, a typist might be required to re-type a corrected draft of a letter and a heavy goods vehicle driver required to complete a series of manoeuvres with an articulated vehicle. For these kind of tests it is important that there are standardised ways of scoring performance and appropriate norms for experienced and inexperienced workers. A com-

60

plication with this form of work sample is that some applicants might become apprehensive of being evaluated and consequently obtain atypically poor results, nevertheless, work samples tend to have good predictive validity.

It is more difficult to create realistic work sample tasks for many managerial jobs, assessing the complex sequences of behaviour entailed in decision making, chairing committees and managing other people. Various exercises have been created for this purpose, however, including in-basket decision making exercises, different types of group discussion or group problem solving, self-presentation tasks and so on. These exercises tend to have lower validities when predicting future job performance than work samples involving psychomotor tasks such as typing and driving.

The Interview

The interview is the most widely used of all selection devices and is also one of the most controversial. It represents the only protracted face-to-face encounter between an applicant and the selector(s) and it has three main purposes. First, to check data already obtained about an applicant through references, the application form, and so on.

Second, to allow selectors to utilise the unique information they gain from a face-to-face encounter (in combination with that obtained through other predictors) to draw valid inferences about the suitability of applicants. Third, it provides an opportunity for the selector(s) to influence directly an applicant's choices. The interview is an opportunity to not only question applicants but also to discuss the job and the organisation. Good applicants may receive job offers from several organisations and the impression they form of an organisation during the interview can be an important determinant of their final job choice.

The interview is also the time when line management take a crucial role in the selection process as it is they who will make the final selection decision for their departments. Here a difficulty arises. Interviewing is a skill (actually a higher-order skill embracing a number of component skills) which can only be developed through training and practice, yet line management (and sometimes members of the Personnel Department) have often had little if any training at interviewing or opportunities to practise what skills they have. Thus even a well designed and conducted selection procedure can founder at this crucial stage if the interviewing and subsequent decision making are handled poorly.

61

Research into interviewing has revealed that the judgements of untrained interviewers frequently differ for the same interviewee and generally have low predictive validity. This is because the typical faults of untrained (and otherwise poor) interviewers include failing to prepare adequately and not structuring interviews in a sensible and consistent manner, failing to obtain appropriate information from interviewees and drawing biased inferences about interviewees, thus leading to poor selection decisions.[11] Each of these problems is examined briefly below.

Preparation and Planning. A common mistake of experienced interviewers is to assume that their skills are sufficient for them to get by with little or no preparation. Yet preparation is crucial. It begins with a statement of the objective of the interview: to determine whether any of the short-listed app- licants is capable and willing to perform the job to the required standards. The person specification provides the 'model' for each applicant and it is import- ant at this stage to decide what information it is necessary to collect in order to determine how well applicants fulfil the person specification. Certain information from the application form or references might also need further clarification. To aid preparation it can be useful to develop an interview form with the items from the person specification listed in one column and a summary of the information known about the applicants with respect to each item in adjacent columns. In this way the 'missing' or ambiguous information for each applicant becomes obvious. Specific questions can then be prepared, unique to an applicant, which need to be asked along with the more general questions asked of all applicants. The purpose of developing a structure is to ensure some standardisation of the interview, that specific topics dictated by the person specification are covered and adequate time is given so that app- licants can ask questions about the job and the organisation.

During the opening phase of the interview it is crucial to establish a good rapport, helping applicants to feel at ease and encouraging them to participate fully in the interview. There is no single way to do this but a friendly approach, attentiveness to the comments of interviewees and providing them with an opportunity to talk about a simple straightforward issue early on, will help considerably. The middle phase of the interview is devoted to the careful questioning of applicants (see below) and it is important to be flexible here ensuring that topics are covered but not necessarily in any fixed order. It is also important that interviewees are given the opportunity to ask questions and to express points of view without letting them dominate the interview to such an extent that the selectors fail to collect the information they need. Before closing the interview, the interviewer(s) should check that all the important questions have been covered and give the interviewees an idea of how and when they will learn the outcome of the selection process.

Collecting Information. Information about applicants is collected through observing them and through asking them questions. Much has been written in recent years about what can be learned from an interviewee's posture, gestures and dress. The average interviewer, however, cannot reliably interpret most of these aspects of an interviewee's behaviour. Nevertheless, it is usually easy to identify nervous candidates and those with little poise in the interview, who are often easily embarrassed by straightforward questions.

The bulk of information is collected through the careful questioning of applicants and *listening* to their answers. The emphasis on listening is vital as the questions asked of an applicant should not simply reflect the topics on the interviewer's *pro-forma* but also be contingent upon the applicant's answers. This is only possible through careful listening.

The essence of effective data gathering during an interview is skilful questioning.[12] Three of the most useful question types which need to be used are *open* questions, *probing* questions and *closed* questions. Open questions take the form "Tell me about . . . ", "How do you feel about . . . ?". They encourage the interviewee to talk because the questions cannot be answered properly with a "Yes" or "No" type response. If the interviewer simply sits quietly after posing the question, or prompts a brief reply with a "Please go on . . .", "Tell me more about . . . ", interviewees speak readily if they have anything to say. The probing question is often the least used of these three question types. It takes the form "Please elaborate upon . . . ", "Tell me exactly what happened . . . ", and it is intended to focus the interviewee upon a specific aspect of an answer he or she has given and to elaborate upon that answer. It is the probing question which frequently distinguishes the ignorant from the knowledgeable, the charlatan from the genuinely competent applicant. Closed questions are those which require simple, frequently one word answers. They take the form "How old are you?", "When did you graduate?", and are ideal for checking facts and for collecting precise information about specific issues. Interviewers can stifle an interview, however, if closed questions are used repeatedly. Such questions can be very effective when used in conjunction with open and probing questions. Open questions get interviewees to talk, often in general terms; probing questions focus their answers on particular issues; closed questions dot the 'i's' and cross the 't's'.

Two other important question types are comparisons and hypotheticals. *Comparisons* take the form "What are the relative merits of A and B?", "Would you prefer X or Y?" and, as long as the 'pairs' are realistic, such questions can expose the beliefs, values and goals of applicants. A *hypothetical* question, such as "What would you do if . . . ?", requires applicants to think about a new topic or situation and can be useful for revealing knowledge, beliefs and probably reactions, but only if the question is realistic and framed within the experience of the applicant.

The kind of questions to be avoided are *leading* and *multiple* questions. The former are phased as follows: "You do agree that . . . ?", "You would be willing to . . . wouldn't you?". Such questions suggest to the interviewee what the interviewer wishes to hear and many interviewees will simply agree with the implied answer although their private view might be different. Multiple questions, "How did you find your time at university and what did you do . . . perhaps you would also mention . . . ?", should be avoided becuase they can be confusing and a thoughtful interviewee will simply answer the question he or she prefers so that a critical question could be overlooked.

It is important to focus questioning upon the past experience and behaviour of an applicant, not simply upon his or her views, as a person's reaction patterns provide some of the most reliable predictive information about him or her. For example, a researcher might be asked to "Tell me about the most difficult phase of the project", "Please describe how you handled the problems" and so on. An interview has been described as "a conversation with a purpose". This could be misleading because in normal everyday conversation comments and questions are often deployed simply for the purpose of developing and reinforcing social relationships, whereas within an interview they are used to make the interviewee think and provide detailed statements about specific topics. These two forms of skill are not substitutable, which is why "good conversationalists" are often poor interviewers. Questioning skills are not easy to develop and it requires considerable practice for them to be used effectively.

Interviewer Biases. Whereas an interviewer's questioning skills determine the quality of the information obtained during an interview, it is the interviewer's *judgements* about that information which determine the quality of the final selection decisions. Bias in the inferences and judgements of interviewers is one of the main reasons why the interview can have poor predictive validity.

There are several well recognised judgemental errors which interviewers often make.[13] One is to stereotype interviewees, that is to inappropriately assign to each a 'character' which is thought (wrongly) to describe members of a group (social, ethnic, religious, political) to which that person belongs. If that 'character' does not approximate closely to the person specification for the job then the applicant is deemed unsuitable. Another common error has been described as the 'halo effect'. This occurs when an interviewer judges a characteristic of an interviewee very favourably and then generalises that judgement to the person as a whole ("If he was in the Guards he must be suitable for the job"). The 'horns effect' reflects the opposite kind of judgement ("I don't think she can handle this job as she does become rather emotional at times"). 'Contrast effects' also influence judgements when several applicants are interviewed in sequence. In this case an interviewer tends to see an 'average' interviewee as being better or worse than he or she really is when the interviewee has been preceded by a series of poor or good applicants. Many judgemental errors exist and the problem for an interviewer is that these errors are often so deeply embedded in his or her thinking that it is difficult to recognise them. This is why formal interview training can be particularly helpful as it should provide a person with useful feedback about such errors.

Some Additional Points. When interviews are criticised as selection devices it is actually a sloppy way of saying that *interviewers* fail to prepare, structure and conduct interviews and make selection decisions in a skilful and objective manner. Once interviewers develop and utilise such skills the interview can become an effective selection device.[14]

As noted earlier, it is sometimes true that line management lack the training and experience to be consistent and effective interviewers. One practice which can help combat this problem is that of conducting *panel* interviews. A panel interview will normally involve three or four interviewers, including one or two from the Personnel Department and one or two from line management. The advantage of such an arrangement is that it allows the interviewing load to be shared, each interviewer discussing with interviewees those subjects about which he or she has most expertise. It also permits the interviewers to check for judgemental biases by sharing their impressions with each other before reaching a final decision.

Board interviews are a particular form of panel interview which are often less satisfactory than one-to-one panel interviews. A Board is often large and composed of people who represent various parties interested in the selection decision but not affected by it. With many interviewers, each can ask only one or two questions so that topics are not explored in any depth or in a coordinated manner and judgements of applicants are necessarily superficial based upon obvious characteristics (e.g. poise, articulateness), rather than upon more important determinants of work performance and past work histories.

Assessment Centres

Assessment Centres refer to procedures for determining a person's suitability for appointment or promotion, not to places! These procedures assess many different attributes/behaviours of a job candidate utilising a variety of predictors and a number of assessors. The aim is to be more comprehensive, more job-related (using work samples and signs) and more objective (consensus of judgements across independent assessors) than is true for traditional methods.[15]

There is a growing use of assessment centres in Britain, particularly by larger organisations. Assessment takes place over a period of days, usually in a residential setting where assessors directly observe individuals working alone or interacting with others in task and social activities. Judgements about the suitability of candidates for jobs have relatively high predictive validities for well designed assessment centres. This improvement is gained, however, at relatively high cost to an organisation in terms of time, personnel and direct expenditure.

The Selection Decision

Some selection decisions are straightforward as one applicant stands out from the rest as being most suitable. It is more usual, however, for there to be several suitable candidates each with slightly different strengths and weaknesses. This often poses a problem for selectors who are unsure about how to weight and combine the different pieces of information into an overall judgement of a candidate. It is crucial at this point to keep the person specification in mind and to distinguish between essential and desirable requirements. Due emphasis should be given to each candidate's past record and to any significant trends in that record. Unless this is done the biases in judgement described above often result in inappropriate criteria being advanced as reasons for selecting or rejecting applicants. It is also the time when deliberate biases, such as 'political' considerations, come to the fore and applicants can be rejected not because they are unsuitable for the job but because their appointment might prove inconvenient for a selector. The value of a panel interview, particularly one comprised of representatives of line management and personnel specialists, is that it is possible for the two functions to bring their separate perspectives to bear upon the final decisions, thus helping to expose and counteract the less deliberate biases in judgement. The end product of the decision making process is usually a rank ordering of candidates according to their suitability for the job. The 'best' candidate is offered the job and one or two others are held in reserve in case the first candidate withdraws. The key processes in a selection procedure which have been described in this section and which result in the final selection decision are summarised in Figure 3.3.

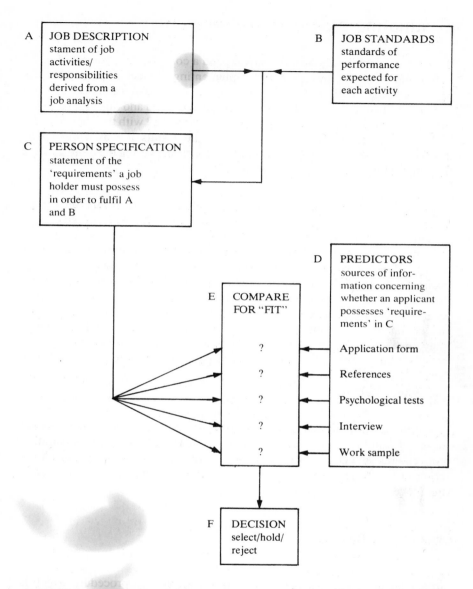

A, B and C are products of the initial conceptual phase of a selection procedure (i.e. developing a person specification). In the subsequent recruitment, screening and selection phases predictive information (D) is collected, compared for 'fit' (E) with the person specification and a decision (F) is made.

Figure 3.3: Key Processes in a Selection Procedure

Evaluating a Selection Procedure

It is not unusual for organisations to expend a considerable amount of time, effort and money in designing and implementing a selection procedure and then not bother to either validate or evaluate it in any systematic way. The terms 'validate' and 'evaluate' are frequently confused and misused so it will help to clarify their meanings. *Validation* is concerned with the question "To what extent has this procedure achieved the results it was designed to achieve?", whereas *evaluation* is concerned with answering the more general but important question "Is this procedure worthwhile?".

There seem to be two main reasons why validation and evaluation are ignored. First, it can be personally threatening for those who design and/or conduct selection procedures to have their efforts assessed. Second, it is extremely difficult to validate and evaluate such procedures because their results often cannot be isolated from the influence of other factors. For example, the obvious criterion to use for validating selection decisions is the future work performance of new employees. Their work performance, however, will not only reflect their ability and motivation at the time they were selected, but also the influence of numerous other factors which come into play once they join the organisation, such as training, the management style of supervisors, changing promotion prospects, etc. Nevertheless, unless a selection procedure is evaluated there is no way of knowing in what ways the procedure might be improved.

The criteria which are typically used to *evaluate* selection procedures include those of validity, reliability, fairness, social acceptability, administrative convenience and cost effectiveness. They are discussed briefly below. Each criterion can be applied to some element (e.g. the interview) or to a phase of the procedure, or to the procedure as a whole.

Validity and Reliability

In a selection context it is the predictive validity of a procedure which is crucial. This entails an assessment of whether the decisions made by selectors result in the appointment of individuals who prove to be competent and motivated employees. If predictive validity is low, an attempt should be made to identify where the invalidity lies. Is it, for instance, because useful predictors are being ignored (e.g. work samples), or are the selectors unable to draw valid conclusions from the data available to them?

It is, of course, crucial that selectors can make predictively valid decisions time and again. In other words, their decision making should be reliable as well as valid. Reliability is a measure of the consistency of decision making. If the quality of the graduate intake into an organisation proved highly variable from year to year it would probably reflect unreliable decision making rather than changes in the quality of the graduates. In order to improve the procedure it would be necessary to identify why decisions proved unreliable. It could be that different people are used as selectors in different years, some being consistently good and others consistently poor in this role.

Fairness

The purpose of a selection procedure is to *discriminate* the good from the poor applicants. It is also a *legal* requirement of any selection procedure that this process is fair. Fairness in this sense means that the procedure should not debar any individual or group of people from being selected on the basis of criteria which are irrelevant to successful job performance. Employment law relevant to selection has been revised considerably in the past two decades (e.g. Sex Discrimination Act, 1975; Race Relations Act, 1976) so that it is now unfair (i.e. illegal) to avoid selecting people to jobs on the basis of their race, skin colour, nationality and ethnic origins, sex and marital status, unless it can be demonstrated that any of these criteria are relevant to job performance. Sex status would be considered valid grounds for discrimination when determining the membership of certain religious orders but would not be accepted normally as a selection criterion for doctors, engineers, nurses or teachers.[16]

At present it is possible to discriminate against job applicants on the basis of their age, religion (except in Northern Ireland), past criminal record and political beliefs without behaving illegally. Such discrimination, however, is viewed by many people as being *unreasonable* (although legal) and is therefore becoming less socially acceptable. Human resource management policies in the field of personnel selection must obviously take account of current legislation and social values. It could prove detrimental in many ways to an organisation if (by accident or design) its selection policies were found to be illegal and/or socially unacceptable.

Social Acceptability and Administrative Convenience

In an effort to improve the validity of a selection procedure it is possible to introduce features which prove counter-productive. An example could be the over-reliance on psychological tests as predictors which might deter potentially good employees from applying for jobs. It could also complicate unnecessarily the administration of the procedure if applicants had to present themselves for several sessions of testing and if the scoring and interpretation of the tests was a time consuming process. Thus it is always useful when designing a selection procedure to consider the likely impact of any aspect of the procedure upon applicants and those responsible for conducting the procedure. Features which are not essential and which are likely to be socially unacceptable or administratively inconvenient ought to be avoided.

Cost-Effectiveness

Many improvements in selection procedures are only achieved through the use of additional resources (time, effort, materials, personnel), all of which incur a financial cost for the organisation. Just as potential improvements in the reliability and validity of selection decisions need to be weighed against the criteria of social acceptability and administrative convenience so potential or actual improvements should also be weighed against the financial costs involved. This is not always an easy calculation to make and requires an estimate of the value to the organisation of any particular appointment. As a general rule, when the predictive validity of decisions is already high, then increased expenditure of time, effort and other resources will only result in marginal improvements and therefore will not be cost-effective. If the predictive validity of decisions is only moderate, however, then it is reasonable to expect that the costs of additional time, effort and so on will be more than offset by the financial benefits which will follow from an improvement in the quality of the selection decisions.

Conclusion

Personnel selection is concerned with locating and recruiting appropriate people to fill particular vacancies as they arise in organisations. It is a crucial aspect of Human Resource Management as it is the point of access to an organisation and poor selection can result in a dearth of employees with appropriate knowledge, experience and skills. Therefore personnel selection should take its direction from the established policies and objectives for managing human resources within an organisation.

Selection procedures can range from brief, simple low cost ones to lengthy and comprehensive procedures which are very expensive to operate. Whatever form a procedure takes three things are essential if it is to be effective.

First, jobs have to a be analysed accurately and thoroughly in order for a detailed person specification to be drawn up for each job. Second, means of obtaining comprehensive and objective data about each applicant, relevant to the person specification, have to be established. Third, selectors must be available who can make reliable and valid predictions about the suitability of applicants for jobs by matching the data about each applicant with the appropriate person specification. The effectiveness of a selection procedure should not be taken for granted, instead each of its phases needs to be evaluated in order to identify whether and how improvements can be made. It must be remembered, however, that an employee's actual work performance does not reflect just the quality of a selector's decisions but also the influence of many other factors operating within the organisation.

References

1   D Torrington (1988), How does human resources management change the personnel function? *Personnel Review, 17*, (6), 3-9.

2   For a discussion of the changing nature of work and organisations see D Clutterbuck (1985), *New Patterns of Work*, Aldershot: Gower; C Handy (1989), *The Age of Unreason*, London: Hutchinson.

3   P Herriot (1987), The selection interview. *In* P B Warr (Ed.) *Psychology at Work* (3rd Edition) Harmondsworth, Middlesex: Penguin.

4   More detailed descriptions of selection procedures and processes can be found in: J McCormick and D Ilgen (1980), *Industrial Psychology* (7th edition) London: George, Allen and Unwin, and M Smith and I T Robertson (1986), *The Theory and Practice of Systematic Staff Selection*, London: MacMillan.

5   J Munro Fraser (1978), *Employment Interviewing* (5th edition) London: MacDonald & Evans; A Rodger (1974), *The Seven-Point Plan*, National Foundation for Educational Research.

6   A Ostell (1986), Where stress screening falls short. *Personnel Management*, September, 34-37, for a discussion of aspects of psychological screening; M Lloyd (1988), The medical examination. *In* E Sidney (Ed.) *Managing Recruitment* (4th edition) Aldershot: Gower.

7   I T Robertson and P J Makin (1986), Management selection in Britain: A survey and critique. *Journal of Occupational Psychology, 59*, 45-57.

Provides a recent review of the use of different predictors in selection procedures in British companies.

8   W A Owens (1976), Background data. *In* M D Dunnette, (Ed.) *Handbook of Industrial and Organisational Psychology*, Chicago: Rand McNally.

9   E E Ghiselli (1973), The validity of aptitude tests in personnel selection. *Personnel Psychology, 26,* 461-477; M Smith and I T Robertson, *op cit.* discuss the predictive validities of various predictors.

10 P F Wernimont and J P Campbell (1968), Signs, samples and criteria. *Journal of Applied Psychology, 52,* 372-376.

11 R D Arvey and J E Campion (1982), The employment interview: a summary and review of recent literature. *Personnel Psychology, 35,* 281-322.

12 P L Wright and D S Taylor (1984), *Improving Leadership Performance.* Englewood Cliffs, New Jersey: Prentice Hall (chapter 4).

13 F Landy and D A Trumbo (1976), *Psychology of Work Behaviour.* Homewood, Illinois: Dorsey Press (chapters 5 and 6).

14 W H Wiesner and S F Cronshaw (1988), A meta-analytic investigation of the impact of interview format and degree of structure on the validity of the employment interview. *Journal of Occupational Psychology, 61,* 275-290.

15 G C Thornton and W C Byham (1982), *Assessment Centers and Managerial Performance.* New York: Academic Press.

16 D Lewis (1983). *Essentials of Employment Law.* London: Institute of Personnel Management; *Butterworth's Employment Law Handbook,* 1984, 3rd Edition edited by P Waddington. London: Butterworth & Co.

Suggested Reading

L J Cronbach (1984), *Essentials of Psychological Testing.* (4th edition). New York: Harper & Row. (A good, comprehensive introduction to the nature and use of psychological tests with a useful description of their use in a selection context.)

M D Dunnette (1966), *Personnel Selection and Placement*. Monterey, California: Brooks/Cole. (An in-depth approach to selection and placement, nevertheless, it is an excellent, readable text.)

M D Dunnette (Ed.) (1976), *Handbook of Industrial and Organizational Psychology*. Chicago: Rand McNally. (An academic handbook which includes a number of 'weighty' chapters on recruitment, selection, etc. Only to be tackled by those who want a thorough and academic grounding in the subject.)

P Plumbley (1976), *Recruitment and Selection*. London: Institute of Personnel Management. (A useful, general and practical book.)

E Sidney (Ed.) (1988), *Managing Recruitment*. (4th Edition) Aldershot: Gower. (A useful collection of papers covering a wide range of topics relevant to personnel selection.)

Questions

1   Critically discuss the following statement: "Personnel selection is concerned with finding the right person to fill the right job".

2   Outline the criteria you would use to assess the suitability of a psychological test for use in a selection procedure. What are the strengths and limitations of tests as selection devices?

3   Discuss the view that interviews are so unreliable as sources of information about job applicants that they are not worth using in a selection procedure.

Chapter 4

Wage and Salary Administration

Angela Mulvie

Introduction

The determination and maintenance of a fair and equitable wage and salary system within an organisation is, arguably, one of the most complex tasks facing the human resources manager. An overriding factor in the success of any organisation in achieving its goals is the application of the employees towards that task. Without an adequate way of rewarding for that effort the organisation cannot hope to motivate for the future. The primary objective of the remuneration system which an organisation adopts is to control and manipulate this relationship between performance and reward within the constraints of the financial position of the organisation.

In Chapter One reference was made to the role of the human resource management specialist in developing appropriate procedures and policies which would integrate fully with the strategic plans of the organisation. The recent adoption of a wider concept of Human Resource Management away from the traditional approach to Personnel Management has placed the emphasis of Human Resource Management firmly on the planning and development contribution the human resource specialist can make to corporate success. Fowler[1] suggests that two main themes exist in human resource thinking:

● every aspect of employee management should be integrated with business management and must reinforce the desired organisation culture

● the organisation should encourage initiative and commitment within its workforce by emphasising the common interests of employer and employed in the success of the business/organisation

As Guest[2] suggests, a number of systems in and around the conventional areas of Personnel Management will operate to achieve these human resource policy goals; one of these systems must therefore be the reward system the organisation uses to achieve the initiative and commitment referred to above. Those organisations adopting a human resource management approach will place greater emphasis on the individual and full utilisation of his/her individual abilities. This in turn implies a need to design reward systems on an individual rather than collective basis with opportunities for the individual to play a greater part in the determination and choice of payment method.

Recent interest in performance management and its operation in both the public and private sectors, and on performance related payment methods on an individual basis are in part a reflection of the growing concern in the field of managing remuneration of finding ways to motivate and reward in a changing environment. In planning and operating payment systems the human resource specialist is faced not only with the internal problems of providing from within available organisational resources, what is perceived by employees to be a just reward for effort, but also with the satisfaction of certain external economic and legislative constraints.

This chapter provides an overview of the operational framework used by organisations in the administration of their wage and salary systems; it outlines some of the different types of payment system available; it considers the process of evaluating different jobs to help establish differences in pay levels; and it considers briefly the statutory and legislative framework in which the human resource specialist must operate in this area of activity.

The Performance/Reward Equation

The factors which influence behaviour and therefore motivation have been described as those which affect the situation people are in: i.e. the extrinsic factors, and those which relate to the characteristics, abilities, needs, qualities, of the individual i.e. the intrinsic factors. As noted in Chapter Five theories of motivation have a number of practical implications for both general and Humnan Resource Managers, not least in the context of reward systems.

The examination of the motivating influence of money has long been of interest to behavioural theorists who have provided us with a variety of explanations of what motivates people in the work situation. The complexities of the motivation process arise because individuals have different needs and different ways of satisfying such needs through establishing and achieving a number of goals. At work such differences have to be recognised and harnessed by management for organisational efficiency by providing a reward system for performance which is valued by organisational members.

Although a positive link exists between motivation and performance it is necessary to recognise also questions of ability, individual role perception at work, the value of a reward system to the individual and his expectations about the relationship between reward and effort. One of the major problems facing the human resource specialist dealing with remuneration is how to reward the poor performer who is not achieving satisfactory work in terms of output, productivity, attitude and cooperation. Within an organisation procedures to deal with such problems through the operation of disciplinary machinery will be available. As a result of increasing interest in finding new methods of motivating staff through rewarding individual effort, many organisations are moving away from traditional incremental pay systems under which everyone achieves the same monetary reward, linked to length of service, towards individual merit/performance related pay.

The importance of money as an extrinsic reward provided by an employer cannot be denied when considering personnel issues of staff recruitment and retention, but it should not be considered as any more significant than the range of intrinsic rewards sought by the employee, such as responsibility, achievement, and recognition. In moving towards a payment system which recognises individual effort some of these intrinsic needs are satisfied.

The wage and salary system is a most powerful influence on behaviour at work. It is essential that the relationship between motivation and performance is known and understood by those responsible for rewarding the employee and by those involved in the design and operation of performance appraisal systems in use in the organisation. Adequate procedures should exist for the administration, monitoring, updating, and refinement of reward methods in the light of organisational and economic change and of the need to keep under review the relationship between performance and reward.

Objectives of a Payment System

In any organisation a number of broad objectives of the pay system can be established. Firstly, for many organisations remuneration is a significant if not the largest element in the cost of production or service. The amount of money available to pay for wages, salaries, and employee benefits may have a major impact on profitability and/or cost effectiveness. It is therefore important that from the employer's viewpoint the payment system ensures a satisfactory level of output at an economic price.

Secondly, it is important that the payment system is economic in terms of what competitors offer within the marketplace. Employers will often exchange information on wage and salary levels with comparable employing organisations in the area and/or nationally as appropriate. In particular, levels of pay will have to be adjusted in line with increases in the cost of living, and the rate of inflation within any government anti-inflationary policy.

A third objective of the payment system is that it should be perceived as a just and equitable reward by employees. This can be achieved in part by the organisation recognising differences in ability, skills, and orientation to work demonstrated by the workforce. Employers will be particularly concerned to maintain appropriate differentials between levels of job according to their relative value. The maintenance of such differentials often becomes the greatest area of concern to staff when job evaluation is introduced, as discussed below.

A further objective of any payment system is to provide opportunities within it for modification and change, not just as the result of economic factors, but also by way of response to employee demands for such change. Trade unions and staff associations will have collective aims of ensuring members' pay matches or exceeds market values; pay increases are awarded ahead of rises in inflation, and any changes to organisational prosperity and conditions are reflected in pay awards made. Information relating to profitability, proposed plans, possible changes to the size and structure of the workforce and work methods will require to be made available. Indeed one reason for rationalising out of date wage and salary structures is to improve this information flow as the basis for future negotiation.

As stated above, the management of pay is a process designed to help the organisation get results. To achieve the objectives of any payment system not only will the administrative procedures of pay have to be in place and operational but also the policy making issues and implications of remuneration will have to have been thought through and integrated into strategic plans. Again this is a major task for the human resource specialist.

Differences Between Wages and Salaries

Although the management of wages and salaries can be seen as one distinct area of personnel activity, certain distinctions can be made between the two which have implications for the climate in which negotiations take place and for the way assumptions are made by both parties regarding employee expectation of reward. These differences have arisen as a result of historical change in industry and the way in which trade union bargaining power has grown and altered in influence. Traditionally the hourly paid or manual worker has been paid per hour for work completed. This rate may be fixed or may vary as levels of output change. The salaried earner has been paid a rate per month/year for work completed with again an opportunity to vary earnings through improved output/quality. Many salaried earners are paid on an incremental basis i.e. basic earnings increase with each year of service.

Differences between ways of rewarding hourly and salaried employees have grown up through custom and practice, through recognition of differences in working conditions and facilities, and through questions of status and promotion opportunities. Whilst many of these differences remain in terms of job content, responsibility and so on, many organisations are looking towards ways of harmonising conditions of employment to provide the same range of facilities and services for everyone.

In most industries today the basis of the manual worker's earnings is his basic time wage i.e. payment for every hour worked/attended. Such basic rates will generally be fixed on a collective basis as the result of bargaining at local or national level, very often as the result of a job evaluation exercise.

Alternatively minimum rates may be set by Wages Councils, whose role in this area is discussed below. A number of additions to this basic pay are usually made:

- **Overtime Pay:** this is paid for work undertaken beyond normal hours and is usually paid at an enhanced rate e.g. time and a half, depending on the time of day.

- **Shift Pay:** this is paid as compensation for inconvenient and changing hours, generally paid as ten to twenty per cent of the basic rate.

- **Special Allowances:** these may be given to an employee having to work in abnormal conditions, circumstances.

- **Bonus:** this may be an extra payment based on the output of the work (paid as part of a payment by results scheme), or it may be an additional payment made to all employees (e.g. as a Christmas bonus as a result of increased profits for the organisation).

- **Cost of Living Allowance:** this may be available for hourly paid employees working in a high cost area.

● **Employee Benefits:** hourly paid staff will be given subsidised conditions and facilities which have a cash value, e.g. meals, overalls, discount purchase schemes.

The basis of the salaried employee's remuneration is also his time rate i.e. he or she is paid generally on a monthly basis calculated as one twelfth of an annual figure which may be negotiated personally on appointment. In many organisations salaried employees will receive an additional payment annually based on the results of a performance review. They may also be in receipt of an additional bonus, based on company profits; they are more likely than manual workers to receive a cost of living allowance; they may enjoy a wider range of benefits and services including for example a company car and subsidised mortgage facilities.

Other major differences between the hourly paid and salaried employee relate to terms and conditions of employment in particular in the question of notice. Wage earners will generally find that their employment can be termianted at shorter notice, assuming the organisation has followed correct procedures. They may also find their promotion opportunities blocked to a greater degree than their salaried colleagues through their own lack of career expectations, and lack of training. Salaried earners will on the whole be seen by their employer as a group with expectations of advancement to a higher level of monetary reward, based on performance, experience, qualifications, seniority and age.

Yet for a number of reasons these traditional differences between wage earners and salaried staff are lessening. As discussed below, the employee benefit package has become a subject for negotiation. In many American and Japanese firms little distinction is made between staff in terms of benefits and services provided; they are seen as much less of a status symbol than once was the case. Trade union pressure in recent years has led to moves towards the harmonisation of conditions of employment and fringe benefits for all employees. Certain legal changes, such as recent equal pay amendments and non-discriminatory legislation, have led employers to look carefully at terms and conditions on offer and provide these on an equal basis, not just between the sexes but between salaried and hourly paid staff.

The Negotiation of Pay Rates

Negotiations over changes to the reward system will normally take place on an annual basis. A claim for increased pay may arise for a number of reasons, generally relating to dissatisfaction over the purchasing power of pay. In entering the negotiating process, management will consider the target settlement it can afford, in the light of some concessions which will have to be made during subsequent discussion. Employees will be concerned with questions of comparability, i.e. looking for at least the same increase as other groups, and traditional relativities, i.e. the maintenance of differences in the relative value of one job to another.

The pay differentials between individuals or groups of employees are determined by the wage and salary structure in operation in an organisation, rather than by different types of payment system. Traditionally blue collar work has been structured into skilled, semi-skilled and unskilled categories with appropriate pay according to the grade of worker. Yet changes in the structure of jobs and their content in response to technological advance have led to a need to rationalise approaches to pay, including consideration of how payments should be made to part-time as well as full-time employees.

During the pay bargaining process management needs to consider what other groups of employees in other companies, services and industries are earning. An exchange of information on current and planned wages and salaries will need to take place with other comparable employers in the area, to provide the organisation with up-to-date information on local labour market conditions and processes.

Since the introduction of much of the employment legislation brought in since 1979 by the Conservative government the bargaining power of certain key groups of employees has been reduced. Within the public sector the government as employer has faced protracted strikes over pay issues in a number of areas. Although incomes policies were encouraged by successive Labour governments in the 1960s and 1970s and have been encouraged on a voluntary basis by the Conservatives since 1979 recent indications show that many employing organisations settle claims within their own parameters of profitability and expansion or business loss and redundancy, rather than within guidelines laid down by government.

Types of Wage Payment Systems

Hourly paid employees will either be remunerated on an individual or group basis. The basic time wage i.e. for the actual number of hours worked will generally account for nearly three quarters of total earnings; the remainder made up of additional payments of one kind or another. As discussed above these may be of a variety of types and may well include an incentive element.

(a) Time Rates

Under this payment scheme the employee is paid a basic rate (per hour, day) for the actual time worked. This basic rate will only vary with changes in the time worked, and does not relate to changes in performance and productivity. Although time rates are simple to administer and are easily understood by both parties, they do not contain the incentive element so important in many production situations, where continuous increases in productivity are necessary.

(b) Payment by Results

Individual payment by results (PBR) schemes which are widely used in the UK are a composite of a basic rate for a job plus a variable payment which is based on output i.e. it is dependent on the personal performance of the employee. Payment is usually based on the amount rather than quality of output. A standard has to be agreed for the work undertaken relating to the time taken to complete the job or the units of production achieved; where this standard is exceeded the bonus payment will be made.

Although PBR schemes have become commonplace, many employers have looked at other ways of paying individuals, for example through the use of measured day work schemes. Research on motivation, in particular in the group situation, has led management to question the idea that opportunities to increase earnings produce greater effort. Problems exist in building and maintaining such opportunities where complex changes in manufacturing technology have to be taken into account.

A number of variations occur within PBR schemes:

● **Straight Piecework:** this is the most common and popular PBR scheme. It is generally used for production work where output and time taken for a job can be easily measured through work study.

● **Differential Piecework:** under this scheme employees can earn bonus through the 'time saved' on a job and this is shared between the employer and the individual i.e. the organisation will retain some part of the bonus as productivity rises.

The obvious advantage of the PBR scheme is the increased productivity from the same number of employees. It can only work where individual employees feel highly motivated to improve their performance level, and is heavily reliant on a steady flow of work through the production line.

However, the administrative costs of running and monitoring a PBR scheme can be considerable. Difficulties may arise in terms of supervisory staff finding themselves with less earning potential than the production workers under their control.

Disputes may arise between individual employees over levels of achievement and it will be necessary for the organisation to maintain an on-going work study programme to take account of changes to work flow and make adjustments to the scheme accordingly. PBR schemes may result in some wages drift where individual earnings rise well above negotiated rates.

In the production situation, problems can arise in paying those who service the production line but do not contribute directly to output achieved; maintenance staff for example are usually rewarded with some other type of bonus. PBR schemes are expensive to install and maintain; the organisation will need a good work-study team to provide their services regularly for this maintenance and updating process.

Group PBR schemes are generally used when it is difficult if not impossible to determine individual performance. The bonus achieved is divided amongst the group which means that group members have to work well together to achieve desired levels of output. While it can be argued that group PBR schemes act as a motivating influence which will bind together group members into a cohesive unit, it is possible that disagreements will arise, membership may change, and as the group size increases individual employees will find it more difficult to understand why changes in earnings overall have been influenced by their own performance.

(c) Measured Daywork

Day work schemes are often seen as an improved alternative to traditional PBR schemes although their popularity of the late 1960s and early 1970s has fallen away. Day work schemes, where again the rate for the job is calculated by work study, are often run for a group of employees rather than for an individual. The incentive element is set on the understanding that an agreed level of output will be achieved. Where this fails to happen the operative will be moved out of the system. In a stepped measured daywork scheme operatives can be moved to a lower level of output in line with their ability. It will be necessary for management to supervise closely under this scheme to ensure a steady flow of work. When compared with an individual PBR scheme, measured daywork is attractive to employers as they have greater control over the cost of wages. Smith[3] describes measured daywork as 'peaceful inefficiency' because although schemes may reduce disputes about incentive payments, they may also reduce the overall level of productivity.

(d) Plant Wide Incentive Schemes

These are essentially a variant of the group incentive scheme mentioned above whereby all employees in an organisation or factory share in some bonus which is linked to levels of output. It is necessary to find some satisfactory way of calculating this bonus, which might be based on total volume of output (where one type of product is made) or total sales value of goods. Because the factory wide incentive scheme provides little individual incentive, and problems can arise with the agreement on indicators of performance, employers may wish to consider an alternative scheme.

Salary Administration

Salaried employees will generally be remunerated on an individual rather than group basis. Whilst many white collar salaried staff will belong to a trade union or staff association who negotiate their pay rates centrally, many others will bargain on an individual basis for the amount of money to be received. Such a figure may fall within a band agreed for that grade of appointment. Within a graded salary structure there exists a sequence of salary ranges or grades, each of which has a defined minimum and maximum. These parameters of the salary bands may be set by comparison with competitors' salary levels and pay structures. Such data can be collected in a variety of ways including large-scale formal salary and benefits surveys, company annual reports, and information and knowledge of the local labour market.

As with decisions relating to hourly paid employees, the Salary Administrator must take into account the organisation's ability to pay, what competitors are offering for comparable posts, efficient manning levels, the use of non-financial motivators, and pressures from relevant trade unions and staff associations.

A number of salary structure types exist, their use often dependent on different approaches to salary progression planning:

(a) Flat Rate

The use of a single rate for individual staff jobs is rare although used for hourly paid workers. This method of payment implies little change in performance with no way of taking account of this through a merit award.

(b) Age Scales

In many organisations, in particular in the public sector, stepped payments are made to employees as they reach a birthday (very often up to the age of twenty-one). Employees paid in this way would be young trainees and an employer would need to take account of the 'going' rate for comparable posts in the local labour market. Where young people are able to meet the requirements of a full adult job at eighteen for example the employer may wish to review the use of 'birthday' increases.

(c) Incremental Salary Scales

This is a most common method of paying salaries whereby a salary range will be set for a particular job with a number of steps within that range. The employee may be appointed to the minimum of the scale or at some stage up it, depending on qualifications and experience. Staff will achieve an annual rise by moving up the scale as a result of length of service rather than by good performance. In this way no distinction is possible in terms of rewarding the good and poor achiever. This may result in a uniform middle level of performance. The high achiever will only be able to progress financially out of the salary band by promotion to a higher paid post.

(d) Flexible Incremental Scales

Some variation in pay for those being rewarded on fixed incremental scales may be achieved by varying the periods between the award of increments, by witholding an increment, or by moving the individual more than one step up the scale. This allows management some discretion in the reward of the good performer.

(e) Merit Rating

Amongst salaried personnel one of the most common ways of remunerating employees is to pay some kind of merit award over and above basic salary as a reward for personal endeavour and progress, and as a motivator for the future. Such merit awards would be given, usually annually, as part of the yearly appraisal of staff performance. Within this appraisal certain factors such as initiative, aptitude, adaptability, and so on are measured in terms of pre-set targets achieved (or otherwise) and a reward for achievement is made in financial terms. It is common practice in many organisations operating merit schemes to separate the interview and discussion on performance review for pay purposes from the appraisal interview. A fuller discussion of performance appraisal and review is found in Chapter Nine.

The current climate in both industry and the public sector is towards a performance management approach i.e. paying for results and achievement. In its application of this approach to many parts of the public sector the government has established an environment in which it has become important to differentiate between ways in which people perform and so reward them accordingly. This particular approach to pay perhaps more than any other has been resisted by the trade unions who traditionally have been suspicious of merit rating schemes which appear to rely heavily on subjective assessments of staff. Yet in many ways the public sector in its moves towards performance related pay is emulating what has been tried and tested in parts of the private sector for some time. Such an approach to reward requires other systems to be in place, in particular an adequate means of assessing performance and results achieved.

(f) Commission

For certain categories of salaried staff, in particular those working in sales, it is common to provide opportunities to earn an additional payment over and above basic salary. This commission may be earned for increased sales volume/orders or for improvements to profits and costs associated with the sales.

In addition to the types of wage and salary systems outlined a number of other ways exist of rewarding both hourly paid and salaried staff:

(i) Profit Sharing

Profit sharing is a way of providing an additional bonus, related to profit, over and above established wages and salaries. While this bonus will rise or fall in accordance with profit levels, rates of pay will remain the same. The amount of profit bonus paid will depend on profit achieved in the previous financial period.

Profit sharing schemes can be either a share scheme type where shares, bought out of profits, are distributed to employees, or a cash scheme where cash payments are linked to profits made. Additionally firms may operate an approved deferred share trust scheme (ADST) whereby the company allocates profit to a trust fund which acquires shares in the company on behalf of employees. Recent finance legislation has led to schemes which meet certain conditions receiving tax concessions, which has led to a greater number of companies introducing such schemes. The 1987 Finance Act allows special tax relief on profit-related pay schemes, provided these are authorised by the Inland Revenue and meet certain conditions. This legislation comes after a series of fiscal initiatives throughout the 1970s and 1980s designed to encourage the spread of profit sharing and employee share ownership.

It is important that the basic wage and salary structure in place is operating correctly before an organisation attempts to introduce a scheme. The extent of profit sharing schemes in the UK is small when compared with the USA, Europe and Japan. Bell and Hanson[4] estimate that over seven hundred schemes are operating in the UK covering over three million employees. Although profit sharing schemes are introduced as an incentive to increase output there will be no immediate 'pay off' in terms of improved morale, better productivity and so on because of the factors involved in making a profit. To many employees the relationship between individual effort and profit is so remote that the influence of schemes on productivity is minimal.

(ii) Bonus Schemes

A bonus may be paid as supplementary to primary salary as a means of motivating and providing extra incentive to the employee – for example, a Christmas bonus.

Job Evaluation

One of the most important factors in determining wages and salaries is deciding how much one job should be worth in comparison with another given that each contains differences in skill content, levels of responsibility, working conditions, and so on. In addition, no two jobs which have similarities in content will be undertaken by individuals with the same levels of competence, skills, attitude and level of motivation. In order to judge these differences in

86

relation to a range of jobs, many organisations use job evaluation to determine how jobs may be placed in a hierarchy of their relative worth in order that employees may be paid fairly.

The Nature of Job Evaluation

"Job evaluation is a method of determining, on a systematic basis, the relative importance of the demands of a number of different jobs in order to build an acceptable and equitable pay structure" (ACAS).[5] It is a process which is concerned with examining the content and circumstances of a job rather than the individual job holder. Regarding the latter, it is important to state that job evaluation is not concerned with how well or badly a job is performed by any one person. The process of performance appraisal, discussed in Chapter Nine, undertakes such an examination. If an employer wishes to acknowledge individual effort or if he values the work of one employee more highly than of another he may reward on a merit basis, over and above the basic rate set for the job.

Yet job evaluation does not exclusively determine wage and salary rates; other factors like the supply of and demand for labour, current market rates both locally and nationally, cost of living indicators, working conditions, the relative bargaining strength of certain sectors of the workforce and the financial position of the employing organisation will all have to be taken into consideration when agreeing appropriate levels of pay.

The Aims of Job Evaluation

One of the main aims of job evaluation is to provide a basis for a wage and salary system that is seen to be fair and equitable to both sides. Decisions made about differences between jobs must be reached in an objective rather than subjective fashion through joint discussion and negotiation. The introduction of a job evaluation scheme will require a joint cooperative effort between management and employees to ensure a common ground for the subsequent negotiation of gradings and wage and salary levels. Where a joint exercise is initiated, less opportunity arises for complaints of arbitrary decisions regarding gradings and so on. Not only must questions of acceptability to both parties be considered however; it is also important that management is seen to introduce a scheme that is both valid (i.e. assessments are made which are representative of the views of those assessing jobs) and reliable (i.e. where assessments take place there is consensus and consistency in the decisions taken).

The majority of job evaluation schemes will be introduced to replace old systems and pay problems caused by historical 'ad hoc' decisions. Where organisational change occurs resulting in a restructuring of jobs, job evaluation may be used effectively to achieve consensus about the reallocation of tasks and reponsibilities which should be accounted for in the payment system.

Before job evaluation can take place a certain amount of preparatory work is required in the form of job identification and job analysis, the latter providing information on the current content and responsibilities of the job. Such information may be collected by questionnaires, interviews and on occasions observation, and written into a job description. The amount of information contained in the job description will depend on the particular job evaluation technique being used, but generally will contain details about

● job purpose

● major tasks, ranked in order of importance with time elements included

● special performance requirements

● working conditions

The responsibility for preparing job descriptions will generally rest with the line manager; where an organisation is using a job evaluation committee members may well scrutinise descriptions as a preliminary function. The committee will also undertake the task of job identification where jobs of a similar nature are grouped for the purpose of evaluation. It is essential that accurate information is collected about what actually happens within a job rather than what is meant to happen or what is thought to happen, in this preliminary stage of evaluation.

Job Evaluation Techniques

Job evaluation schemes are generally of two kinds: analytical and nonanalytical. In the former jobs are broken down into a number of aspects each of which is considered as part of the whole job for comparative purposes. In the latter comparisons are made between complete jobs. Following the introduction of the Equal Value amendments in 1984 many organisations have had to look very carefully at the type of job evaluation scheme in operation. Although many cases involving major issues of interpretation of the legislation are only now reaching a stage of resolution, judgements are being made in favour of analytical rather than non-analytical schemes. Indeed the whole issue of job evaluation schemes, their operation and updating is having to be addressed by many employers unwilling to risk judgements against them in equal value claims taken to an Industrial Tribunal.

The three non-analytical schemes generally found are:

(a) Ranking

The ranking method considers the worth of one job against another, within a group of perhaps twenty-five to thirty jobs maximum, placing the jobs in some sort of rank order of importance. The criteria for assessment will include such factors as responsibility, supervision, level of required initiative, and so on. Although ranking requires limited expertise in job evaluation and is easy to understand and administer it is highly subjective and fails to differentiate degrees of difficulty between jobs.

(b) Paired Comparisons

This is a refinement of the ranking method whereby each job is ranked against every other job, and points are awarded accordingly to whether overall importance of a job is seen to be of greater worth (two points), equal worth (one point), or less worth (zero points). Jobs are placed in rank order according to the total number of points achieved. The number of pairs to be considered is calculated as $\frac{n(n-1)}{2}$ and generally about twenty jobs would be the maximum number considered.

(c) Job Grading/Job Classification

This method establishes a grading structure into which individual jobs are then slotted. The committee will decide how many grades will be created and what each will contain. Individual jobs considered as typical of each grade are chosen as 'benchmarks', which are then used as a comparison with other jobs. Although a simple method to operate and understand, job grading is still a subjective means of evaluating one job agains another and it does not allow a complex job to fit easily into one grade.

The major analytical schemes in job evaluation are:

(a) Points Rating

Points rating has become one of the most popular methods of job evaluation used in the UK, primarily as it is seen as one of the least subjective methods available. A numerical value is given to the 'worth' of each job evaluated. Each job is split into factors and subfactors. For example, a skill factor might be split into education/training/job experience required/manual dexterity. Points are awarded for each factor according to a predetermined scale. A number of benchmark jobs are chosen as a measure of validity to assist in the comparative process. The factors identified are usually weighted so that some are given greater emphasis than others. The choice of factors and weights may prove difficult and it can be argued that such a choice is only made in a subjective fashion relying heavily on the personal judgement of committee members. The points assigned on each factor for each job are added to give a rank order expressed in points for all the jobs in that job group or 'family'. However, it can be used in a variety of situations and has proved popular as a method of job evaluation.

(b) Copyrighted Systems

A number of these systems are available from firms of management consultants. One of the better known is the Hay Chart Profile Method. In this method a points scale is used, based on three factors of problem-solving, know-how, and accountability.

(c) Factor Comparison

In this method, which is not commonly used, the job is analysed under five main headings: mental requirements, skill requirements, physical requirements, repsonsibilities, and working conditions. The evaluation takes place by allocating monetary values to these factors, based on current rates, thus bringing money into the discussion of job evaluation and subsequent negotiation that will take place.

Introducing a Job Evaluation Scheme

The success of any job evaluation scheme will depend in large part on its acceptability to all parties as a means of determining a basis for discussion/negotiation on pay. The involvement of both management and employees at all levels in the organisation is important to create an atmosphere of trust and respect. One useful way of achieving employee representation and commitment is through the establishment of a job evaluation committee whose membership comprises representatives from management and the workforce; generally human resource specialists or their nominee will deal with the administration of procedures.

Where an organisation has not used job evaluation before it may engage a firm of management consultants for assistance. Another useful source of help would be the Advisory, Conciliation and Arbitration Service (ACAS) who may provide an independent assessor.

Approaching job evaluation as a joint management/employee exercise will lead to a more objective consensus and greater acceptability of a scheme which can then form the basis for subsequent determination of gradings and wage levels. Every scheme should have an appeals procedure built in to allow any individual or group, who feels their jobs have been underevaluated in relation to others, to present their grievances.

Once a scheme has been agreed and introduced it will be necessary to undertake regular reviews of the scheme to allow for any changes in job content and circumstances to be taken into account and modifications made accordingly. The introduction of equal opportunity and sex discrimination legislation and the outcome of recent tribunal cases have meant that employers must scrutinise their schemes for required adjustment.

Where a job evaluation exercise results in a number of upgradings the total wages bill may increase. It is not common practice to reduce an employee's pay level where job evaluation has resulted in a downgrading; rather, new elements may be built into the job to maintain the reward level.

The Legislative Framework of Payment Systems

A number of statutory requirements exist relating to the payment of employees. These must be taken into account in administering the wage and salary system in operation. Some examples of the main issues are discussed below.

(a) Employment Protection Rights

Aspects of pay affected by the Employment Protection (Consolidation) Act 1978, amended by the Employment Acts 1980, 1982 and 1988, include

- written particulars of terms of employment (including rate of pay, or way it is calculated, and pay period)

- itemised pay statements

- guaranteed payments (where employees are not provided with work throughout a day during any part of which they would normally have worked)

- issues of medical suspension and payment for same

- payment for allowable time off e.g. for trade union duties

- redundancy payments

(b) Statutory Sick Pay and Statutory Maternity Pay

Statutory sick pay, brought into effect by the Social Security and Housing Benefits Act 1982 and associated regulations, requires employers to take over the role of the State in certain circumstances in paying sick pay to their employees. This payment is dependent on the employee satisfying rules and regulations regarding periods of incapacity, periods of entitlement, qualifying days, and rules on the notification of absence (this latter at the discretion of the employer).

Statutory maternity pay (SMP) was introduced from April 1987 and is payable to employees who take maternity leave or leave entitlement and who satisfy certain conditions. Like SSP, SMP can be reclaimed by the employer from the government by way of deductions from National Insurance contributions, provided it is paid properly. The right to return to work after the birth of a child is unaffected by the SMP scheme as the two provisions are quite separate. Where a woman is eligible to receive SMP payment this must be done whether or not she is entitled to return to work after the confinement.

(c) Equal Pay Legislation

The 1970 Equal Pay Act, which came into force in 1975 and has been subsequently amended by the Equal Pay (Amendment) Regulations 1983 and the Sex Discrimination Act 1986, established the right of men and women to equal treatment as regards terms and conditions of employment including pay, when they are employed on the same or broadly similar work or work, which though very different has been given equal value under a job evaluation scheme or work which is of equal worth in terms of the demands and requirements of the job. The legislation applies to men and women in both full-time and part-time employment. Where employees feel they have a grievance which cannot be solved at employer level claims for equal pay can be taken to an Industrial Tribunal in the normal way. Such a claim may include a request for arrears of remuneration or damages in respect of contravention of the legislation. Arrears of pay and damages for cases brought under the 'equal value' provisions can only be backdated to January 1984, the date on which the regulations took effect.

(d) Statutory Wages Regulation

In many cases terms and conditions of employment including levels of remuneration are the subject of collective agreements reached by voluntary methods. However for certain industries and trades, statutory regulation of wages exists to ensure that adequate levels of remuneration are achieved. This regulation is undertaken by Wages Councils which developed originally from Trade Boards set up at the turn of the century to recommend improvements in rates of pay in a number of so-called 'sweated industries', where traditionally rates of pay had been kept to a minimum. During and after the Second World War there took place a major extension of these Boards, which became known as Wages Councils, following legislation in 1979. The operation of these Councils is governed now by provisions under the 1986 Wages Act which repealed earlier legislation.

Traditionally the function of the Councils was to fix a statutory minimum rate of pay and terms and conditions of employment where no satisfactory voluntary mechanism existed. By the early 1960s some three and a half million workers were covered by fifty-three Councils, plus an additional four hundred thousand agricultural employees covered by two agricultural Councils. During the 1970s a number of Councils were disbanded; the remainder covering mainly the retail, hotel and catering, and clothing industries. For some time the Conservative government has considered the reform of these Councils to remove a number of statutory burdens placed on employers, to simplify the regulations relating to pay, and to provide new employment opportunities by encouraging more recruitment. The main argument put forward is that the Councils act as a block to flexibility on which jobs growth depends. A consultative paper issued in February 1989 is presently under discussion. Concerns about the proposals have come in the main from the trade unions and the Equal Opportunities Commission which has argued that abolition would hinder progress on women's pay at precisely a time when

93

more female labour needs to be attracted into the marketplace.

The 1986 Wages Act also removed the statutory right of manual workers to be paid in cash (as had been the case for many years under the provisions of the Truck Acts). This has meant that employers have had to look at the whole question of procedures for administering payment systems.

(e) Income Tax

Apart from the normal deductions to be made from wages and salaries in respect of income tax, deductions may also be required in respect of expense payments and fringe benefits. Many employers provide a wide range of fringe benefits and services to their employees as part of the remuneration package. Under the various Finance Acts certain benefits and services are liable to income tax, whilst with others certain limits are set before tax is payable. In particular the government has favoured the encouragement of employers to set up profit sharing and profit-related pay schemes as noted above.

The statutory regulations which affect the administration of pay are complex and it is important that Human Resource Managers have amongst their staff someone who can advise on this issue to ensure that both employees and employer achieve their objectives of satisfactory reward at least cost.

Conclusion

Within the field of wage and salary administration a number of factors have to be considered in developing, maintaining and updating payment systems. Not only will trade union and employee representative pressure affect the decisions to be made, but also such things as custom and practice, labour market conditions, and changes in legislation will affect the decisions made in this area.

Increasingly the human resource specialist, as part of the decision making process in many organisations, will have a crucial role to play in advising on reward systems. As the pool of qualified labour shrinks, more attention will have to be paid to the development of strategies not only for recruiting but also for retaining staff. Whilst remuneration may not be the only motivator in the workplace it will remain an important one and employing organisations will have to look towards new ways of paying people at work. Any changes to established pay practices however will have to be made with care and always with the economic capabilities of the organisation.

References

1   A Fowler, When Chief Executives Discover Human Resource Management (Comment), *Personnel Management*, January 1987.

2   D Guest, Personnel and Human Resource Management: Can You Tell The Difference?, *Personnel Management,* January 1989.

3   I Smith, *The Management of Remuneration* IPM/Gower 1983.

4   W Bell and C Hanson, *Profit Sharing and Profitability: How Profit Sharing Promotes Business Success*, Kogan Page 1987.

5   ACAS, *Job Evaluation, Advisory Booklet No. 1*, H.M.S.O.

Suggested Reading

G McBeath and D Rands, *Salary Administration,* Business Books, 3rd ed., 1981.

G F Thomason, *Job Evaluation: Objectives and Methods,* IPM, 1981.

M Armstrong, *A Handbook of Personnel Management Practice* (esp. Chs. 20-28), Kogan Page 3rd ed., 1988.

K Puttick et al., *Wages and the Law, Shaw & Sons/IPM, 1989.*

Questions

1   What main problems face an employer in designing wage and salary systems?

2   What are the main issues an organisation has to consider when introducing job evaluation as a means of regularising wage and salary systems?

3   What is the place of profit sharing within a wage and salary system?

Chapter 5

Motivation and Job Satisfaction

Peter L. Wright

Introduction

To be successful, organisations need the commitment of their employees. Two kinds of commitment are important. One is a commitment to the achievement of the goals of the organisation. The other, which is particularly important in the case of employees who are making a significant contribution towards these goals, is a commitment to remaining a member of the organisation, rather than taking valuable knowledge and skills elsewhere. Gaining such a commitment is no easy matter. This is particularly true today, when managers are faced with far reaching changes in the age composition of the labour force, in attitudes towards work, in employment opportunities and so on. There is no simple set of rules which can be applied to achieve commitment within organisations. Rather, what is required to be able effectively to influence employee's work behaviour and attitudes is a more fundamental understanding of what motivates and what satisfies people at work.

In this chapter, we shall attempt to answer two main questions. Firstly, what determines the levels of motivation and job satisfaction which people experience at work. Secondly, what effects do these levels of motivation and job satisfaction have on important aspects of their work behaviour, such as levels of work performance, labour turnover and absenteeism. The aim is not to provide a review of the whole field of motivation and job satisfaction. It is to lay the foundation for suggesting practical guidelines which can be used to influence motivation and job satisfaction and, through them, people's work behaviour.

Motivation and the Management of Human Resources

In general terms, motivation is concerned with the forces which instigate, give direction to and sustain behaviour. In other words, motivation is what arouses people into action, determines the goals towards which these actions are channelled and influences the vigour and persistence with which such goals are pursued. More narrowly, in organisational terms, the motivation to work can be defined as the willingness to expend effort on a particular task in order to attain an incentive or incentives of a certain type. This definition is a useful one from our point of view, because it focuses attention on one of the key factors which influence work performance – the amount of effort the individual is willing to put into his or her work.

There are, of course, a great many other factors apart from motivation which influence levels of work performance. These include such things as whether the workers concerned have a clear understanding of the goals they are intended to achieve, their level of ability, the difficulty of the task, the feedback they receive concerning their performance, and so on (see Chapter 6). In effect, these factors put people in a position where they *can* perform the task to the expected standard. However, whether they *will* do so will depend upon whether they are sufficiently motivated to be willing to expend the effort necessary to perform the task and perform it well.

Thus, motivation is a vitally important subject both for managers in general and the Human Resource Specialist in particular. It is important to managers in general because it can be a major influence on their subordinates' work performance, and how well subordinates do their jobs will in turn have a major impact on the manager's own effectiveness and how easy a managerial life he or she has. Thus all managers need to have a good general understanding of motivation to motivate their subordinates to do their jobs well. Motivation is an important subject to the Human Resource Specialist for three main reasons. Firstly, like any other manager, the Human Resource Specialist will need to motivate his or her own subordinates to work effectively. Secondly, a major part of the Human Resource Specialist's job is the design, implementation and administration of Human Resource systems which have important motivational implications. Examples include incentive systems, performance appraisal, job evaluation, training, recruitment and so on. Some of these systems are intended to influence motivation directly in one way or another, but in each case, people's motivation will also influence the way in which they respond to the system. Thirdly, the Human Resource Specialist needs a good understanding of motivation because he or she may need to advise senior management on the likely motivational consequences of actions which they may propose to take. For example, overlooking a popular internal candidate for promotion could have widespread adverse motivational consequences among his or her fellow managers, who take the decision as a sign that their own dedication and loyalty might similarly be overlooked in the promotion stakes.

To function effectively in all these areas, the Human Resource Specialist needs to have a good understanding of what motivates different people, what factors influence their level of motivation and what steps can be taken to enhance motivation or maintain it at a satisfactory level. Two main types of motivation theory have been put forward in an attempt to answer these questions, need theories and process theories. We will examine each in turn.

Need Theories of Motivation

Needs provide the force which instigates motivated behaviour in the first place. They produce a feeling that we lack something necessary for our physiological or psychological well being, and make us agitated, restless or dissatisfied until we do something to dissipate the need. Need theories of work motivation are based on the assumption that if we can identify the different needs which motivate human behaviour and discover how these can be fulfilled within the working environment, then we will have discovered how to motivate people at work.

A wide variety of different needs have been identified. In the late 1930's, Murray and his colleagues listed no less than twelve physiological needs, including the needs for air, water food, sex, etc. and twenty-eight psychological needs, such as the needs for achievement, affiliation, recognition, dominance, power, autonomy, play, and so on. In the early 1940's, Maslow suggested that there were five main classes of human needs, physiological, safety, social, esteem and self-actualisation needs. He further suggested that these needs formed a hierarchy, with physiological needs at the bottom and self-actualisation at the top. If the lower order needs are unfulfilled, he argued, they will dominate behaviour, but once they are fulfilled, they no longer motivate, and people work their way up the hierarchy to esteem and self-actualisation needs. However, the research evidence provides little support for this idea, and in any case Maslow's original theory was hedged about with so many qualifications and exceptions that it is difficult to see how any clear cut conclusions can be drawn from it.

An influential need theory of the 1950's was Herzberg's motivator-hygiene theory of job satisfaction. Herzberg argued that job satisfaction and dissatisfaction were caused by two entirely different sets of factors. Factors such as supervision, salary, interpersonal relations and working conditions, he said, did not influence job satisfaction. Improving them would decrease job dissatisfaction but would not produce job satisfaction in a positive sense. The only way to produce job satisfaction, and thus increase motivation, according to Herzberg, was to make the work itself more interesting and improve such things as opportunities for achievement, recognition, responsibility and advancement. This process of actually building into people's jobs greater scope for personal achievement and its recognition, more challenging and responsible work and more scope for individual advancement and growth, Herzberg called job enrichment.

The theoretical and practical aspects of Herzberg's work have fared quite differently as far as subsequent research is concerned. The motivator-hygiene theory has been evaluated in a great many research studies and the majority fail to support it. It appears that factors causing job satisfaction and dissatisfaction do not divide neatly into two separate categories, as Herzberg suggests. On the other hand, it has been shown that job enrichment can have beneficial effects on both the quantity and quality of work output. In other words, the major weakness of Herzberg's theory was not in claiming that job enrichment could increase motivation, but in claiming that it was the *only* way to increase motivation.

Indeed, from the mid 1960's, there was growing acceptance of the view that early motivation theorists had greatly underestimated the complexity of human motivation. Not only are people motivated by a wide variety of different needs, but they are also highly variable. Whilst each individual may have his or her own hierarchy of needs, arranged in his or her own particular order of importance, this order will vary from individual to individual, and even within the same individual over time or in different situations.

The importance of individual differences is clearly recognised in current approaches to job design. One example is Hackman and Oldham's Job Characteristics Model, described in more detail later, in which it is suggested that employees' reactions to enriched jobs will depend upon the extent to which they value the fulfilment of higher order needs. However, the role played by individual differences in the motivation to work has much wider implications for managerial practice. Quite simply, it means that no theory of human needs can tell us what motivates a *particular* individual or group of individuals. People differ, and what motivates one individual or group may not motivate another or motivate them to a different extent. Motivation theories can undoubtedly be useful in identifying the range of human motives and explaining how they affect behaviour. But if a manager wishes to know what motivates a particular individual or group, there is no substitute for studying that particular individual or group, and finding out what it important to them, and therefore motivates their behaviour.

An understanding of people's needs, however, is only the first step towards predicting and influencing their work behaviour. Needs provide only a partial explanation of motivated behaviour. Knowing that someone has a need for money, for example, will not in itself tell us what he or she will do to fulfil this need. The response may be to work harder (if this will result in increased pay); put in for promotion; look for another, better paid job; take an additional part-time job; become apathetic because there does not seem to be any way of earning more money, and so on. Thus, predicting which particular course of action will be selected in any one situation requires more than an understanding of human needs. It also requires an inderstanding of the *processes* whereby these needs are converted into motivated behaviour. It is this subject which is taken up in the next section.

Process Theories of Motivation

The portrait of human motivation presented by need theorists is largely an emotional rather than an intellectual one. People are motivated to fulfil their needs without apparently devoting too much thought to the process. Process theories of motivation represent an attempt to redress this balance. The emotional aspects are not ignored, but greater emphasis is placed on the role of cognitive processes than in need theories.

A variety of different process theories have been put forward. Most are partial theories, in that they attempt to explain only one aspect of the motivational process. Locke, for example, has concentrated on the effects of goals on work performance. On the basis of extensive research, he and his colleagues have been able to show that gaining commitment to hard, precisely defined goals produces higher performance than simply asking people to 'do their best'.

The importance of goal setting has also been recognised by proponents of Organisational Behaviour Modification, who base their approach on Skinner's learning theory. They suggest that a combination of precise goals, feedback on gaol achievement and positive reinforcement for good performance, such as praise, will have a major impact on productivity. In one study where these ideas were put into practice, for example, it was estimated that the company saved $2 million over a three year period.[1]

Another partial theory is Adams' equity theory which is concerned with the effects of perceived fairness of rewards on work behaviour. According to Adams, people who believe that their rewards are unfair in relation to those received by others will take steps to restore a sense of equity. Based on this theory, it has been suggested that people who believe that they are underpaid will fell resentful and decrease either the quantity or quality of their output, whereas those who believe that they are overpaid will feel guilty and increase the quantity or quality of their output. The research evidence firmly supports the first prediction, and this has obvious implications for the Human Resource Manager. However, people who are overpaid do not always react as the theory predicts. Some may feel guilty and improve their performance, but others may restore feelings of equity in more convenient ways, such as changing their perception of their contribution or finding a more favourably rewarded group with which to compare themselves.

Apart from these partial theories, there is one process theory of motivation which attempts to provide a comprehensive framework within which it is possible to explain most aspects of work motivation. This is expectancy theory and the remainder of this section will be devoted to describing this theory in some detail.

The first major expectancy theory of motivation was put forward by Vroom,[2] although later writers, such as Porter and Lawler,[3] have both added to and modified the original theory in certain respects. The main principles of expectancy theory are presented in diagrammatic form in Figure 5.1. Variables in 'solid' boxes represent those included in expectancy theory itself. Those in 'dotted' boxes show how other concepts, particularly those from other motivational theories, can be incorporated within an expectancy theory framework. According to expectancy theory, the level of work motivation is determined by two main factors, value of incentives and effort-incentive expectations.[4] Incentives are anything which the individual may receive as a result of achieving a particular level of performance. They include not only positive outcomes, such as more money; greater security; enhanced promotion prospects; social acceptance; a sense of achievement; but also negative outcomes, such as loss of pay; damaged promotion prospects; social rejection; boredom; tiredness; headaches; loss of leisure time, and so on. These positive and negative incentives can be regarded as things which fulfil or prevent us from fulfilling our needs. Thus, just as people have different needs, the value of incentives will be different for different people. Some people may place a higher value on money, others on security, friend-ship, prestige, achievement, and so on.

Effort-incentive expectations refer to the strength of the individual's belief that he or she will receive, or avoid, such incentives by expending effort on a particular task. This is made up of two components. First, there are the individual's beliefs about the level of performance which he or she can reach, and second the individual's beliefs about the incentives which are likely to result from achieving that level of performance. According to expectancy theory, if any of these terms are zero, then motivation will also be zero. Suppose, for example, a sales representative is told that she will enhance her promotion prospects if she reaches the target of 500 units sold in each quarter of the following year. This will not motivate her if any of the following apply:

● Her effort-performance expectations are zero. She does not believe that she is capable of selling 500 units in each quarter of the following year, no matter how hard she tries.

● Her performance-incentive expectations are zero. She does not believe that she would be promoted even if she reached the target.

● The value of the incentive is zero. She does not want to be promoted, but would prefer to continue as a sales rep.

However, providing all these variables are above zero, the individual concerned will be motivated, and the higher they are, the more motivated he or she will be, and the more effort he or she will be willing to put into the task in question.

The amount of effort the individual puts into the task is one of the factors which will determine what level of performance he or she achieves. Other factors include:

Goal Clarity. The extent to which the individual has a clear understanding of the objectives he or she would be attempting to achieve with respect to the task in question.

Ability. The extent to which the individual has the necessary knowledge and skills to perform the task well.

Resources. The extent to which the individual has the equipment, support staff, raw materials, etc. necessary to perform the task well.

These factors, together with effort will determine the level of performance the individual achieves. Having achieved this level of performance, the individual will then receive certain incentives. Two broad classes of incentive can be distinguished, intrinsic and extrinsic. Intrinsic incentives are those which arise directly from the task itself, such as a sense of achievement, feelings of

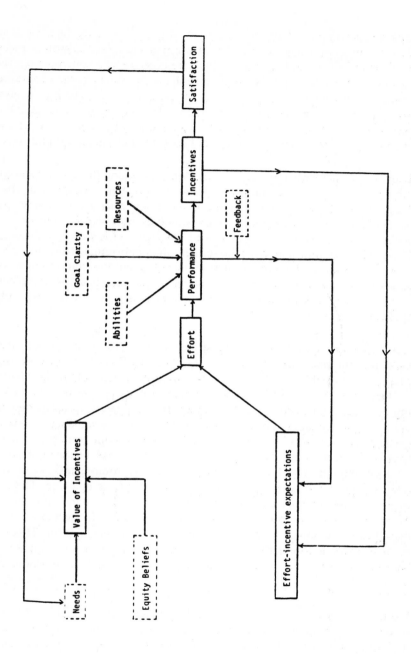

Figure 5.1: An Expectancy Model of Motivation and Job Satisfaction

103

pride and accomplishment, satisfaction at a job well done. In effect, we award these to ourselves if we feel we have performed a task well. Extrinsic incentives, on the other hand, are those which are given to us by other people, and include such things as money, social acceptance, praise, promotion, and such perks as a bigger office or a named car parking space. Having received whatever incentives accrue from performing the task, the individual will then experience a certain level of satisfaction, which may be high or low depending upon the extent to which they come up to the individual's aspirations.

Thus far, we have assumed that the individual is doing the task for the first time. However, there are many tasks which we do over and over again. In so doing, we get first-hand information of about how easy it is to achieve particular levels of performance, what incentives one actually receives for achieving these levels of performance and how satisfying such incentives are. This additional information may in turn modify our original effort-incentives expectations, or our feelings about the value of incentives, thus affecting our level of motivation. To complete the model, therefore, it is necessary to build in various feedback loops to show that in many cases we are dealing with a cyclical process.

It is, however, possible to distinguish between two different types of feedback. In some cases, we may receive 'intrinsic' feedback from the task itself. That is, it is possible to assess one's own performance and obtain an accurate evaluation of the standard achieved, whilst actually performing the task or immediately after completing it. Such information can obviously affect our beliefs about the amount of effort required to achieve a satisfactory level of performance, and this is shown in the solid feedback line from performance to effort-incentive expectations in Figure 5.1. Sometimes, however, it may be difficult to tell how well or how badly we are performing a task, or we may take actions which have repercussions of which we are unaware. Thus, we may not know whether we have achieved an acceptable standard of performance, or worse still, mistakenly believe that we have. In such cases, feedback from an external source of information can be very useful. This may come from the individual's immediate superior or a specially designed feedback system. Such 'extrinsic' feedback is shown separately in the dotted box in Figure 5.1.

Using expectancy theory, it is possible to analyse the effects of different incentives on work performance and explain why they have the effects they do. The effectiveness of money as a motivator, for example, can be explained as a function of both its value as an incentive and the ease with which it can be linked with performance. Where a job has an output which can be counted (e.g. amount produced or amount sold), then it is possible to link specified amounts of additional pay to level of output, as in a piecework system. Thus, there can be high expectations that improved performance will lead to additional earnings, resulting in increased motivation for people for whom money is a valued incentive.

Many jobs, however, do not have a single output which is easily counted. The Human Resource Specialist is one example. Alternatively, the output may not be under the sole control of the job holder. For example, a Production Manager whose department has a decline in productivity of 10% could be a poor performer or someone who is coping magnificently with the adverse effects of a strike. In such cases, performance cannot be measured directly. Organisations wishing to relate pay to performance therefore tend to give merit increases based upon superiors' assessment or evaluation of performance in a personnel appraisal system. This makes the link between performance and incentives much more intangible. If the appraisees trust the judgement and objectivity of the appraisers then the system may have the desired effect. On the other hand, if they believe that the appraisers are incapable of recognising good performance or that they give out merit increases on criteria other than performance, then this will undermine their effort-incentive expectations and their faith in the appraisal system. Thus, instead of motivating employees, the system may produce dissatisfaction, resentment and frustration. Because of problems such as these, some motivation theorists have serious reservations about the value of merit increase systems based on human judgement.[5]

Turning next to social relations, this is an incentive which has high value for many employees, but it is not one which organisations can easily link to performance. The main source of incentives, such as a feeling of belonging or being socially accepted, is the work group to which the person belongs. They, not management, will decide what types of behaviour will be rewarded with social acceptance and, as the Hawthorne studies showed, the work group may use social control to hold performance down rather than increase it. Thus attempting to improve social relations at work, e.g. by providing better social facilities, will not necessarily improve work performance. It may, however, improve job satisfaction which, as we shall see, may have other beneficial organisational effects.

Finally, there are the incentives which satisfy higher order needs. Some of these, such as promotion and recognition, are extrinsic; that is, they are within the power of the organisation or individual managers to give or withhold. Thus they can be made contingent upon performance, and when used in this way can be a powerful source of motivation for people who value such incentives.

Many of the incentives which fulfil higher order needs, however, are intrinsic. It is impossible to give someone a sense of achievement or the satisfaction of doing an interesting job. Nor is it possible to withhold such things. In effect, people award such incentives to themselves. All the organisation or individual manager can do is to redesign the person's job so that it offers the opportunity to experience such things as challenge, responsibility, interest, achievement and so on. On such jobs, however, there is a strong, natural link between performing well and receiving such incentives. One can only get a sense of achievement by achieving something; experience a sense of responsibility by behaving responsibly; or enjoy an interesting job by taking an interest in it. Thus, on intrinsically motivating jobs, people who value the fulfilment of higher order needs will monitor their own performance and reward themselves when they achieve what they consider to be a satisfactory level of performance. For this reason, they develop strong expectations that good performance will yield valued incentives, which explains why job enrichment can be an effective motivational technique for employees with strong higher order needs.

Research into expectancy theory hs provided evidence that the basic central core of the model does have some validity. Mitchell[6] reviewed 22 studies in which an attempt had been made to show that job effort was determined by a combination of what we have called value of incentives and effort-incentive expectations. He found that the average correlation between expectancy theory predictions and job effort was around 0.35. This is high enough to suggest that value of incentives and effort-incentive expectations do have a significant effect on effort. Nevertheless, it still leaves a great deal of the variation in effort to be accounted for. Part of the problem is undoubtedly methodological. Such variables as expectations, values and effort are very difficult to measure precisely and accurately, so there could be large amounts of error involved in attempts to test the model.

However, it is unlikely that methodological problems alone are responsible for expectancy theory's failure to predict job effort more accurately. Another contributory factor is almost certainly the fact that the basic expectancy model does not include all the variables which influence effort. This has led expectancy theorists to develop more and more complex models, often incorporating concepts and processes from other motivation theorists, in an attempt to provide a more comprehensive explanation of the motivation to work. The fact that so many other theoretical concepts can so easily be 'grafted on' to expectancy theory is both one of tis major strengths and major weaknesses.

It is a strength in that it allows virtually all motivation theory to be incorporated within one theoretical framework. Thus the whole of need theory can be included in the model by making needs one of the major influences on value of incentives. Equity theory can be included by arguing that people's beliefs about whether incentives are equitable or not may also influence their value to them. Goal setting theory can be incorporated by assuming that goal clarity influences performance, and if targets are explicitly linked to promised rewards, this could affect effort-incentive expectations too. Finally, feedback can be incorporated into the model, either as intrinsic feedback stemming directly from performing the task itself or as extrinsic feedback from some external source.

Thus expectancy theory serves the useful function of providing us with an overall picture of how the various different aspects of work motivation inter-relate and interact with each other. Unfortunately, however, this does not make the theory able to predict levels of work motivation any more accurately because all these additional concepts are also difficult to measure, and their precise relationship with expectancy theory variables is difficult to establish. This in turn makes it difficult to carry out a rigorous test of the model. Lawler and Suttle[7] comment rather sadly that "At this point in time, it seems that the theory has become so complex that it has exceeded the measures which exist to test it".

Furthermore, it is questionable whether even the more complex versions of expectancy theory include all the variables which influence human moti-vation. Expectancy theory seems to assume that people rationally work out their preferences and expectations (either consciously or unconsciously) in order to decide how much effort to put into a task. As Locke[8] points out, however, much of human motivation is not rational but is, instead, impulsive, emotional, neurotic or habitual, and no account is taken of such factors in expectancy theory. Whilst Locke's criticism is justified, it must be pointed out that this is also a problem for other cognitive theories of motivation, including his own goal setting theory. Irrational behaviour is by its very nature unpredictable. Certainly there are theories which can *explain* irrational behaviour after the event – psychoanalysis is a prime example – but such theories are notoriously bad at *predicting* what irrational behaviour will occur before it happens. It is arguable, therefore, that it is better to concentrate, as expectancy theory does, on the more rational aspects of human motivation, which are to some extent predictable and therefore controllable, rather than attempt to deal with the irrational aspects which by their nature are difficult either to predict or influence.

In summary, then, expectancy does not provide a final answer to the problems of work motivation. It does not include all the factors which influence work motivation nor, due to measurement problems, can it provide precise predictions of levels of work motivation. What it does do, however, is to provide a framework within which it is possible to identify the major controllable influences on work motivation and give some indication of how they are related. This makes it an extremely useful tool for the analysis of motivational problems. In effect it provides a checklist of the factors which need to be taken into account when attempting to influence levels of work motivation. There may well be others, but unless *at least* these factors are taken into account, there is a danger that one of the key variables in a particular situation may be overlooked, and consequently an attempt to influence motivation will misfire. In Chapter 6, the motivational principles described in this chapter are incorporated into a checklist, which is intended to help managers to analyse performance problems and identify potential solutions to them.

Job Satisfaction and the Management of Human Resources

Job satisfaction, and its converse job dissatisfaction, may be defined as the extent to which a person's general attitude towards his or her present job is either favourable or unfavourable. In addition to overall job satisfaction, it is possible to break down the person's attitude towards the job as a whole into more specific attitudes towards particular facets of the job, such as pay, supervision, security, social relations, working conditions and so on.

From the Human Resource Specialist's point of view, two main questions arise with respect to job satisfaction. What steps can be taken to improve job satisfaction and what effects does job satisfaction and dissatisfaction have on employees' work behaviour. We will examine each in turn.

Improving Job Satisfaction

Based on a review of research into job satisfaction, Vroom[2] suggested that the type of job which people typically find satisfying is one which provides "high pay, substantial promotional opportunities, considerate and participative supervision, an opportunity to interact with one's peers, varied duties, and a high degree of control over work methods and work pace". Thus, one way to improve job satisfaction would be to attempt to provide jobs with the characteristics which Vroom describes. However, as Vroom points out, people differ greatly in their motives, values and abilities, and this is likely to have an effect upon the type of job which they would find satisfying. Thus, providing the kind of job which would satisfy the 'average' or 'typical' worker would not necessarily satisfy everyone. Because of individual differences, different workers may experience different levels of job satisfaction within the same working environment. It follows that another way to approach the problem of improving job satisfaction would be to attempt to match the characteristics of the job to the needs of the workers concerned. Various different ways of achieving this end have been suggested.

Job Satisfaction Surveys

Not only may employees within a particular organisation have needs which differ from those of the 'typical' or 'average' worker, but their perception of the extent to which existing job characteristics fulfil these needs may also differ from those of management. Thus, providing the type of job which management *thinks* would be satisfying to them may not in fact improve their jobs in ways which the workers concerned would find most desirable. In many respects, therefore, it would be useful to carry out a job satisfaction survey to discover which aspects of their jobs the employees themselves feel are least satisfactory, before making any changes. However, it should be noted that such a survey will raise expectations that things will be improved, and as is pointed out in Chapter 6, failure to act on the results of the survey could make job satisfaction even worse.

Individual Job Design

In many jobs, particularly at the managerial level, the job content is to some extent flexible. This is sometimes seen quite clearly when a new job holder is appointed and does ostensibly the 'same' job in a quite different way from the previous incumbent. Certain core job activities may have to be performed, irrespective of who does the job, but outside these there may be many other activities over which the job holder can exercise some degree of choice. Such activities might include sitting on committees, liaising with other departments, carrying out special projects, attending conferences and so on. Thus, managers who identify the preferences of subordinates with respect to such 'peripheral' activites, and take them into account when allocating them between subordinates, are likely to enhance their general level of job satisfaction.

Group Job Design

With more routine, interdependent jobs, it is much more difficult to design jobs to suit individual needs. Nevertheless, it may still be possible to take into account the needs of the job holders as a group when designing jobs. In their Job Characteristics Model, Hackman and Oldham[9] suggest that certain core job characteristics produce favourable psychological reactions on the part of employees and these in turn lead to beneficial work and personal outcomes (see Figure 5.2). They also suggest, however, that the strength of the rela-

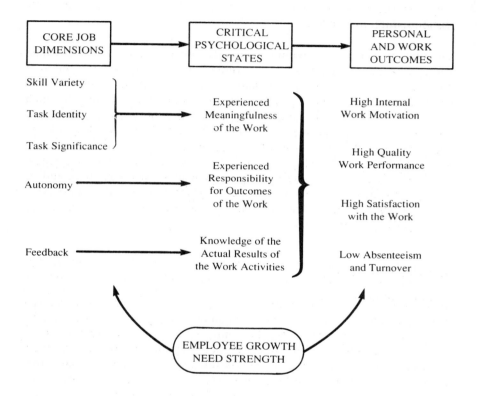

Figure 5.2: The Job Characteristics Model (from Hackman and Oldham, 1976)

tionship will be moderated by the Growth Need Strength (GNS) of the employees concerned. Employees with high GNS (those who value the fulfilment of higher order needs) are more likely to react favourably to enriched jobs than those with low GNS. The research evidence supports this conclusion. Higher levels of job satisfaction and work performance are found amongst high GNS employees than those with low GNS when jobs are high

110

on the core job characteristics described in Hackman and Oldham's model.

Nevertheless, the model still has two limitations. It does not tell us what to do when employees on the same job have highly different levels of GNS. If they do, then obviously a job designed to suit those with high GNS will be less satisfying to those with low GNS. The model also does not tell us what to do if the majority of the group has low GNS. It tells us how to enrich jobs to suit high GNS employees, but not how to design jobs which would be satisfying to those with low GNS.

Optional Work Systems

A system which would overcome the first of the above problems was introduced by Motorola in one of its departments. A group of 60 employees on an assembly line were given the choice of either remaining on the assembly line or moving to an enriched job where they assembled the whole product on their own. At first, only a few chose the enriched jobs, but eventually about half the employees moved over to the new method of production. Giving the workers the choice of the type of work they did appeared to have beneficial effects for both them and the organisation. Absenteeism and labour turnover went down and product quality improved.

However, it must be admitted that this is an isolated example involving a relatively small group of workers. Running two parallel production lines would not be a practical solution for large scale production departments, particularly if competitors are manufacturing equivalent products cheaply using conventional productions methods. Thus, in many cases, it may not be economically feasible to vary jobs to take into account individual needs. Even if the job itself cannot be modified, however, there may still be steps which can be taken to provide a more flexible working environment.

Flexible Working Hours

There has been a considerable growth in recent years of 'flexitime' systems which allow employees to choose, within certain limits, the times at which they work. Typically, employees are expected to work a set number of hours in any one week, and there is a 'core' time during the day when everyone is expected to be present. Outside this, however, there is a broad time band within which the workers can choose the hours which they work to suit there own needs.

Cafeteria Wage Payment Systems

The conventional type of wage and salary payment system provides for a particular level of pay, with standard deductions, benefits, holiday entitlements and so on. However, this ignores individual differences between employees with respect to the types of benefits they would prefer to receive. Thus, some might prefer straight salary with no deductions, apart from statutory ones, whereas others might prefer a larger pension, health insurance and so on, with their contributions deducted from their pay. Systems which allow employees a choice about such matters have been called 'cafeteria' systems, because, like cafeterias, they allow people to select what they want from a range of alternatives, rather than having to take a set menu. Research in the U.S.A. has shown that allowing employees to choose the type of benefits they receive, rather than imposing a standard system, can increase pay satisfaction without increasing the monetary cost to the organisation. However, it must be noted that, because there are more statutory deductions in the U.K., there is also less scope for flexibility in the way in which wages and salaries are paid than in the U.S.A.

Flexible Leadership Styles

Modern leadership theorists tend to argue that there is no one best way to manage people.[10] The most appropriate leadership style will depend upon the situation. Situational factors which determine the most appropriate leadership style include such things as the nature of the task, the amount of authority the manager has, whether the manager has all the relevant information, and the preferences of the subordinates. Thus, managers can, within certain limits, enhance the job satisfaction of subordinates by selecting leadership style, e.g., directive or participative, task or person centred, which matches the preferences of the subordinates concerned.

Selective Recruitment

So far, we have been considering ways of changing jobs or the working environment to match people's needs. However, there is another way of achieving a better fit between job characteristics and people's needs, and that is to select employees whose needs fit the jobs which the organisation already has. The accurate identification of potential employees' needs during the selection phase is something which requires considerable skill (see Chapter 3). One alternative which has been suggested in recent years is the 'realistic job preview'. This gives potential employees a realistic description of the job, rather than the highly flattering picture usually given in job advertisements, thus allowing them to make a more rational decision about whether the job would be suitable from their point of view. Typically, realistic job previews reduce the number of applicants for a job, but those who do apply and are selected tend to be more satisfied and remain in it longer.[11]

Organisational Consequences of Job Satisfaction and Dissatisfaction

Job Satisfaction and Work Performance

Early theorists tended to believe that a satisfied worker would be a productive worker. However, the accumulated research evidence has shown that this is not necessarily so. Correlations between job satisfaction and work performance vary widely, but the average correlation has been found to be in the region of 0.14, a figure which Vroom described as being so low as to have little theoretical or practical significance.[12] Such findings are very damaging for theories like Herzberg's which claim that job satisfaction leads to higher levels of productivity. However, they are quite consistent with expectancy theory. In effect, expectancy theory argues that it is anticipated rather than current satisfaction which influences performance. That is, a worker is motivated to expend effort on a task to the extent that he or she believes that this will result in obtaining valued incentives, and hence feeling satisfied. Porter and Lawler[3] therefore argue that the way to improve performance is not to increase everyone's satisfaction and make everyone happy, but to ensure that the best performing employees are the most satisfied, by providing a strong link between levels of performance and the incentives received.

Job Satisfaction and Labour Turnover

Studies of the relationship between job satisfaction and labour turnover have consistently found this relationship to be negative. As one might expect, the more satisfied workers are with their jobs, the less likely they are to leave them. There are, of course, other factors involved, a major one being the ease with which the worker can obtain another job. This will depend on such things as the state of the labour market and the extent to which he or she has skills for which there is high demand. Thus, a satisfied worker may move to what he or she believes will be an even better job, whilst a dissatisfied worker may remain in the same job because he or she cannot get anything better. Nevertheless, other things being equal, it does appear that increasing levels of job satisfaction does lead to lower levels of labour turnover.

Job Satisfaction and Absenteeism

Studies of the relationship between job satisfaction and absenteeism have produced inconclusive results. The relationship tends to be negative, but is very weak and variable. One recent review suggests that job satisfaction typically accounts for less than 4% of the variance in absenteeism.[13]

Thus, attempts to decrease absenteeism solely by increasing levels of job satisfaction seem unlikely to be particularly effective. A more promising approach would seem to be to attempt to *motivate* employees to attend work more regularly. This is the view taken by Steers and Rhodes.[14] They suggest that attendance motivation will be influenced by the following factors:

1   Work related attitudes, e.g., job satisfaction

2   Economic and market forces

3   Organisational control systems, e.g., rewards and punishments for attendance and non-attendance

4   Personal factors, e.g., family size, age, etc.

5   Absence culture and work group norms

Steers and Rhodes further suggest that actual attendance also will be influenced by perceived ability to attend. This in turn will be influenced by:

1   Illness and accidents

2   Family responsibilities

3   Transportation problems

The full model is presented in diagrammatic form in Figure 5.3.

The major advantage of this model is that, like expectancy theory, it can be used as a diagnostic tool to pinpoint the key problems and find solutions. It may be that, in a particular instance, work attitudes are a major contributory factor in absenteeism and steps to improve job satisfaction are in order. In other cases, the problem may lie elsewhere, and steps such as the introduction of rewards for good attendance, day care centres for children, a company bus or a company health programme could be more effective.

114

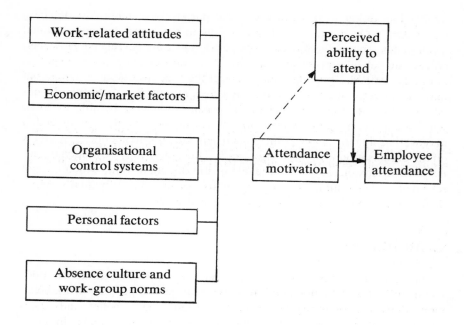

**Figure 5.3: An Organising Framework For Understanding Absence Research
(from Steers and Rhodes, 1984)**

Job Satisfaction and Industrial Unrest

There has been surprisingly little research into the relationship between job
satisfaction and industrial relations problems, such as strikes, go-slows,
stoppages, working to rule and so on. Common sense would suggest that
dissatisfied workers would be more likely to take such actions, but apart from
some research which shows that dissatisfied workers are more likely to join
a union and more likely to vote for union representation, there is little or no
firm evidence on this important question.

However, there is research which throws light on certain related types of
behaviour. Dissatisfied employees are less likely to perform what have been
called 'citizenship behaviours', such as helping co-workers, cleaning up the
work place and taking good care of company resources.[15] Conversely, they
more frequently indulge in behaviours such as complaining about the boss or
the organisation to outsiders, ignoring the boss, taking undeserved breaks,

115

deliberately doing work incorrectly, and purposely damaging or defacing equipment.[16] On the face of it, this seems to contradict the conventional wisdom that job satisfaction and work performance are not related. However, citizenship behaviours are activities which are outside the employee's job as normally defined. Thus, they may benefit the organisation as a whole, but may not directly affect the employee's own output. Similarly, employees taking actions to the detriment of the organisation may be able to do so without it affecting their own performance in any observable way. Indeed, it may well be that the whole point of such behaviours is to get one's own back on the organisation *without being caught*. Thus, there may be hidden organisational disadvantages to high levels of job dissatisfaction, which are not revealed by conventional research methods, because the individual's output on his or her own job remains apparently unaffected.

Conclusion

In this chapter, we have described the main factors which influence motivation and job satisfaction and how they in turn affect people's work behaviour. Because people vary so much in their needs, values, beliefs and expectations, it is impossible to suggest a single, generally applicable solution to all problems of motivation and job satisfaction. What satisfies and motivates one person may not satisfy and motivate another. The principal aim of this chapter, therefore, has not been to suggest solutions to problems of motivation and job satisfaction. Rather it has been to enhance the understanding of these subjects, in order to enable Human Resource Specialists and other managers to analyse such problems and identify more effective solutions for themselves. This is a theme which will be taken up in the next chapter, when we shall be concerned with the question of improving work performance in more general terms.

References

1 E J Feeney (1972) Performance audit, feedback and positive reinforcement. *Training and Development Journal*, November, 8-13.

2 V H Vroom (1964) *Work and Motivation*. Wiley.

3 L W Porter and E E Lawler (1968) What job attitudes tell about motivation. *Harvard Business Review, 46*, 118-126.

4 These concepts are given different names in different versions of expec-

tancy theory. Valence, value of rewards, expectancy and effort-reward expectations are common alternatives.

5   See, for example, H H Meyer (1975) The pay for performance dilemma. *Organizational Dynamics,* Winter, 39-50.

6   T R Mitchell (1974) Expectancy models of job satisfaction, occupational preference and effort: A theoretical, methodological and empirical appraisal. *Psychological Bulletin, 81,* 1053-1077.

7   E E Lawler and J L Suttle (1973) Expectancy theory and job behavior. *Organizational Behavior and Human Performance, 9,* 482-503.

8   E A Locke (1975) Personnel attitudes and motivation. *Annual Review of Psychology, 26,* 457-480.

9   J R Hackman and G R Oldham (1976) Motivation through the design of work: Test of a theory. *Organizational Behavior and Human Performance, 16,* 250-279.

10 P L Wright and D S Taylor (1984) *Improving Leadership Performance.* Prentice-Hall.

11 A more detailed discussion of many of these methods of matching the job content and environment to individual needs can be found in E E Lawler (1974) For a more effective organization – Match the job to the man. *Organizational Dynamics, 2,* Summer, 19-29.

12 Vroom, *op. cit.* For an extensive, more recent review, see M T Iaffaldano and P Muchinsky (1985) Job satisfaction and job performance: A metaanalysis. *Psychological Bulletin, 97,* 251-273.

13 R D Hackett and R M Guion (1985) A re-evaluation of the absenteeism-job satisfaction relationship. *Organizational Behavior and Human Decision Processes, 35,* 340-381.

14 R M Steers and S R Rhodes (1984) Knowledge and speculation about absenteeism, in P S Goodman and R S Atkin (Eds) *Absenteeism: New Approaches to Understanding, Measuring and Managing Employee Absence.* Jossey Bass, 229-275.

15 T S Bateman and D W Organ (1983) Job satisfaction and the good soldier: The relationship between affect and employee 'citizenship'. *Academy of*

Management Journal, 26, 587-595.

C A Smith, D W Organ and J P Near (1983) Organizational citizenship behavior: Its nature and antecedents. *Journal of Applied Psychology, 68,* 653-663.

16 P E Spector (1975) Relationships of organizational frustration with reported behavioral reactions of employees. *Journal of Applied Psychology, 60,* 635-637.

Suggested Reading

For a collection of original articles and commentaries covering the whole field of work motivation and job satisfaction, see:

R M Steers and L W Porter (Eds) (1987) *Motivation and Work Behavior,* 4th Ed. McGraw-Hill.

Questions

1   An understanding of human needs provides a necessary but not sufficient basis for influencing the motivation to work. Discuss.

2   To what extent has expectancy theory enhanced our ability to understand, predict and influence the motivation to work?

3   What are the implications of job satisfaction research for the management of human resources?

Chapter 6

Managing Unsatisfactory Performance

Peter L Wright and David S Taylor

Introduction

A common theme which runs throughout this book is the identification of practical methods to influence the behaviour and attitudes of people at work. This concern can be seen in the different chapters on selection, training, motivation, staff appraisal, and so on. In order to deal with such topics in any depth, it is necessary to cover them in separate chapters, which may erroneously give the impression that such topics represent problems which can be looked at in isolation. Real life, however, does not segment itself as conveniently as the chapters in a book, and material from all these chapters may be relevant to the solution of a single real life problem. The aim of the present chapter is to present an integrated scheme for the analysis of performance problems which draws together material from many different aspects of Human Resource Management.

Maintaining, and where possible improving the level of performance of subordinates is a major aspect of the manager's job. It is particularly important where the subordinate's performance falls below expected standards, but a significant contribution to organisational effectiveness can also be made by discovering ways to improve the performance of people who are already performing their jobs satisfactorily. Furthermore, although there are exceptions, many of the methods which can be used to bring unsatisfactory performers up to standard can also be used to make satisfactory or good performers even better. Thus, whilst we use the term 'performance problem' for the sake of convenience in this chapter, it is worth noting that the term 'opportunity for development' would be equally applicable in many cases.

The Three Stages of Performance Improvement

In order to improve performance at work, whatever the current level of performance may be, three steps are necessary. The manager concerned must define precisely what aspects of performance it would be beneficial to improve, discover the reasons why performance is not satisfactory or not as good as it could be, and identify effective actions which can be taken to achieve the desired improvement in performance.[1] If any of these steps are omitted, then the attempt to improve performance is unlikely to be successful. If the performance problem is incorrectly defined in the first place, then much time and effort can be wasted attempting to solve the wrong problem. If the real reasons for the problems are not understood, then an inappropriate solution to the problem is likely to be chosen, such as trying to motivate someone who lacks the ability to do the task well in the first place. If effective actions to solve the problem are not identified, then the result may be increased understanding, but we cannot be sure that this will have beneficial effects in organisational terms. The individual may know *why* his or her performance was unsatisfactory, but not have a clear idea of *what* to do to improve it. We will now examine these three steps in more detail.

Identifying Performance Problems

Where performance is obviously unsatisfactory it will be relatively easy to identify that a performance problem exists. Quantity or quality of output may be\below laid down minimum standards. Costly mistakes may have been made. There may have been complaints from other members of the organisation, or from people outside the organisation, such as customers, clients, suppliers, government inspectors, and so on. On the other hand, it is less easy to identify potential areas for improvement when performance is satisfactory or good. Unless there are some obvious minor blemishes, a review of the employee's performance as a whole may be necessary. In an appraisal interview, for example, there will typically be some form of review of the employee's 'strengths' and 'weaknesses' (although we would not recommend the use of the term 'weakness' in the interview itself) which may reveal areas for further development. In yet other cases, an area for improvement may not even relate to the individual's present job, but may be concerned with knowledge or skills the individual may need for some future job or to cope with new developments such as changing markets or changing production methods.

However, identifying that there may be a need for performance improvement is not the same as identifying what it is. For example, the fact that a customer has complained about the arrogant manner of a sales representative may indicate that there is a performance problem, but it does not tell us exactly what the sales representative did to produce this impression. It could be any one of a number of things, such as accent, manner, style of dress, the use of particular words or phrases, and so on. Telling the sales representative to be 'less arrogant' will have little effect if he or she is unaware of the source of the problem. Thus, it will be necessary to identify precisely what the problem is before trying to solve it. Furthermore, even if we know what the problem is, this does not tell us whether it is worth spending time and effort trying to solve it. Both these points will be taken up later.

Causes of Unsatisfactory Performance

Early writers on work performance tended to assume that it was influenced by a relatively small number of factors. For example, Maier's[2] much quoted formula, put forward during the 1950's, suggested that:

$$Performance = Ability \times Motivation$$

This formula serves the useful function of drawing attention to two of the major factors influencing work performance. It also says something of the relationship between them. The fact that the relationship is multiplicative suggests that there is little point in attempting to increase someone's ability if their motivation to do the task is zero, nor in attempting to motivate someone who does not have the ability to do the task in the first place.

Nevertheless, there are clearly other factors, apart from ability and motivation, which influence work performance. If one were to have a major operation, for example, then the services of a highly gifted, highly motivated surgeon would be very desirable, but the presence or absence of sterilised instruments, a fully equipped operating theatre and a back up team of anaesthetist and nurses could also have a major effect on his or her performance. In an attempt to provide a more complete picture of the factors influencing work performance, therefore, more and more complex formulae began to appear. For example, Campbell and Pritchard,[3] suggested that:

Performance = f (aptitude level x skill level x understanding of the task x choice to expend effort x choice of degree of effort to expend x choice to persist x facilitating and inhibiting conditions not under the control of the individual)

This formula undoubtedly gives a more comprehensive description of the factors influencing work performance than Maier's, but it does have a number of drawbacks as a diagnostic tool. Its apparent complexity would tend to discourage managers from using it. It does not give any indications of the actions which might be taken to solve the problem once its causes have been identified. Finally, the mathematical nature of the formula is largely spurious. The variables listed undoubtedly do influence performance in some way, but they are extremely difficult to measure and the relationships between them are quite complex. For instance, having a high skill level may actually impair performance on a relatively simple task, because the individual finds the task boring and consequently may not be motivated to perform well. In practice, therefore, it is unlikely that one could use such a formula to predict effort simply by inserting precise numerical values for the terms on the right hand side of the equation. This can reduce the formula's acceptability to scientifically trained managers, who may take the view that because it cannot be used like a 'real' scientific formula, then the whole idea is bogus.

An alternative approach is simply to list factors influencing work performance. Several such lists have been produced, including those of Miner (see Table 6.1) and Steinmetz (see Table 6.2).[4] Such lists avoid some of the problems of the formulae described earlier, but they are not without limitations. For example, the practical value of Steinmetz's list is limited by the fact that it is quite long, and includes many factors that the manager can do little or nothing about, such as sex and senility. It also omits others which the manager can do something about, including lack of feedback. Similarly, relevant factors such as lack of clear targets and lack of feedback are omitted from Miner's list, despite its length. Furthermore, whilst both Miner and Steinmetz discuss methods of improving work performance, they do not link specific remedial actions to each of the suggested causes of poor performance. Thus their lists may help managers to have a better understanding of the causes of poor performance, but they do not provide specific guidance on what to do to solve a performance problem once it has been identified.

Identifying Solutions to Performance Problems

Mager and Pipe's Flow Diagram

Many of the problems outlined in the previous section were overcome by Mager and Pipe[5] by the use of a flow diagram (see Figure 6.1). Mager and Pipe suggest that the first step in analysing performance problems should be to describe the 'performance discrepancy', i.e. the difference between someone's actual performance and his or her desired performance. Next the flow diagram suggests that the manager should examine the consequences of

122

Table 6.1: Steinmetz's List of Possible Causes of Poor Performance

Managerial and Organisational Shortcomings

Lack of proper motivational environment
Personality problems
Inappropriate job assignment
Improper supervision
Lack of training
Failure to establish duties

Individual, Personal Shortcomings of the Employee

Lack of motivation
Laziness
Personality clashes
Dissatisfaction with job assignment
Failure to understand one's duties
Chronic absenteeism
Alcoholism
Mental illness
Chronic illness
Senility
Sex

Outside Influences

Family problems
Social mores
Conditions of the labour market
Governmental actions
Union policies
Climate

Source: Steinmetz (1969)

Table 6.2: Miner's List of Factors Leading to
Ineffective Performance in Business Organisations

Intelligence and Job Knowledge
> Insufficient verbal ability
> Insufficient special ability other than verbal
> Insufficient job knowledge
> Defect of judgement or memory

Emotions and Emotional Illness
> Continuing disruptive emotion (anxiety, depression, anger, excitement, shame, guilt, jealousy)
> Psychosis (with anxiety, depression, anger, etc., predominating)
> Neurosis (with anxiety, depression, anger, etc., predominating)
> Alcoholism and drug problems

Individual Motivation to Work
> Strong motives frustrated at work
> Unintegrated means to satisfy motives
> Excessively low personal work standards
> Generalized low work motivation

Physical Characteristics and Disorders
> Physical illness or handicap, including brain damage
> Physical disorders of emotional origin
> Inappropriate physical characteristics
> Insufficient muscular or sensory ability

Family Ties
> Family crisis
> Separation from an emotionally significant family
> Social isolation
> Predominance of family considerations over work demands

The Groups at Work
> Negative consequences associated with group cohesion
> Ineffective management
> Inappropriate managerial standards or criteria

The Company
> Insufficient organisational action
> Placement error
> Organisational over-permissiveness
> Excessive span of control
> Inappropriate organisational standards or criteria

Society and its Values
> Application of legal sanctions
> Enforcement of cultural values by means not connected with the administration of the law
> Conflict between job demands and cultural values as individually held (equity, freedom, morality, etc.)

Situational Forces
> Negative consequences of economic forces
> Negative consequences of geographic location
> Detrimental conditions of work
> Excessive danger
> Problems in the work itself

Source: Miner and Brewer (1976)

124

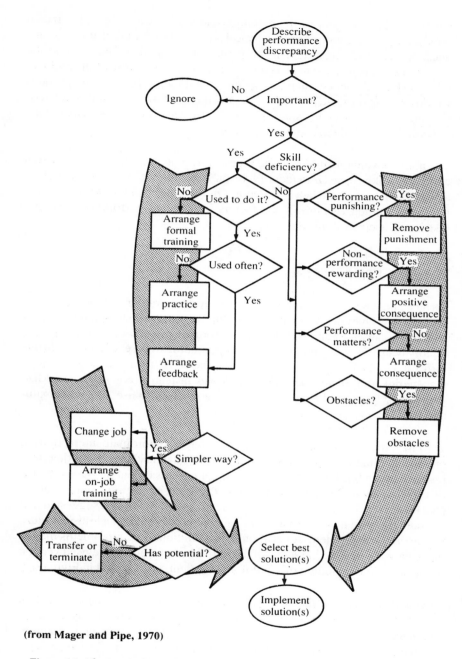

(from Mager and Pipe, 1970)

Figure 6.1: Mager and Pipe's Flow Diagram for Analysing Performance Problems

the discrepancy, and only do something about it if these are important. It then asks whether the cause of the problem is a skill deficiency. If it is, various questions are used to establish the nature of the skill deficiency and the remedial actions which can be taken in each case. If the cause of the problem is not a skill deficiency, then it is assumed that the problem is one of motivation or some obstacle preventing satisfactory performance, and again various questions are used to establish the specific cause of the problem and the remedial actions which can be taken in each case.

The major advantage of Mager and Pipe's flow diagram is that its step by step approach makes it easier to identify the precise cause of the problem, and the actions which can be taken to solve it. On the other hand, it does present a relatively limited account of the factors influencing performance, largely restricting itself to skills and motivation.

Wright and Taylor's Checklist

Wright and Taylor[1] attempted to overcome this problem by developing a revised flow chart based on Mager and Pipe's work, which included various additional causes of and solutions to performance problems. However, this rapidly became a very complex diagram, spreading over several pages. In this form, it would have been much too cumbersome to use as a convenient managerial tool. They therefore developed instead a one page checklist, which they felt would be easier to follow and easier to use in practical situations.

The checklist grew out of our interest in manager-subordinate interactions in one-to-one situations, such as personnel appraisal interviews. It was therefore restricted to individual, rather than group or organisational problems. It also restricted itself to problems arising from the job itself. Subsequent use of the checklist, both as a training technique and in real life situations suggested that it would have been useful to include 'personal factors' as an additional cause of performance problems, even though the solution to such problems may in many cases be beyond the scope of the individual manager. A revised version of the checklist, including this additional element, is presented in Figure 6.2.

The checklist suggests that the first step in analysing a performance problem is to define the problem in behavioural terms. That is, the manager should stipulate, as precisely as possible, what it is that the subordinate is doing or not doing which is adversely affecting his or her work performance. This helps to avoid one of the major pitfalls in attempting to improve work performance, that of defining a subordinate's performance problem in terms of

Figure 6.2: Checklist for Improving Work Performance

1 What is the problem in behavioural terms? What precisely is the individual doing or not doing which is adversely influencing his or her performance?

2 Is the problem *really* serious enough to spend time and effort on?

3 What reasons might there be for the performance problem? (see column 1)

4 What actions might be taken to improve the situation? (see column 2)

Possible Reasons for Performance Problem	Possible Solutions
Goal Clarity. Is the person fully aware of the job requirements?	Give guidance concerning expected goals and standards. Set targets. MBO.
Ability. Does the person have the capacity to do the job well?	Provide formal training, on the job coaching, practice, secondment, etc.
Task Difficulty. Does the person find the task too demanding?	Simplify task, reduce work load, reduce time pressures, etc.
Intrinsic Motivation. Does the person find the task rewarding in itself?	Redesign job to match job-holder's needs.
Extrinsic Motivation. Is good performance rewarded by others?	Arrange positive consequences for good performance and zero or negative consequences for poor performance.
Feedback. Does the person receive adequate feedback about his/her performance?	Provide or arrange feedback.
Working Conditions. Do working conditions, physical or social, interfere with performance?	Improve light, noise, heat, layout, remove distractions, etc., as appropriate.
Personal Problems, e.g. stress, substance abuse, family problems, etc.	Provide counselling if sufficiently skilled. Call in specialist helper.

5 Do you have sufficient information to select the most appropriate solutions(s)? – if not, collect the information required, e.g. consult records, observe work behaviour, talk to person concerned.

6 Select most appropriate solution(s).

7 Is the solution worthwhile in cost benefit terms?
   a If so, implement it.
   b If not, work through the checklist again, or relocate the individual, *or* reorganise the department/organisation, *or* live with the problem.

8 Could you have handled the problem better? If so, review own performance. If not, and the problem is solved, reward yourself and tackle the next problem.

a personality defect, such as laziness, lack of confidence or arrogance. This is not to say that personality has no effect on behaviour. It undoubtedly does. However there are two good reasons for defining performance problems in terms of behaviour rather than personality. The first is theoretical. Although personality influences people's behaviour, it is by no means the only determinant. The environment also has a major impact. Thus people with quite different personalities may behave in quite similar ways when in certain environments, such as at a funeral service. Conversely, even though their personalities do not change, people often behave quite differently in different situations, for example, at a formal meeting compared with an office party.

The second reason is practical. By the time we are adults, our personalities are relatively stable. Thus bringing about a change in personality is extremely difficult and is not something which managers have the expertise to do effectively, nor perhaps would it be ethical for them to attempt to do so. Thus, deciding that the problem is someone's laziness, lack of confidence, lack of foresight or aggressive nature renders the problem unsolvable. Further, we do not observe such personality traits directly. They are inferences based on observation of behaviour. The individual has done, or failed to do, something to give us this impression of his or her personality, for example, sat around doing nothing when there was work to be done, failed to speak up in a departmental meeting or failed to order essential supplies on time. These rather more precise behavioural descriptions are much less complex to tackle. They are aspects of behaviour which a manager can probably get a subordinate to change if the right approach to the problem is used.

Having defined the problem in behavioural terms, the next step, as in the Mager and Pipe flow diagram, is to ask whether the problem is really serious enough to spend time and effort on. If the behaviour in question has little effect on the individual's work performance or that of others, then expending a great deal of time and effort in an attempt to change it would hardly seem to be an effective use of the organisation's resources. Of course, there may be times when we feel obliged to do so, for reasons of expediency. The organisation may demand compliance with apparently meaningless rules, or our immediate superior may insist on his or her own foibles being imposed on our subordinates. By the same token, however, it may be useful to examine our reasons for believing that a performance problem exists. It is all too easy to say something is bad for morale, bad for the company image, will upset people, or will give a bad impression, but will it? In some cases, such feelings may be justified but there is always the possibility that they are merely rationalisations designed to provide a justification for our own foibles or assumptions about correct behaviour.

128

Assuming the problem is seen as a significant one, the next step is to review possible causes and potential solutions. In many respects, it is probably better to work through all the possible causes first, before thinking about solutions. In this way, you are less likely to get sidetracked before completing a thorough analysis. For ease of presentation, however, we will consider them together here.

Goal Clarity

The individual may not know or may misunderstand the requirements of the job. For instance, the individual may not realise that a certain task is part of the job, may not know what standard of performance is expected, or may mistakenly place greater emphasis on one part of the job rather than another (for example, stressing quality of output when quantity is more important or vice versa).

If so, some guidance is necessary concerning the job requirements, priorities and expected standards. Depending on how the individual is likely to respond, such guidance may range from a quiet word pointing out that some aspect of performance is important to a more rigorous goal setting exercise, say in a performance appraisal interview. Alternatively, if the problem is widespread, a more formal system such as Management by Objectives (MBO) for the unit as a whole may be appropriate. Research by Locke and his colleagues (see Chapter 5) has shown that goal setting can be a highly effective method of improving work performance, particularly when combined with appropriate feedback. A survey of 17 goal setting programmes revealed a median improvement in performance of 16%.[6]

Ability

The individual may lack certain skills or knowledge required to do the job well. If so, and the individual appears to have the capacity to acquire such skills or knowledge, then some form of training (see Chapter 7) or development (see Chapter 8) may provide a solution to the problem.

Task Difficulty

Looking at the problem the other way round, the task may be too difficult for the job holder to be expected to perform it effectively. It may be more complex, involve more different aspects or involve shorter deadlines than the individual can cope with. Alternatively, the goals which the individual has been set, whilst clear, may be inappropriate. They may have been set at too high a level or they may conflict. For example, the job holder may have been set high goals for both quantity and quality of output, either of which can be achieved, but only at the expense of the other. Thus, whatever the individual does, performance will be below standard in one area or the other. If it is decided that task difficulty, rather than lack of ability is the source of the problem, then simplifying the task or setting lower performance goals may be appropriate solutions.

Intrinsic Motivation

The individual may not be motivated to perform well because he or she does not find the task rewarding in itself. That is, the job does not provide the interest, stimulation, opportunities for achievement, feeling of pride, etc. which the job holder would like to experience. In order to provide such intrinsic motivation, it will be necessary to redesign the job in some way so that it provides more challenge, more responsibility, more intrinsically interesting work, and so on (see Chapter 5). A survey of 13 job enrichment programmes showed a median improvement in performance of 17%.[6]

	Good Performance	Poor Performance
Rewards	(1)	(2)
Negative or Zero Outcomes	(3)	(4)

Figure 6.3: Extrinsic Rewards and Work Performance

Extrinsic Motivation

The individual may not be motivated to perform well because he or she believes that good performance will not be rewarded, or may even be punished by other people, e.g. superiors, colleagues, customers, etc. (see Chapter 5). Wright and Taylor[1] suggest that a simple 2 x 2 diagram may help in the analysis of the effects of extrinsic rewards (see Figure 6.3). To encourage good performance, the majority of items should be in quadrants 1 and 4. That is, good performance should result in many positive outcomes for the individual concerned and few negative ones, whilst the reverse should be the case for poor performance. Yet one often hears of good performers being punished and poor performers being rewarded. For example, conscientious employees may be given disliked and tedious tasks, because they are the only ones who can be relied upon to do them well, whilst 'difficult' employees are not given disliked tasks because it is not worth the trouble this would cause. Similarly, poor performers may not be given difficult tasks to do because they would only make a mess of them. If the nature of the reward system is such that it does not pay to be a good performer, it is only to be expected that extrinsic motivation will be low. Under these circumstances, we suggest that the manager should examine all the rewards at his or her disposal – verbal recognition, more interesting work assignments, not being given last minute onerous assignments, time off, visits to conferences, salary and promotion recommendations, etc., and ensure that they go to the good performers rather than the poor ones. The research evidence indicates that rewards and punishments administered appropriately (i.e. contingent on performance) cause increases in performance. Conversely, administered inappropriately or not at all, they are likely to produce many dysfunctional effects, including declining productivity and feelings of inequity and dissatisfaction.[7] Where monetary rewards can be clearly linked to measurable levels of performance, this can have a marked impact on performance. A survey of 15 studies of payment by results systems showed a median improvement in performance of 35%.[6]

One area of performance which senior management may wish to consider in relation to their own reward behaviour is staff development itself. There are undoubted benefits for the manager who takes the time and trouble to develop his or her own staff, but there are also potential costs. For example, good subordinates may be lost through promotions and transfers, and there may be correspondingly less time to spend on the achievement of short-term goals. Thus, if senior management say they want managers to develop their staff, but actually reward the more visible behaviours with easily measurable outputs, whilst ignoring staff development, then many managers will inevitably feel that it is not in their interest to spend much time on long-term staff development.[8]

Feedback

Poor performance may occur because the individual does not receive adequate feedback concerning his or her standard of performance, and thus does not realise the need for improvement. In that case, some form of feedback concerning the level of performance achieved will be necessary. This may be carried out informally in discussion with the individual concerned, or if there is a general problem of lack of feedback, it may be appropriate to set up a formal feedback system providing data on levels of performance directly to the employees in question. During the early 1970s, Emery Air Freight estimated that they had saved two million dollars over a three year period by using a combination of goal setting, feedback and recognition.[9]

Resources

The individual may not be able to perform well because he or she lacks the necessary equipment, staff, raw materials or support services. If this is the case, the manager will need either to provide the necessary resources or, in fairness, accept a lower standard of performance than otherwise might be expected.

Working Conditions

The individual's level of work performance may be impaired by adverse conditions, such as inappropriate levels of noise, temperature, humidity, interruptions, hours of work, and so on. As with resources, the manager will need either to improve working conditions, or accept a lower standard of performance than might have been expected.

Personal Problems

The individual's work performance may have been affected by factors not directly concerned with work, for example, family problems, stress, substance abuse (alcohol, drugs, etc.), lack of social acceptance, and so on. In such circumstances, unlike the cases we have previously discussed, there are no ready-made 'solutions' to the problem. Easing the person's work load may be appropriate as a temporary expedient, but obviously does not provide a viable long term solution. Furthermore, telling someone how to solve their personal problem is usually not very effective. A solution which would work for the person giving advice may be inappropriate or unacceptable for the person with the problem. What the manager can do, providing he or she has the necessary skills, is to carry out a counselling interview. That is, allow the person to talk through the problem, and allow them to reach their own solutions, *without giving advice*. However, if the manager feels that he or she lacks the skills to do this effectively or the problem is too severe for the manager to provide effective assistance, then it will be more appropriate to call in outside help. This may come from specialist counsellors, either within or outside the organisation or from groups such as Alcoholics Anonymous who provide help with specific types of problem. Given that occupational stress is a quite prevalent problem, it may also be worthwhile providing training in stress management for those managers who feel they would benefit from it.[10]

Identifying Specific Causes of and Solutions to Performance Problems

As we have seen, the same performance problem may have a large number of possible causes and solutions. Thus, if one of the main causes of a performance problem is outside the range of factors normally considered by the manager concerned, there is a danger that it will be overlooked, with the result that an inappropriate or less appropriate solution is selected. This is particularly likely to be the case when narrow, simplistic assumptions are made, such as "all poor performers are lazy" or "performance problems can be solved by treating people with consideration and concern". Such assumptions undoubtedly match reality some of the time but, given the complexity of human behaviour, they also result in the manager being wrong much of the time.

The primary aim of the Wright and Taylor checklist, therefore, is to encourage managers faced with performance problems to consider a wider variety of options with respect to possible causes and potential solutions than they might otherwise have taken into account. It appears to have been successful in this respect. An experimental study showed that a group trained in the use of the checklist identified significantly more possible causes and potential solutions when analysing a performance improvement case than did an untrained control group.[11]

Having generated such possible causes and potential solutions, however, the next thing which the manager must do to solve the problem is to identify from all these possibilities the most significant causes of the problem and the most appropriate remedial actions which can be taken. To do this, it may be necessary to gather further information. In particular, the individual concerned may have information which would throw additional light on the problem and ideas concerning ways in which it could be solved. Nevertheless, even when the manager has collected all the available information concerning the problem, identifying its true causes and the most appropriate solutions may be no easy matter. This is a difficult enough task in itself, but it is likely to be made worse by the fact that it is often a source of conflict between superior and subordinate. As Mitchell and O'Reilly[12] point out, there is a tendency for people to a) think that their own behaviour is cased by external forces, whilst seeing that of others as being caused by internal forces, and b) attribute their successes to themselves and their failures to forces beyond their control. These two biases combined mean that superiors are likely to blame poor performance on causes within the subordinate (e.g. lack of ability, poor motivation, malice, etc.), whereas the subordinate is likely to attribute poor performance to external factors (e.g. lack of resources, poor cooperation from others, overwork and, if pushed, lack of support from the superior).

Mitchell and O'Reilly suggest that one way to reduce the effect of such biases is to collect data on the consistency, consensus and distinctiveness of the poor performance. That is, the manager should ask whether the subordinate has performed the task poorly before (consistency), whether other subordinates perform the task poorly (consensus) and whether the subordinate has performed poorly on other tasks (distinctiveness). The greater the distinctiveness and consistency, and the lower the consensus, the more likely it is that the causes of the poor performance are internal. Conversely, the lower the distinctiveness and consistency, and the higher the consensus, the more likely it is that the causes of poor performance are external. Such rules are not foolproof. They assume that all the subordinates concerned are working under exactly the same conditions, and this may not be the case. For example, a manager might treat one of his or her subordinates quite differently from the others without being aware of it. Alternatively, an individual may consistently perform poorly, in comparison with his or her work mates, because the other members of the group refuse to cooperate with the individual, but help each other. Nevertheless, in many cases, the rules we have outlined will provide useful guidelines for analysing whether the causes of a performance problem lie within or outside the individual concerned. Furthermore, a knowledge of the biases which typically occur in such situations should help the manager to counteract his or her own biases, and to have a better understanding of the defensive reactions which subordinates often exhibit in relation to performance problems.

If it appears that the problem is one which has its roots at the individual level, then it is necessary to decide which of the various possible causes are relevant in the case under consideration. A useful place to start is motivation. Mager and Pipe[5] suggest that a motivational problem exists when an individual who is not performing satisfactorily could do so if he or she had to. The question to ask, they suggest, is "Could the individual do it if his or her life depended on it?" If the answer is "Yes", then the problem is a motivational one. One point worth noting, however. People may *claim* they would perform a job badly, because this is a more acceptable excuse for avoiding it than simply saying that they do not *want* to do it. A manager told us of a subordinate who said that he was dubious about taking on a routine administrative job because he would probably not be very good at it. The manager replied that he would give the subordinate the job for a year, and if he performed it well, would then take him off it. If, however, the subordinate performed badly, taking him off the job would deprive him of the opportunity to develop new skills, and he would therefore be left on the job. Thus, it no longer paid to be incompetent and the subordinate's doubts about his abilities suddenly disappeared. If subordinates claim lack of skill as a reason for not doing something, it would therefore be worthwhile to check, using the 2 x 2 diagram (Figure 6.3), whether there are not also sound motivational reasons for not *wanting* to do it. If there are, then changing the reward/punishment system or changing the nature of the job may be a more appropriate solution.

Similar problems may arise with respect to resources and working conditions. These are both a convenient focus for deeper more underlying motivational problems. It may be difficult for the individual to articulate things relating to the job itself which demotivate and dissatisfy. By contrast, it is easy to point to a low status company car or obsolete word processor as factors causing poor performance. In some cases, such things may be genuine sources of concern. In others, however, they may be symbols of a deeper dissatisfaction, and it is not unknown for people's dissatisfaction to get *worse* when given the improvement in resources or working conditions they asked for. They convinced themselves that such improvements would solve the problem, only to find that when they got them, the job was actually no better, and despair is the result. Thus it would be sensible, when there are complaints about resources and working conditions, to probe more deeply to find out whether there are other problems which might be the root cause of the complaint.

Identifying whether goal clarity is a problem is relatively straightforward. The manager can ask the subordinate what he or she thinks are the goals of the job and see whether the subordinate's perceptions match his or her own. Where they do not, then differences can be explored and resolved. This may not always help in attributing blame for past mistakes. One of the authors mastered very early in National Service the "What me Sarge, no Sarge, nobody told me Sarge" response, which can be quite difficult to break down or disprove. Nevertheless, clarifying goals for the future can, at the very least, ensure that this excuse will not work next time.

Similarly, feedback problems can be relatively easily identified by asking the subordinate what feedback he or she receives concerning levels of performance, how soon after the event it occurs, how useful it is, and so on.

This leaves task difficulty and abilities. These are, in many respects, opposite sides of the same coin. The task may be too difficult for the individual, given his or her abilities, or the individual's abilities may be insufficient to cope with the difficulty of the task. There is also the possibility that the individual finds the task boring because it is not difficult enough, and therefore is not motivated to perform well. Thus, such problems can be solved in a variety of ways, such as increasing the abilities of the individual, replacing the individual with someone of greater (or lesser) ability or changing the difficulty level of the task. The solution chosen will depend, at least in part, on the relative difficulty of these alternatives. For example, there is little point in deciding to replace the individual with someone more able, if such a person would be difficult to obtain or prohibitively expensive to hire.

Finally, if it is decided that lack of ability is the cause of the problem, it is still necessary to decide *why* the person lacks ability. As Mager and Pipe point out, someone may lack ability because they never had it in the first place or because they used to have the ability but have become 'rusty'. It is therefore useful to ask whether the individual used to be able to perform the task well. If the answer is "Yes", the solution may be a refresher course or quite simply an opportunity to practise the task more frequently, rather than a full training programme designed for beginners.

In this section we have concentrated upon ways of solving a performance problem at the individual level. It must be recognised, however, that by no means all performance problems can be solved in this way. It may be, for example, that the individual is unable or unwilling to develop the skills necessary to perform the job satisfactorily or has needs which the organisation cannot fulfil or cannot fulfil at an acceptable cost. In such cases the 'solution' may be to relocate or dismiss the individual. Alternatively, if the problem is a general one, in that similar performance problems arise with respect to other members of the organisation, then steps to solve the problem at the group or organisational level may be more appropriate. This might take the form of improving the organisation's recruitment and selection system or the introduction of some form of organisational development. The latter method will be taken up in the next section.

Solving Performance Problems at the Group and Organisational Level

A decision to investigate organisational and individual effectiveness usually arises when a line manager, Human Resource Specialist, or other key personnel, believe that an individual or group of individuals or the organisation as a whole, could be performing more effectively than they are presently doing. Our checklist approach is a 'bottom up' approach: that is, it initially looks at the behaviour of individuals in an attempt to improve their performance and, if this is unsuccessful, then suggests undertaking a more global investigation. An organisational development (OD) approach reverses this. OD specialists would tend to take a 'top down' approach where diagnosis starts at the organisational level and works down to the individual level. Our reasoning in taking a 'bottom up' approach is that it may solve a problem with less disruption, and at a lower cost, than the 'top down' approach.

The OD approach, however, is likely to be more appropriate when it is believed that although individuals may not be performing satisfactorily, tackling the problem at the individual level may be ineffective. This may be because groups of employees are exhibiting poor work performance or dissatisfaction. As a result, senior personnel may feel that unique individual variables are not the cause, but rather that more pervasive influences are affecting performance detrimentally such as the work structure, organisational design or culture, inequitable reward systems, lack of cooperation between groups and so on. If this is the case, then attempting to solve problems at the individual level is unlikely to achieve success and a broader OD approach to the problem will be more appropriate.

As with the checklist approach to individual performance problems, an OD approach will follow the stages of diagnosis, intervention and evaluation. However, whereas an individual approach to problem solving is generally tackled by the job holder's line manager, OD approaches require the involvement of an OD specialist. Where an organisation has a professional OD specialist within its Human Resource management team, he or she will act as an internal consultant for OD problems. Where this is not the case, because of the broad range of special skills required for the application of OD, an external OD consultant will be required to assist the organisation through the change process. In this latter situation, some careful thought will be needed both in appointing an external consultant and in applying OD techniques. The process of OD is usually both time consuming and expensive.

A second problem can arise in the problem solution stage. Some OD specialists have been criticised for their too rigid application of favourite techniques such as sensitivity training, grid techniques or MBO (management by objectives), when other approaches may be more effective in overcoming the problem. Alternatively situations have arisen where key people within the organisation have believed that they knew what the problem was and have therefore sought a consultant to apply a particular remedy, even though their original diagnosis may have been incorrect. Another organisational factor relates to the acceptance of an OD specialist's recommendations. An organisation will waste both time and money, and perhaps exacerbate employee dissatisfaction, if after employing an OD specialist, it is unwilling to accept the diagnosis and recommendations generated or apply the interventions for inappropriate reasons. Several examples exist where this has occurred. One situation of increased dissatisfaction occurring among employees was experienced by a company which employed one of the authors. An initial agreement was made to feed back the results of a survey based on interviews and a questionnaire. On receipt of an analysis of the survey, senior management reversed its decision to feed back the results to the employees. As a result, dissatisfaction was expressed and the company experienced several serious production disruptions over the next few months. Consequently it is essential that an 'open climate' exists, or is willing to be accepted, for implementing OD activities.

Modern OD Techniques

All OD approaches are aimed at introducing planned change, based on preliminary diagnosis, to improve an organisation's effectiveness (see Chapter 13). Performance diagnoses can occur at three levels of analysis, the organisational level, the group (interpersonal and intergroup) level and the individual job level. Various factors are influential at each of these levels and, as a result, different OD interventions can be implemented depending on the problem(s) diagnosed. Table 6.3 indicates some of the major variables of influence under the headings of Unit of Analysis, Influential Components and Possible Interventions. Further details concerning many of these methods of organisational development can be found in Chapters 8 and 13.

Conclusions

In this chapter, we have attempted to show the wide variety of different factors, both individual and organisational, which can be involved in the solution of performance problems. We also presented guidelines designed to help managers with the difficult process of deciding which, from all the

Unit of Analysis	Influential Components	Possible Interventions
Organisational Level	Technological factors Organisational structure Data communication and feedback systems Human resource systems Organisational culture	Work organisation Quality-of-work-life programmes Structural design (division of labour) Function design (coordinating functions) Survey feedback Organisation confrontation meetings Manpower planning; selecting, training and developing human resources; reward systems; goal setting Open systems planning Strategic planning Developing a corporate culture
Group Level	Task design – for interactions both between and within groups Group member attributes – demographic and other individual differences Group performance norms and expectations Interpersonal relationships within and between groups	Work design Team building Process consultation Johari Window Sensitivity training Survey feedback Selection, training and development Grid training MBO, goal setting, reward systems, quality-of-work-life Third party intervention Transactional analysis
Individual Level	Skill requirements Task meaningfulness Responsibility for outcomes Autonomy for working practices Feedback of job performance Individual differences	Job design, quality-of-work-life Career planning and development, training MBO, goal setting, reward systems Stress management Grid training, sensitivity training Selection see also Fig. 6.2 – Checklist for Improving Work Performance

Table 6.3: Organisational, Group and Individual Factors in Unsatisfactory Performance

available alternatives, are the most likely causes and the most appropriate solutions. However, we did not present a flow diagram or checklist which would tell the reader how to identify the 'correct' solution to a performance problem. We have refrained from doing so for two reasons. Firstly, it will be apparent that reaching solutions to performance problems is often not a clear cut matter. In many cases, it involves gathering information from a variety of sources, including the subordinate concerned, weighing the evidence and coming to a considered judgement, rather than working through a series of simple yes/no questions. Secondly, there may be several different actions which can be taken to solve the same problem. Some may relate to the organisational environment and some may be things the individual can do. As we have noted, the subordinate may wish to blame the problem on the environment whilst the boss may be tempted to blame it on the subordinate. However, there may be no need to choose between the two. The sophisticated manager may, in effect, say to the subordinate: "You, as my subordinate, have every right to expect that I do my best to provide you with a working environment which will enable you to do your job well. On the other hand, no one can expect that an ideal environment will exist all the time. Therefore, I, as your boss, have the right to ask you to develop your abilities so that you will be able to perform the job well, even in less than ideal circumstances. Now let us see what we can do to achieve both these objectives". In other words, rather than looking for *the* solution to a performance problem, it will often be more appropriate to attempt to develop a balanced package of remedial actions.

References

1   P L Wright and D S Taylor (1984) *Improving Leadership Performance*, Prentice-Hall.

2   N R F Maier (1955) *Psychology in Business*, Harrap.

3   J P Campbell and R D Pritchard (1976) 'Motivation theory in industrial and organizational psychology', in M D Dunnette (ed.) *Handbook of Industrial and Organizational Psychology*, Rand-McNally.

4   J B Miner and J F Brewer (1976) 'The management of ineffective performance', in M D Dunnette (*op cit*).

    L M Steinmetz (1969) *Managing the Marginal and Unsatisfactory Performer*, Addison-Wesley.

5   R F Mager and P Pipe (1970) *Analysing Performance Problems*, Fearon.

6   E A Locke, D B Feren, V M McCaleb, N K Shaw and A T Denny (1980), 'The relative effectiveness of four methods of motivating employee performance', in K D Duncan, M M Gruneberg and D Wallis (eds) *Changes in Working Life*, Wiley.

7   P M Podsakoff (1982) 'Determinants of a supervisor's use of rewards and punishments: A literature review and suggestions for further research' *Organizational Behavior and Human Performance, 29*, 58-83.

8   M Sashkin (1981) 'Appraising appraisal: Ten lessons from research for practice, *Organizational Dynamics*, Winter, 37-50.

9   E J Feeney (1972) 'Performance audit, feedback and positive reinforcement, *Training and Development Journal, 26*, 8-13.

10 For a more detailed discussion of the nature of stress and its treatment at an individual level in organisations, see A. Ostell (1986) 'Where stress screening falls short', *Personnel Management*, September, 34-37, and A Ostell (1988) 'The development of a diagnostic framework of problem solving and stress', *Counselling Psychology Quarterly, 1*, 189-209. Organisation-wide strategies for managing employee stress are discussed in D P Torrington and C L Cooper (1977) 'The management of stress in organisations and the personnel initiative', *Personnel Review, 6*, 48-54.

11 D S Taylor and P L Wright (1982), 'Influencing work performance: The development of diagnostic skills' *Journal of Management Development, 1*, 44-50.

12 T R Mitchell and C A O'Reilly (1983) 'Managing poor performance and productivity in organizations', in K D Rowland and G R Ferris (eds) *Research in Personnel and Human Resources Management*, Vol 3, JAI Press.

Suggested Reading

A number of the references noted above can be recommended for further reading. Further details of the main approaches to performance improvement described in this chapter can be found in Mager and Pipe (1970) and Wright and Taylor (1984) Chapter 2, and useful reviews of the whole field are provided by Miner and Brewer (1976) and Mitchell and O'Reilly (1983). A more detailed account of the various factors influencing work performance than was possible in this chapter can be found in G Dessler (1980) *Human Beha-*

vior: Improving Performance at Work, Prentice-Hall.

Questions

1 What are the main factors which influence work performance? How would you decide which were the most likely causes of a performance problem?

2 What are the relative merits of Mager and Pipe's Flow Diagram and Wright and Taylor's checklist as means of analysing and solving performance problems?

3 Indicate how organisational factors can influence individual performance at work.

Chapter 7

Training

David S Taylor

Introduction

Human Resources training and retraining is one major approach used by work organisations to maintain and improve the competence of its workforce and increase its adaptability to changing organisational needs. It attempts to develop any combination of physical, social and cognitive skills in order to achieve new or more effective ways of behaving. The skills of a company's human resources are essential components for its success. Consequently, training and retraining, where implemented as an organisational development strategy, should be seen as an integral part of an organisation's investment plan. The organisation's human resources are the possessors of the skills and knowledge required to produce and develop the products or services provided by the organisation. The benefit to it of a highly skilled workforce is that it will be better placed to defend, maintain or increase its success in its market environment.

If we look at the role of human resource development in general there is a continuum of training and development needs to be fulfilled. In the short term, new job incumbents need immediate training. Present incumbents may need retraining or additional training to fulfil short term projects and departmental objectives. In the medium term, business trends need to be assessed to provide guidance for changing skill requirements. Career needs and succession planning will also need attention. In the longer term any long range strategic plans will need consideration for anticipation of future skill requirements and manpower plans and these translated into training needs. Several aspects of this continuum are considered in other chapters. Chapter 2 is concerned with manpower planning which will influence longer term training strategy, and recruitment and selection (Chapter 3) is an alternative to training since if people are available in the labour market with the required skills then an organisation can choose whether to train or recruit. The previous chapter on

Managing Unsatisfactory Performance indicates the importance of training as one potential short term remedial factor. Training also impinges on the next chapter on Management Development and the broader organisational views expressed in Chapters 12 and 13. To avoid overlap then, this chapter will look specifically at how training can be developed systematically to ensure that an organisation's human resources achieve the required knowledge, skills and attitudes in an efficient and cost effective way. It will begin by looking at attitudes to training and training trends. The training context will then be briefly considered followed by a description of a systematic approach to training. Three phases will be distinguished – the assessment phase, the training development phase and the evaluation phase. Since the chapter is aimed at the general reader, more emphasis is placed on the assessment and evaluation phases than on specialist training techniques relevant in training development.

The Present Situation

It is interesting that although almost all companies and their senior executives when asked, will extol the importance of training, the reality relating to the investment in, and practice of, training is different. In terms of cash investment, The Industrial Society[1] from a sample of 134 firms of various sizes and covering a broad section of the industrial, commercial, financial and Public Service sectors, found that 65 per cent of the surveyed firms spent less than 0.5 per cent of their annual turnover on training their employees. Further, a recent report by Coopers and Lybrand Associates,[2] based on an investigation of training activities and attitudes in British Companies, found among other things, that "Except in some service sectors, training was not seen as an important contributor to competitiveness . . . and . . . few companies saw a direct link between training activities and profitability . . . " (p. 4). A comparison study of 45 matched firms in Britain and West Germany supports the link between productivity and training investment. Daly et al,[3] found an average differential of 63 per cent in productivity (range from 10 per cent to 130 per cent) between the two countries in favour of West Germany. The authors of the inquiry attributed much of the difference to skill factors achievable through training. In comparison, the British workers were poorer in machine maintenance procedures, they were slower at diagnosing faults in machinery and lacked the skills necessary to repair faults where they were diagnosed. Supervisory skills were also implicated. Production foremen in all the 16 German firms visited had basic craftsmen qualifications, 13 had a Master craftsman qualification and the other 3 were in the process of acquiring this. In Britain of the 16 firms visited, in only 2 cases had apprenticeships been served. The foremen from the remaining 14 firms had no formal qualifications and *there was no intention within the companies to provide training for their achievement*. The authors concluded that a broad policy initiative is required to combine and improve technical and managerial skills in British manufacturing industry.

One distressing finding of the Coopers and Lybrand study was the widespread ignorance of top management regarding the comparison of their company's training performance with that of their competitors even in the U.K., let alone overseas. Perhaps the best indicator of the perceived attitudes of top managers to training is the statement of several training managers and personnel directors relating to the cost of training, that "it was better that the full costs of their firm's training should not be made known to the board because, if it were, the board might wish to reduce it." (p. 10). It seems that in most companies, only in the case of management training was some interest expressed at board level. Companies which did possess a positive attitude towards training tended to be those for whom the impact of *not* training showed up rapidly, for example in the service sector where customer – staff contact influences customer loyalty, or where shrinkage is a major influence on profitability, or in companies in which training is seen as an essential part of a general ethos of caring for, developing and retaining staff. In all these cases training is seen as an *investment* rather than as an *overhead* to be reduced when hard times occur.

It is also interesting to note the different approaches to training during a recession between Britain and other countries. Whereas in Britain during the recession in the early 1980's training expenditure was reduced, in Germany and Japan short time working was seen as an opportunity to undertake training rather than reduce it.

A major influence for the implementation and maintenance of training activities is top management commitment, according to a research team from Warwick University.[4] A positive culture for training, expressed through top management commitment, is a critical requirement. "In a quarter of [their] sample of twenty firms, the belief of the chief executive in the value of training was a prime moving force, while in others top management endorsement and support generally was a major asset." (p. 29) They also note, however, that a positive culture for training also requires structures to translate the philosophy into practice, otherwise a 'planning gap' between practice and good intentions will interfere with its implementation.

In summary, during the early to mid 1980's training in Britain was not seen generally as a key element in a company's corporate strategy except perhaps for management training. However, recent evidence seems to indicate that

145

formal training activities have increased in the last few years.[5] This increase, according to the authors, has occurred as a result of heightened competition, changes in product design, the provision of new services or improvement of existing ones, and changes in manufacturing processes.

An additional stimulus to training may occur as a result of the shift in the labour market from surplus to shortage due to the decline of 16 to 19 year olds of about 25% by 1995. This situation is likely to be favourable for female employees in many organisations, for example Esso, Littlewoods and GEC Marconi, are providing special programmes to attract and retain women employees. It is worth pointing out that organisations that take a positive approach to training and career development usually recruit better quality staff and retain them.

On the negative side, it is still probably true to say, however, that a minority of British firms view training expenditure as an investment rather than as an overhead cost to be minimised. The relationship between training and its benefits such as better quality, increased flexibility, and possibly higher productivity, must be recognised for it to be seen as an investment. In countries such as West Germany and Japan where this relationship is recognised, provision of long term finance at relatively low rates of interest, through close cooperation between banks and industry, provides a positive climate for training. Such cheap long term loans are generally not available to companies in Britain, probably as a result of the success of financial institutions in profiting from short term loans and investment. As a result, many firms and particularly smaller ones, refrain from training – to some extent because they fear trained employees will be 'poached' by other companies, but also because they believe suitably trained people will be available in the labour market when needed. However, the skill shortage that is likely to develop during the 1990s may leave many companies with major problems unless they prepare for the scale and speed of its occurrence. Failure to do so may create a situation where at best the situation is alleviated through paying for additional overtime working, sub-contracting work out where possible or accepting lower standards of quality. At worst the skills may become obsolete because firms may lose their markets to foreign competitors.

The importance of financial incentives to stimulate training activities, however, is questionable according to Pettigrew, Sparrow and Hendry.[4] From their survey they found in general that grants made no difference, or only marginal difference, to the training the recipients do. Organisations apparently made the decision to train first and then sought for ways of defraying costs. If this is the case, then the major impetus to create an improved investment in training activities within industry and commerce should be one which

146

tackles the beliefs of top management, since it is their commitment which is most critical to a positive approach to training.

Responsibility for Training

In the majority of companies interviewed in the Coopers and Lybrand report, the responsibility for training was delegated to branch or division managers with support from personnel and training, and it was suggested that neither the training managers themselves nor senior executives viewed the training activities as being a major factor in the competitiveness of their companies. As a result, it is understandable why training and training departments and their personnel are seen to have relatively low status and why training is not seen as an important investment contributing to a skilled workforce.

The training function can be seen to have two roles. There is a *reactive* role in which the training department provides the necessary expertise or skill in response to requests from line managers and supervisors. In this sense it is a service function providing managers with support to help them fulfil their needs for an effectively trained workforce. The second role is a *proactive* one in which the training specialists are involved in suggesting and where necessary implementing training to fulfil not only short term organisational needs but also longer term corporate plans and strategies.

The reactive role stems from the responsibilities of the line managers and supervisors for the training and development of their staff. Each manager and supervisor is usually accountable to senior management for the performance of his or her staff. As a result they must bear the responsibility of identifying the training and development needs of their subordinates. In addition, the line managers will need to allocate time and resources for training, where resources may include space and equipment for internal courses and budget allocation for either internal or external courses. Finally managers and supervisors should be responsible for the evaluation of the results of training in terms of assessing how their trainees subsequently perform in their job. In this situation training is viewed as the responsibility of the managers and supervisors, with the training specialist performing the reactive role of assisting managers and supervisors in clarifying training needs, developing training courses and evaluating their success.

Having noted that however, there are many managers who do not see training as their responsibility, not because of any logical or managerial reason, but largely because they have not considered training as a major influence on the achievement of their subordinates in organisational terms. The human resource management specialist may need to persuade line management of this – that basically training is their responsibility and the training function is there to advise and provide specialist assistance. Where the responsibility for training has been delegated to branch or division managers with support from senior personnel and training specialists, it can be relatively easily established. One problem may arise, however. Line managers are often subject to relatively short term objectives linked to productivity and profitability. This may discourage them from improving or upgrading their subordinates' skills through training, because they may not achieve output targets if personnel are 'off the job'. To avoid this, devolved responsibility for training must be backed by senior management and means to overcome the budgetary and time restraints provided.

Where training and human resource development is seen as a major source of investment by senior management, the proactive role of the training function will be easier to implement. For this proactive role, the training specialist needs to be involved at board level during the development of the organisational objectives; that is, its present and future needs derived from some form of strategic review. However, this has seldom occurred although hopefully the trend towards viewing training and development of all levels of employee, besides management, as a board level topic, will increase and add impetus to this involvement.

Human Resource Management and Training

The Training Department has usually been viewed as an integral part of the organisation's human resource function. However, in small organisations where no human resource specialist exists, training will be the responsibility of the owner. In medium and large organisations, however, with specialisation of functions occurring, the training function will exist as part of the human resource development area.

The argument for the close integration of training within Human Resource Management rests on the need to closely interrelate the various activities of recruitment, selection, development and training.

However, this does not necessarily require the training specialist to report either to the Personnel Manager or the human resource specialist. Alternatives include reporting to the Chief Executive or to a senior line manager. In areas where the impact of training or not training shows up rapidly, as in the service sectors, the Chief Executive may have a personal interest in it and as such require the training specialist to report directly to him or her. This also

148

serves to provide additional status to training.

Senior line managers may be responsible for training in those organisations where emphasis on training is given to a particular category of employees such as sales. If training is restricted in such a way, then the training personnel will usually report to the Sales Manager. This approach leads to the training being closely related to the needs of the department.

However, an important advantage in closely co-ordinating training and other human resource activities is that it results in more appropriate training based on a coherent policy of Human Resource Management.

Training Benefits and Costs

It was noted earlier that many organisations perceive training expenditure as an overhead rather than as an investment. However, if training is to be viewed as an investment, it must lead to some identifiable return like any other sort of investment. Consequently what an organisation needs to know is what are the benefits of systematic training and at what costs? It is difficult to identify *precisely* the outcomes from training. Training is one ingredient in the performance mix which is influenced by motivation, job design, equipment design, company policy, supervision and so on, as well as skill. Nevertheless, a systematic approach to training can achieve or influence the following:

- The speed of learning. Systematic training should achieve reduced learning time and higher skill levels thereby reducing learning costs.

- Improved performance of existing employees. Job incumbents can, through training, up-date and improve their work performance. This should result in increased productivity through increased working speed, reduction in working errors, or both.

- Decreased supervision. A well trained workforce should require less supervision and allow increased delegation. This releases management time for planning, organising and development activities.

- A more flexible workforce. Training can increase the range of skills of its employees so that, where acceptable, employees can cover for absent or sick colleagues or rotate jobs for various purposes, including that of increasing motivation levels.

- To ensure for succession. To prepare people within the organisation to fulfil its future needs for supervisory and managerial succession at all levels. This can influence turnover, since employees are less likely to leave if they believe that promotional opportunities are available.

● Improved company morale. An organisation which views training as an essential ingredient in caring for, developing and retaining its employees is likely to be one with high morale. It is also more likely to be receptive to change resulting in increased flexibility in response to external situations.

To these may be added individual factors such as increased self-fulfilment in achieving higher levels of skill which will lead to increased self esteem and greater job satisfaction. Also, at the national level, a country's international competitiveness and economic performance is significanty influenced by its skilled workforce and, as a result, its standard of living.

However, it must be remembered that although an organisation's positive approach to training can influence many of these factors, it cannot be a substitute for inadequate job design or poor supervisory and managerial practices leading to low motivation and morale.

It is relatively easy to measure the *costs* of providing training but what is a problem, for which there exists no simple formula, is the measurement of the *financial outcome* of training to the organisation. This latter requires a cost analysis of some sort, which attempts to estimate the effects of training on a company's profit statement. The costing of the provision of training involves calculating both fixed and variable costs. Fixed costs involve such things as capital and running costs of maintaining a training centre; the cost of the training personnel and equipment costs. Variable costs will be influenced by the number of courses run; equipment and materials used on a course; visiting speakers and so on. One could also include in the latter any costs incurred due to employees being non-productive during the period of their training, either through having to replace them or through lost production.

Once the costs have been determined, the problem is how to measure the economic results of the training to the organisation. In some situations, at the operator level, training costs can be compared with increases in productivity. For example Jones and Moxham[6] in assessing the results of a new training system on sewing machinist skills showed that the training resulted in:

a   Reduced training time to achieve a set standard (from 17 to 7 weeks) b   Reduced labour turnover (from 70 to 30 per cent) and

c   Increased output of about 30 per cent.

A cost-benefit anaylsis can then be used to convert this into a financial statement.

The effects of training cannot always be so precisely identified however, especially at the supervisory and managerial levels. Improving a manager's skill in staff development techniques would be seen as having longer term rather than short term influences. In the longer term, for example, it may be influential in reducing turnover, improving morale and reducing costs for management succession. In order to produce a cost-benefit analysis however, what time scale do we choose and on what do we base our 'guesstimates' relating to the monetary values of the outcomes? Nevertheless if the investment value of training is to be demonstrated, estimates of the benefits in cost terms will be necessary. One needs to treat the figures with care however. Figures, whether based on real or estimated outcomes, are often used out of context as 'hard facts'. It should be remembered that estimates are approximations and not certainties.

Earlier, in looking at the benefits of training, it was noted that organisations are not the only beneficiaries of planned training. In addition benefits accrue to the individual and to the nation. This was earlier recognised in that historically individuals paid for their apprenticeships, or more recently received low wages whilst serving them. Also recently, national funds have been available as an impetus to training. The Institute of Personnel Management proposed that learning costs should be shared by its beneficiaries in appropriate proportions although without any real guidelines as to how that was to be calculated. Nevertheless few would disagree with the proposition of shared costs. Since however, employers are intimately concerned with profit, national pressure and incentives are needed to encourage them to train more. Because of the difficulties which can occur in carrying out cost-benefit analyses, the value of training as an investment rather than as an overhead may not always become apparent, especially if some of the returns on investment are long term rather than short term. Because of this, some form of motivation for training involvement needs to be stimulated at the national level.

We shall discuss additional approaches to the evaluation of training in a later section.

The Training Process

Training can, and occasionally does develop without any real attempt either to see whether the content is appropriate to the needs of the job holder, or whether the training methods are effective for learning that content. Frequently training, especially at the managerial level, is not based on an assessment of training needs. Training may be implemented because it is thought to be a 'good thing' or fashionable. Sensitivity, or 'T group' training during the late 1960s and early 1970s was of this kind.

Such 'fashions' will benefit some managers, improving their communication skills and general understanding of people. However, it is rather like a shotgun approach to target shooting. Inevitably some of the lead pellets will hit the target but a large number will miss. Even where training appears relevant to fulfil a perceived need, its success is frequently assessed on the basis of how much the participants enjoyed it, without any attempt being made to see whether it has actually brought about any real change in the employee's job behaviour. In an attempt to avoid or minimise such situations, it is essential to implement a systematic approach to training course development, the aims of which are:

● To increase the effectiveness of training by reducing learning time to achieve specified performance levels.

● To improve the job performance levels of present employees.

● To ensure for succession. That is to prepare people within the organisation to fulfil its future needs for skilled manpower.

A SYSTEMATIC APPROACH TO TRAINING

A systematic approach to training is one which is planned specifically to meet defined training objectives. This does not mean it is any more elaborate or expensive than unsystematic training. On the contrary, planned training is more likely to be cost-effective and because it is systematic it is more likely to be comprehensible to non-specialists and as a result to gain more commitment.

A systematic approach involves three major phases:

152

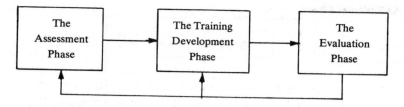

Figure 7.1: The Three Phases of a Systematic Approach to Training

1   The assessment phase, which focuses attention on the training needs and training objectives of the organisation.

2   The training development phase which is concerned with how the training objectives are to be achieved.

3   The evaluation phase which attempts to answer two questions. The first is, "how far have we achieved our original training objectives?" and the second, "how valid were our original training objectives for the needs of the organisation?".

Each of these three phases can be further subdivided as illustrated below in Figure 7.2.

1   The Assessment Phase

The assessment phase focuses attention on the training needs of the organisation from which the objectives of training can be specified. It involves then two main components. The identification of training needs and the specification of training objectives. Each will be looked at separately.

The identification of training needs. Before the objectives and content of training can be specified, what training needs to be done, and where, should be identified. That is, the organisation must look at what is presently happening and what should or could be happening. Any differences between the two may give some indication of training needs. It should be remembered, of course, that training is not the only influence on organisational success. Selection procedures, work design, resources and company policies concerning supervisory practices and payment systems, amongst others, can all influence organisational success. It is important to distinguish between the various causes of any discrepancies between actual and desired situations otherwise incorrect solutions will occur that can create negative attitudes to

153

1. Assessment Phase

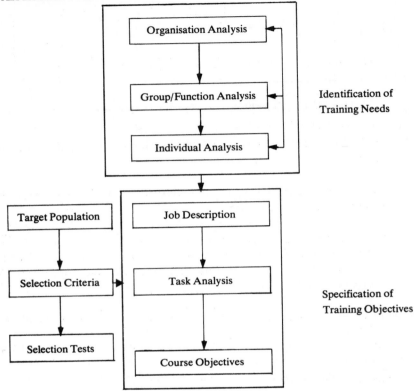

Organisation Analysis

Group/Function Analysis

Individual Analysis

Identification of
Training Needs

Target Population

Job Description

Selection Criteria

Task Analysis

Selection Tests

Course Objectives

Specification of
Training Objectives

2. Training Development Phase

| Training Unit Outlining | Training Unit Sequencing | Final Content Selection | Training Procedures Selection |

3. Evaluation Phase

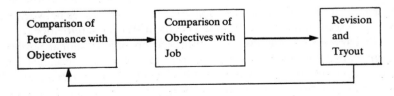

Comparison of Performance with Objectives

Comparison of Objectives with Job

Revision and Tryout

Figure 7.2: The Components of a Systematic Approach to Training

154

training. Anecdotal evidence exists of many 'failed' training programmes where in most of these cases, training was not the best approach to solve the stated problem. For example low productivity being related to lack of skill when the reward structure at worst penalises individual effort or at best fails to reward it, (see chapter 5 on motivation). Another area involves situations in which despite successful training the newly learned skills cannot be applied on the job, (for example training supervisors in participation techniques which cannot be applied subsequently because of the nature of the organisation and expected role of the supervisor). A thorough training needs analysis may then highlight problems outside the training area, which need to be solved before training solutions can be successfully implemented.

Training analysis can be carried out at three levels, the organisation level, the group/functional level and the individual level. The three levels are interconnected and include some overlap. Analysis at the organisational level often will reveal training needs at the group level which in turn will lead to training requirements for individuals. Similarly an analysis at the individual level, for example poor sales performance, may indicate at the group level, production problems of poor quality control or at the organisational level a product which is obsolescent indicating a need for innovation.

An organisation analysis sets out to determine where, within the organisation as a whole, any training emphasis is required. Since organisations have limited resources all organisational problems cannot normally be dealt with simultaneously. Consequently one aspect of the organisational analysis is to arrange priority in terms of tackling those problems first, whose solution would provide the greatest organisational benefit. It is important in carrying out the analysis to state any deficiencies or problems as problems, rather than as perceived solutions. There is a tendency for managers to state organisational performance problems in terms of their solutions. For example, a reduction in sales might be expressed as 'a need to retrain our salesmen in more aggressive techniques'. That may be a correct solution, but on the other hand it could be a problem of pricing policy, of an obsolescent product, or of poor quality. By stating the solution, further analysis or discussion is cut short. Providing training to achieve that solution may not eliminate the problem and a lot of money may be wasted in the process.

The importance and frequency of organisation analyses will be influenced by the context in which a company operates. The context can be seen as a continuum. At one end organisations exist in a rapidly changing market affected by frequent changes in technology, scientific discoveries or market conditions, for example in the areas of consumer electronics and computers. At the other end, organisations operate in a relatively stable commercial or technological environment, such as the banking or furniture manufacturing areas. The need for frequent analyses will be greater in the former case than in the latter, as will be their importance for organisational success.

The contents of organisational analyses overlap with procedures which should normally be covered by the corporate planning and strategic review processes. These include reviews of organisational goals and objectives, of the company's strengths and weaknesses and of its manpower plans and skills inventory. Personnel records relating to strikes, turnover, absenteeism, accidents, productivity, customer complaints and so on, may also be indicators of corporate or strategic problems. Consequently the organisation analysis will probably involve discussion at board level and should include senior management from all the major functional areas, marketing, production, finance, etc.

The important objective of the organisational analysis is to decide whether the company is meeting its stated objectives. If it is not, the reasons for failure should be sought and the extent to which they can be influenced by training determined.

The group or function analysis involves looking at particular departments, functional areas or groups of people to assess whether any of these require training. For example sales training, training in production planning, training for computerisation in the wages and salaries department, or interpersonal skills training for middle managers, may all be possible outcomes from a group or function analysis. Here the achievement of departmental or functional goals is the expected outcome, including those relating to future changes in those areas. The latter includes not only changes due to technical or technological innovations and their implementation, such as the introduction of computers into production planning but also personnel changes due to promotion and succession requirements. Indicators which may trigger a group or function analysis might include such factors as failure to achieve set objectives, observed shortages of expertise and skill, an ageing work group or morale factors such as high turnover or absenteeism. However, as training plans are generally reviewed on an annual basis for budgetary reasons, the analysis at this level is likely to be reviewed annually.

Individual need for training, as well as being revealed by the previous two levels of analysis, can be assessed at *the individual level*. Indicators at this level might include failure to achieve standard output, or any lack of success in achieving expected targets or, in the case of managers and supervisors, poor group maintenance, low morale, expressed dissatisfaction and high turnover.

156

Besides production figures and other forms of direct information, such as complaints, information at the individual level can be obtained through performance review and development interviews. Potential reviews will provide information relating to succession planning and the needs of particular individuals for this.

Two types of approaches to analysing training needs are probably apparent from the previous discussion. Firstly the *General Survey* in which training needs are identified usually through discussion between managers and supervisors. Problems that arise due to failure to achieve organisational objectives, group or individual targets provide the stimulus for discussion, as well as changing environments, markets and employee profiles.

Although these surveys are usually verbal, through discussion or interview, they need not be and questionnaires can be developed to do much of the basic information gathering.

The advantage of some sort of general survey is that all or most managers and supervisors are being involved in the process of training from the beginning, with the probable result that they are more likely to be both cooperative and supportive of future training programmes.

The second type of information gathering source relating to training needs is the interview; either the performance review to assess individual performance, or the potential review to consider potential for promotion. It is important not to do both in the same interview for reasons discussed in chapter 9 on performance review.

The third method not previously mentioned in this chapter although relevant to selection processes also (see chapter 3) is the use of job description and task analysis techniques to explore both the detailed requirements of a job and the knowledge and skills required to achieve success in the job. The latter analysis will lead to a description of training requirements. Any discrepancy between these and the skills of the job holder will suggest the training needs of the individual.

From the research evidence available it appears that a systematic analysis of training needs is seldom done. Without such an approach, however, it will be difficult for companies to integrate their training into their present and future corporate plans and business strategies. Training based on a sound analysis of needs is more likely to be valid and soundly based. It is therefore one of the most important stages in training course development.

Specifying training objectives. In some cases, the specification of training needs may describe the required behaviour change. However, this will usually be in a rather general form such as, 'be able to carry out an appraisal interview' or 'improving typing skills', or 'be more effective in handling difficult patients'. Before developing the training programme however, we need to know what the trainees already know and can do, and what they will need to know and be able to do at the end of the course. The difference between these two will determine the objectives and content of training. This applies equally to employees already in post and to those about to be hired. In the latter case it is important to note that we can set our selection criteria at whatever standard we wish, assuming we will be able to attract applicants. The more stringent our requirements, in skill and knowledge terms, the less training we will need to do. The level at which we set our selection criteria may depend upon what group of people we want or can realistically attract, that is, upon our target population. If no pool of people exists with the skills we require, or we would have difficulty attracting people with those skills, our target population may be school leavers. If that is so, we might want only those with a GCSE pass at grade C in mathematics, in which case this would become part of our selection criteria. In the case of engineering apprentices this might enable us to reduce the amount of mathematics teaching required in the training course. At this stage then there is an interplay between selection and training. Similarly, as a result of our assessment of training needs we may realistically say that the probability of selecting people to carry out the job is low. In this case, we may decide to redesign the job, in order to increase our chances of recruiting people who will successfully carry out the various tasks.

So as a result of our assessment of training needs, we will be in a better position to decide whether or not training will be the best solution to achieve those needs. These decisions will influence our objective setting.

Assuming we decide to go ahead with training and we know what the content of training will be, we need to specify the objectives. In specifying training objectives it is important to ensure that wherever possible, they should be *observable* and *measurable*.[7] As far as possible then, training objectives should state in the necessary detail

- what the trainee will be able to do as a result of training

- the normal operating conditions in which the behaviour will occur and,

- the standard of acceptable performance against which the trainees' behaviour is to be judged.

158

An objective which states that 'at the end of the training course a manager will understand the process of communication' is inadequate. It fails to fulfil any of the three criteria. It may be adequate as a starting point for the design of training, as a basis for discussion about the proposed content, but even then, the use of the word 'understand' can be misleading. Will the manager in 'understanding' need to be able to design a communication system, or use one, or describe how it operates or, more likely, be able to communicate effectively to ensure that messages are received and acted upon in the way intended by the communicator? Consequently the use of such words as know, understand, or appreciate creates insufficient precision. Instead words such as solve, identify, perform, etc. should be used.

The process leading to the specification of objectives will usually start with a job description. A job description will probably be held in personnel records. It is a narrative statement mainly describing the content of the job; any measures of performance; the conditions under which the work is done and the position of the job holder in the organisational hierarchy. However it does not provide details about the observable behaviour involved in doing the job. To achieve this, the job description is broken down into specific tasks, duties and responsibilities. These are then analysed to determine the knowledge, skills and, where appropriate attitudes, needed. This latter process is called task analysis. (It is worth noting that there is no single acceptable title for this analysis and it is referred to by names other than task analysis, such as job analysis and job specification.)

The training objectives are then derived by comparing what the job requires in terms of skills knowledge and attitudes with the trainees' present attributes. For new recruits the total content of the task analysis will probably form the basis of the objectives, whereas for more experienced individuals, this will be less so.

Specifying training objectives can be a time consuming and difficult process. It has nevertheless two outstanding advantages. The first relates to the training itself. If a copy of the training objectives are given to the trainee prior to it, the total effectiveness of training will be enhanced. Secondly, well written objectives based on the three criteria noted earlier in this section, will enhance and simplify the process of evaluation.

2 The Development Phase

Whereas the assessment phase is concerned with *what* one intends to achieve through training, the development phase is concerned with *how* one intends to achieve it. It involves taking the information generated through the previous analysis as the content and breaking it down into training units. These units should then be sequenced in such a way that learning is enhanced by ensuring some sort of logical order of content. That is, that each piece of provided information or skill occurs at the right time, such that it can be easily integrated with previous learning.[8]

When the content has been decided upon, the training techniques to be used will need to be selected. Should one use simulators, or real practice? How much lecturing content should there be, or would seminars be preferable? Would learning in groups compared to setting individual tasks reduce learning time? There are numerous training techniques and the final choice will depend on the skill to be learned, the cost of the different procedures (for example simulation can be expensive, but so can real practice on sophisticated machines easily broken by trainees) and of course on what is available.

Other decisions to be taken by the trainer include *where* the training will take place, and *when* it will take place. In general, training can be carried out on-the-job, off-the-job or, as in the case of most apprenticeship training both on- and off-the-job. On-the-job training involves job instruction given usually be the employee's supervisor or a specially selected experienced employee. Most training is performed on-the-job. Techniques used include demonstration – commonly called 'sitting next to Nellie' – in which the trainee watches or is told how to carry out a task and then given a chance to do it; coaching, similar to demonstration but usually involving more guidance and counselling, and planned experience whereby over a period of time, the trainee experiences doing different jobs in a planned way to develop the necessary skills through job assignments and problem solving. Planned experience can involve the use of programmed instruction and computer assisted instruction. These techniques usually combine learning both on and off the job by providing basic information regarding functioning followed by on-the-job exercises to practise control. Off-the-job techniques are usually simulation exercises. They include equipment simulation (e.g., flight simulators) and situational simulations (e.g., business games, case studies and role plays). An important factor in off-the-job training is how well the skills learned in simulated situations transfer to on-the-job performance. For equipment simulation, usually the closer the correspondence between the simulator and actual equipment the greater the transfer. For non-technical skills such as problem-solving, interviewing and supervisory skills, an additional factor, that of a supportive organisational climate, can influence transfer to the job. Each approach has its value and their advantages and disadvantages must be considered in the light of the course content and the needs of the trainee. Factors which can impinge on the decision might include the

160

safety of the trainee, the cost of breakdown due to incompetent control on both the organisation and on other employees and the safety of others such as the general public. Even where such issues are not relevant, in company, on-the-job training will only be the answer when sufficient time can be allocated for an instructor to provide the necessary amount of time and individual attention to the trainee, especially in the early stages of learning.

The issue of when training should occur depends on the status of the trainee. For new recruits, it will be immediately after recruitment in most cases. However, for those already in post, there is a need to consider when the training will best integrate with their work, with other training needs and with the output or productivity needs of the departments to which they belong.

A final point worth mentioning relates to the motivation of the trainees. New employees presenting themselves for training will exhibit varying levels of enthusiasm ranging from a high level following a deliberate choice of jobs to perhaps reluctance where little or not choice has been involved. In any event, they will have already formed initial attitudes towards their training. Their early experiences on the training programme may or may not fulfil their early anticipations and as training progresses they will develop fresh attitudes not only about their chosen job, but also about the organisation they have joined. The way training is conducted, the behaviour of the instructors and other company personnel and the facilities provided all offer cues from which the trainees will formulate their attitudes and motivation towards the company, their chosen job and their training. Motivation is an important factor also in training and retraining present employees. Their attitudes about the company can be enhanced or damaged by the organisation's approach to training which in turn can influence the success or failure of a training course. There is abundant anecdotal, as well as some research evidence to indicate that training programmes can fail, whatever their technical merit, if they are auto-cratically developed and implemented. There is thus a strong need to involve people at all levels, to solicit information and advice and to keep people informed subsequently of progress.

3   The Evaluation Phase

The final phase in any systematic approach to training is the evaluation phase. It is necessary for at least three reasons.

First, evaluation indicates the overall effectiveness of training in achieving what it set out to achieve, that is whether it met its set objectives. This provides feedback for the trainers and may indicate areas for improving future training.

161

Secondly, evaluation information provides data which can be presented to senior managers regarding the effectiveness of the training department's operations. From this, the senior managers can then make decisions regarding the adoption and support of training activities. If employers and senior managers are to believe in the value of training and its relationships to organisational success, training operations should be justifiable in cost effectiveness terms and evaluating training will provide a basis for this.

Thirdly, the evaluation process can influence the trainees themselves. Letting trainees know that evaluation will occur is likely to influence their approach to training and their behaviour during training, especially if their success in learning the content will have some influence on their future positions within the company. As noted earlier, providing trainees with a set of training objectives will help them know what they need to learn and giving them feedback on their progress is likely to have a motivational effect on their learning. Also giving trainees an opportunity to comment upon the content of training and the techniques used may enhance their future attitudes both towards future training and the company itself.

This third point indicates that evaluation exercises will affect the nature of the situation. Observing and measuring trainees' behaviour will affect the behaviour if the trainees are aware of it. Asking trainees about their reactions to the course will polarise their thoughts and testing their learning will influence their efforts.

Having noted these three organisational advantages, evidence tends to indicate that evaluation is not given sufficient emphasis by companies and little notice is taken of the results. What evaluation does take place is usually conservative and inaccurate. It is conservative because trainers are usually concerned about the ratings they receive at the end of a programme of training, since they could reflect badly on themselves and their efforts. Understandably they want good ratings irrespective of the effect of the programme on the trainees' learning. The ratings can be inaccurate because the type of evaluation, usually some form of questionnaire, is given to trainees who are usually on an end of course 'high'. They are less likely therefore to consider carefully the effect of the training on their future organisational behaviour. Also, the trainees themselves may be wary of making negative comments for fear of some form of retribution. As a result, they are more likely to criticise contextual factors like accommodation, organisation or conditions rather than the content and techniques of the training or company training policy. These factors negate the function of evaluation for the organisation which is to ensure relevant training; to improve where possible the professional skills of the trainers and to provide senior management with information regarding the role of training in the corporate strategy of the organisation.

Following the question of 'Why evaluate?' comes the question 'How to evaluate?'. As a feedback process it has three parts:

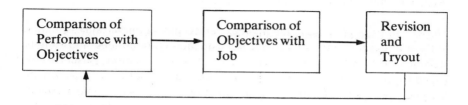

Figure 7.3: The Three Components of Evaluation

In comparing what trainees can do differently as a result of the programme, with its objectives, trainers can assess how successful the training has been in achieving what it set out to achieve. This is termed 'internal validation'. It is concerned with how successful training has been in achieving its laid down objectives.

However, answering this question does not indicate the relevance of training to the organisation. If a thorough analysis of training needs has been carried out prior to the development of the training programme and the objectives have been realistically based on those needs, it is likely that the training will be relevant. There are however examples of training having a zero or negative effect on job performance, for example sales staff who as a result of training courses subsequently perform no better or marginally worse. To check this, it is necessary to measure subsequent job performance to assess whether the training has achieved the organisational needs for more skilled operatives; better sales people, or more effective managers. This has been termed 'external validation'. Were the training objectives realistically based on training needs and did training fulfil them? Validation is important because some overall measure of evaluation, such as an increase in profit or productivity, may be caused by other factors such as changes in pay policy; supervisory practices; improved machinery or a change in market conditions. The term validation is becoming less used and it is generally assumed under the broad umbrella of evaluation. Nevertheless the *processes* of validation must be performed if evaluation is to have any value.

As a result of validation and evaluation, indicators will emerge relating to training effectiveness. As a result the content may need revision and the

163

whole process of evaluation repeated. It should be seen therefore as a continuous process and not a single 'one off' event.

The previous section implied that evaluation can occur at different points. The training literature usually distinguishes four *levels of evaluation*. These are the reactions level, the learning level, the job behaviour level and the organisational level.

The reactions level refers to the trainees perception, opinions and evaluation of the training content and methods used and their feelings about the training staff and their presentation and behaviour. This information is usually collected by questionnaire, although interviews of selected trainees can also be used for depth of information. The information gained can provide a general view of the impact of the programme and also more particular information, where necessary, such as a comparison of its effect on younger as compared to older trainees, male and female or any other distinguishing features between groups of trainees. Information can also be collected at different points in time. It may be that a trainee's view of the programme can change due to the events that occur over time. It has been noted already that an end of course 'high' usually occurs and trainees reactions may change subsequently. It will be useful to check this by carrying out the evaluation at two points in time: immediately after training has finished and subsequently, perhaps three to six months later.

Assessment at *the learning level* is concerned with measuring the extent to which trainees have learned the content of training – its laid down objectives. It may be related to a change in an individual's knowledge, skills or attitude. The assessment technique will depend upon what is being assessed. Tests of attitude will require numbered scales or rankings of importance. For knowledge, essay questions, multiple choice or true-false questionnaires can be used. Skill learning on the other hand will require some form of performance measures, such as ability to assemble units, handle difficult customers or perform a disciplinary or appraisal interview.

Again tests can be performed at different periods of time, in this case, usually to test retention of the learning. As a result of these, especially for little practised skills or techniques, it may be necessary to provide refresher courses.

It is expected that learning which occurs on a training course will be transferred to the work situation. This may not always be the case for various reasons and evaluation at *the job behaviour level* may indicate the source of the inhibitory factor. For operator tasks it may be easier to do this. Lack of

164

transfer may well point to inadequate training content – poor teaching; low fidelity simulation or insufficient practice. However for social skills as in managerial and supervisor training the reasons for poor transfer may be more difficult to pinpoint. Other non-training features may be influential here such as the lack of reward or even negative consequences occuring as a result of implementation. A poor supportive climate may make implementation difficult.

Information relating to on-the-job behaviour changes can be achieved through various techniques, the most common being managerial or supervisory rating. However, others which could be used in the right organisational climate include rating by peers or subordinates. At the operator level simple output figures may be sufficient, providing account is taken of any abnormal operating conditions which may be influencing productivity or output at the time the assessment occurs. Whatever form of assessment is used it is important that it should occur some time after the end of the training programme to allow for any adjustment period. This is particularly important when the training has occurred off-the-job. A 'sleeper effect' or time lag can occur between the trainees learning and demonstration of it.

Evaluation at *the organisation level* is an attempt to assess the effects of training on the overall functioning of the organisation. This can be demonstrated in numerous ways and some attempt to predict these should be made during the design of the programme. Indicators can include increased productivity; improved quality; reduced learning time and therefore costs; reduction in damage or errors and those related to personnel criteria such as reduced turnover and absenteeism and improved cooperation.

These four levels can be seen to form a hierarchy, or continuum of effect. Training can fail at any of these levels. For instance trainees may react well but fail to learn, or they may learn well but be unable to apply the learning. They may behave differently but without any effect on other people or the organisation. Consequently evaluation should occur at all levels. If the job behaviour or organisational level is ignored we may be measuring only superficial changes whereas if we fail to evaluate at the reactions or learning level, any changes that occur cannot be safely ascribed to training.

However, two major criteria for deciding the extent of evaluation are the cost of the evaluation process, and the usefulness of the results. For example, a simple end of course questionnaire is relatively cheap but produces only low quality information, whereas quantitative data collected at all levels, though of great value in terms of information gleaned, will be expensive in both terms of costs and time.

The thoroughness and cost of the evaluation process will be influenced by the thoroughness with which the previous two phases have been carried out. The more thorough the assessment and development phases, the more observable and measurable will be the results, and the more precise and simple will be the evaluation process.

The Design of Evaluation Procedures

A factor which may be apparent from the previous section is that a continuum of evaluation criteria exists relating to the certainty of the inferred influence of a training programme on subsequent work performance. That is we can assume a causal relationship between training and improved individual or organisational performance, or assume an inferred relationship but be uncertain whether other factors, such as some form of better working conditions or improved supervisory practices, have made a contributory influence to the improvement in performance. The extent to which we can assume causality depends upon the design of our evaluation procedures.

In order to make causal inferences there is a need to measure the knowledge, skill or attitude level both before and after training. That is, in technical jargon, there is a need to use both pre and post-tests. There is also a need to use control groups, that is groups of people of similar age, experience etc., who do not experience the training at all or who only experience part of it. This helps to ensure that any differences which occur in performance cannot be ascribed to other variables which subsequently might affect work performance. This process however is rarely carried out. The methodology requires a minimum number of people for many of the more sophisticated experimental designs. Rarely are the necessary number of trainees available.

Carefully designed evaluation procedures should not be discouraged however and whenever possible the more sophisticated experimental designs should be used. Where this is not possible it is still essential to collect data of some sort. Despite the view that simple pre-test post-test designs are unacceptable because causality cannot be inferred, they do provide data which can help both to evaluate present courses and improve future ones. Even a post-test on its own can provide data, albeit at a low level of sophistication, which can help course assessment. If simple designs such as the pre-test, post-test, or post-test only are used, using the post test at two points in time, such as immediately after the course and six months later, will enhance the value of the data collected.

A final factor which can make the design of evaluation procedures more or

166

less easy is the sophistication of the measures which can be taken. For example although at the operator level output changes may be measurable in terms of the number of units produced, at the supervisory or managerial level it may be very difficult to enumerate changes in for example interviewing skills or participative management techniques. In these latter cases the performance changes may be only assessments by self, superiors, peers or, in rare cases, subordinates.

It is worth stressing that some data is better than none, but the more sophisticated the data the more sophisticated the inferences that can be made. Evaluation is an essential procedure not only as a feedback device for improving training courses and their outcomes, but also because the information is essential to justify the value of the training department activities to senior managers and the organisation as a whole.

Conclusion

An organisation's employees are among its most important and expensive assets and their skills are essential for its success. Nevertheless in many organisations, there is widespread ignorance among top management of their own training investment. In some companies it is not seen as a key element in their corporate strategy and the link between training and profits are not always recognised. As a result, training tends to have a relatively low status. To overcome some of these problems, training needs to be seen as an investment for an organisation, and as such to become of concern at board level.

To help achieve this, training managers must themselves become more effective both at a reactive and proactive level. Close integration of training with human resource management policy is one requirement. Nevertheless the basic factor which will enhance the status of training is its proven success in creating a more skilled workforce which enhances the success of the organisation.

Training staff must prove the value of their training activities to the organisation and this is only likely if the training they provide is systematically developed, implemented and evaluated.

References

1   The Industrial Society, *A Survey of Training Costs*. The Industrial Society, 1985.

2 Coopers and Lybrand Associates, *A Challenge to Complacency*. A report to the Manpower Services Commission and the National Economic Development Office, November 1985.

3 A Daly, D Hitchens and K Wagner, 'Productivity, Machinery and Skills in a Sample of British and German Manufacturing Plants', *National Institute Economic Review*, February 1985, Vol III, pp 48-61.

4 A Pettigrew, P Sparrow and C Hendry, 'The Forces that Trigger Training', *Personnel Management*, December 1988, pp 28-32.

5 C Hendry, A Pettigrew and P Sparrow, 'Changing Patterns of Human Resource Management', *Personnel Management*, November 1988, pp 37-41.

6 A Jones and J Moxham, 'Costing the Benefits of Training', *Personnel Management*, April 1969, pp 22-28.

7 R F Mager, *Preparing Instructional Objectives*, Belmont, California, Fearon Publishers, 1975.

8 R F Mager and K M Beach, *Developing Vocational Instruction*, Belmont, California, Fearon Publishers, 1967.

Suggested Reading

The two R F Mager references, *Developing Vocational Instruction* and *Preparing Instructional Objectives* are excellent books, being informative and easy to read.

Other texts include:

J Kenney and M Reid, *Training Interventions*, Institute of Personnel Management, London, 1986.

K R Robinson, *A Handbook of Training Management*, 2nd edition, Kogan Page, London, 1985.

A C Hamblin, *Evaluation and Control of Training*, McGraw-Hill, London, 1974.

Questions

1 Indicate some of the factors which influence the decision to implement organisational training.

2 Describe the main characteristics of a systematic approach to training.

3 What advantages accrue as a result of evaluating training? Why can it be difficult to do?

Chapter 8

Management Development

Christopher Molander

Introduction

In this chapter we shall describe the nature of Management Development (MD), illustrating its scope and thereby attempting to dispel the oft held view that MD is 'about sending people on courses'. This naturally leads on to a discussion of where the responsibility for MD lies – with the line manager rather than the personnel department. There are practitioners in the personnel field who would say that such a view has represented best practice for many years. Certainly the writer has maintained that view over the last twenty years. Recently, however, increased interest in HRM has led to a restatement of this important principle.

A 'model' will then be introduced to help the reader decide what type of MD activity is likely to be most appropriate in different situations. This will be followed by a description of those techniques which are likely to become most useful in the future.

The Nature of Management Development

It is important early on to clarify what Management Development means in practice and what is its role in a work organisation. Let us begin with a definition:

'Management Development is a conscious and systematic process to control the development of managerial resources in the organisation for the achievement of organisational goals and strategies'.

At first reading this definition may appear unhelpful. But its value lies in its generality. Organisations work in different environments and as a result have different cultures and structures and are faced with different problems. Not only is this true for any one organisation in general, but within an organisation, divisions and functions are faced with their own peculiar problems and have developed a climate and structure to meet their specific needs.

There can therefore be no one 'right' recipe for Management Development. It will need to vary from organisation to organisation, and indeed within organisations. As problems differ, so different managerial development efforts will have to be devised to cope with them. Management development activity which will pay off in terms of improved managerial performance will need to be contingent, or dependent, upon an assessment of the prevailing needs experienced by management at a particular time and within a particular division of an organisation. Hence, to do more than produce a very general definition of Management Development might do more harm than good, since the identification in practical terms of the problems a manager's subordinates face is an important first step in planning development.

There are, however, a number of key words which the reader will do well to remember. Any effective management development effort requires to be part of a planned strategy – a 'conscious and systematic process' which has the clear purpose of helping managers meet 'organisational goals'. In other words random activities stemming from a multitude of objectives (for example, keeping training departments busy), and which are not necessarily in line with the climate and style of the organisation, are likely to be at best a waste of time and money, and at worst positively harmful. Much of what passes for Management Development has the characteristic of randomness, and is sometimes controlled by individuals who have neither the authority nor the influence to ensure that there is likely to be an effective outcome of their efforts.

The risk of randomness is increased the further away MD planning occurs from the 'coal face'. Some of the largest and most prestigious organisations in Britain develop MD strategies without any significant line management involvement. The analysis of needs and the planning of initiatives have been left to experts who jealously guard their professional skills. The experts are mentally and physically far removed from the work place. They have neither the knowledge to develop nor the power to implement 'tailor made' MD strategies designed to meet specific operating needs. Integrated and valid MD activities are likely to follow only from the closer involvement of line management in the MD process.

In general, management development activities can be focussed at one of three levels; the individual, the group or the organisation. The manner in which these activities are introduced by line management can either be prescriptive or consultative. The following table seeks to show this more clearly. In order to clarify the point further, a number of examples have been given within each of the six possible boxes of types of development activity. Many more could be given, so the examples should not be taken as exhaustive.

FOCUS

		INDIVIDUAL	GROUP	ORGANISATION
STYLE	**PRESCRIPTIVE**	E.G. General Management Courses Qualification Courses Some forms of Appraisal	E.G. Some forms of Team Building Project based learning Some forms of Management by Objectives	E.G. Some forms of Management by Objectives Some forms of Organisation Development
	CONSULTATIVE	E.G. Counselling Coaching Needs analysis Career planning Specified experience Task related Courses	E.G. Analysis of problems Identification of needs Role negotiation Action learning Some forms of Team Building	E.G. Organisation Analysis and Feedback

Table 8.1: Types of Management Development Activity

The two dimensions of this table – the focus and style – are important to the understanding of the dimensions of Management Development.

Focus

It is commonly felt by managers that Management Development has for its purpose the change in behaviour of an individual – and indeed that is its objective. This change in behaviour may be brought about by providing the manager with new knowledge, for example in some aspect of his profession, or by providing him with new skills, say in the area of 'Human Relations'. What is often overlooked, however, is that some behavioural change – better performance; different attitude to the job; greater useful output and so on can be brought about more effectively by changing the environment in which the individual works.

172

It is often the case that managers perform less well than they might, not because they lack the capacity or the inclination, but because there are constraints surrounding their role which either prevent them from behaving differently or encourage them to behave in the way they do. Take for example the behaviour of an individual in a team meeting. It might be said that X can be relied upon to be destructive at departmental meetings, and to engage in destructive argument some days and withdrawal behaviour on others. Does she need training in interpersonal skills? Or are there other issues which provoke the behaviour? A recent example of just this problem arose in a team meeting with an O & M unit. As a result of a team building exercise, it was discovered that the behaviour of the individual in question stemmed from a role clash with two other senior managers for whom the unit provided a service. This clash meant that she was unable to do a significant proportion of what she thought was her job, and others saw her as idle and 'biding her time' until she could take early retirement. Her behaviour in the meetings was much more related to the sheer frustration caused by the lack of job clarity than to any 'personal difficulty'. In this case, a restatement of departmental objectives and the accompanying redefinition of individual roles was sufficient to modify the observed behaviour. The behaviour was symptomatic of a problem and not the problem itself. Dealing with symptoms is seldom helpful. The root cause of the problem remains, and one set of symptoms will often be replaced by another. The purpose in giving this example is to demonstrate that in helping managers develop, it may be more effective to take as the target for change, not the individuals, but the circumstances in which they find themselves. Change the immediate 'environment' and the behaviour may change itself.

A second example may help further to make the point. Most organisations or divisions within them may be said to have their own culture or climate. By this is meant a set of assumptions about what is proper with regard to attitudes and behaviour at work. These assumptions and values are reflected not only in the way people behave but in the way they are managed. For example, many managers are apt to comment: 'What we need here are a few more self starters – people prepared to take initiative, to take risks and not just to live by the rule book, getting by without thinking'. In practice, however, the managerial style of the unit may be such as to reward precisely the opposite sort of behaviour. Risk taking, especially when things go wrong, may be followed by such retribution that the individuals concerned will 'keep their head down'. If they 'read' the organisational climate as one which rewards pedestrian rule following behaviour, and which is disturbed by those who take initiative, then in their own interests they will naturally adapt their behaviour to fit perceptions of the climate.

Frequently, the organisation's 'espoused' culture is at variance with the 'actual' culture. Managers are quite capable of reading the culture for what it really is and adapting their behaviour accordingly. Why take risks when you observe that those who don't on the whole indulge in such creativity do at least as well, if not better than those who do?

So the target for change of a management development effort may go beyond both the individual and the group and legitimately be seen as the organisation itself. But the principle is the same. Behaviour in individuals may often be more usefully affected not by taking them as the target for change, but the culture in which they work.

To many readers, this may seem far removed from Management Development as they know it. Indeed it is the case that some forms of MD operating at the organisation wide level are akin to Organisation Development. Management Development can in certain circumstances stem from Organisation Development activities. Those readers who are unfamiliar with the latter concept should read the appropriate chapter of this book.

Style

The second dimension in table 8.1. was labelled 'Style'. Just as management development activities can produce change in behaviour by changing the individuals' immediate work group, or the division or organisation in which they work, so change can be introduced prescriptively or as a result of consultation. In recent years for example, some organisations have attempted to introduce appraisal systems. Frequently the need for such systems is experienced not by potential appraisers but by the Personnel Department. Sometimes little or no consultation takes place with those who would have to appraise and still less with those who are about to be appraised. However sophisticated the scheme, months of effort can be wasted if managers lack the commitment to make it work. As a result many schemes have been abandoned.

Increasing interest is being shown in appraisal by line managers and there is marked evidence of a return to performance related pay. Such developments are symptomatic of the need to integrate personnel policy with the operating demands of the organisation. An emphasis to be found in the principles of HRM as opposed to the more traditional Personnel Management is the greater need to reward performance. This will lead to the introduction of more rigorous performance related appraisal systems, as well as of course to more imaginative payment methods designed to win the 'hearts and minds' of managerial employees. The more traditional non directive approach favoured by many Personnel Managers is likely to become less common.

Management by Objectives springs to mind as another obvious example of a technique of Management Development often introduced in a prescriptive way. If the 'user' is not committed to the scheme, or still more if the scheme is perceived as being out of line with the way the organisation runs, then no amount of administrative effort will compensate. Several organisations have experimented with MBO; few can be said to have introduced it successfully, in such a way that it is still used, and seen as a valuable technique for improving motivation and performance. Later we shall say more about MBO. My purpose in mentioning it briefly now is to provide an illustration of prescriptive Management Development.

Any system of Management Development which is introduced without taking into account the expressed needs of the user or 'client' may be said to be prescriptive. It is by no means the case that all prescriptive introductions of management development activities are inappropriate. New employees for instance may require certain types of training and development and certain posts may require the possession of a particular qualification. In these cases prescriptive Management Development is appropriate. But where new ideas are being introduced, or the active involvement of those being developed is crucial yet uncertain, then prescriptive approaches are likely to be unnecessarily difficult to sustain – especially when the prescription appears to emanate from the Personnel Department.

In contrast, the consultative approach may in some, though not all, circumstances, have more to offer. Appraisal systems, counselling, job rotation and career planning for example require the active involvement of the manager being developed. Who knows individual needs best – the subordinate or the boss? In all probability the one will have information which the other does not have. The boss may have a more detached view of the subordinate's strengths and weaknesses, and yet still be basing these views on limited and erroneous experience. The subordinate may be expected to have more reliable information of what aspects of the job motivate and those which do not; what she does well and not so well and of the direction in which she would like a career to develop. In such cases a consultative approach in which both the boss and the subordinates share information, identify problems and aspirations and mutually agree a planned development programme, is likely to be more appropriate.

In other words, managers who take seriously their responsibility for developing their subordinates will need to take account of the options open to them in deciding strategy.

A great deal of what passes for Management Development in business organisations may be said to fit into the top left hand box of table 8.1. It is prescriptive and aimed at the individual as the target for change. Indeed many managers when asked to define Management Development reply that in essence it is 'sending managers on courses'. Whilst individual prescriptive development has a real role to play, it can be over-played. The initiation of other types of development activity which provide a thrust for change aimed away from the top left hand corner is timely.

The argument of this chapter so far has been based on the notion of choice. From it we can deduce three major possible ways in which change in the individual can be encouraged – which is the purpose of Management Development. The first type of general management development activity is based on the proposition that individual behaviour can be changed directly by the provision of training, for example, knowledge acquisition through job rotation and specific courses, or through feedback on performance. Here the target for change is the individual directly.

The second type of management development activity reflects the view that the individual's behaviour is a function of the values and attitudes held. If these can be changed, behaviour will change itself. This we may call the psychological approach. Team building activities which aim to clarify the group's objectives and to reduce the degree of conflict between members may in certain cases produce attitude change in the individual. Similarly conflict between groups may be reduced by confrontation of difficulties and reallocation of responsibilities.

A third approach is more sociological. The target for change is here seen to be the way in which work is organised and the structures set up to get it done. Work procedures can be more or less enabling or constraining. If the job itself offers little opportunity for taking responsibility, for example, it is little use exhorting managers to behave responsibly. Far more effective are changes in job content – not the amount of work to be done, but the quality of work experience which is offered.

If Management Development itself has been slow to become established much more so has this latter approach to it. The reasons are not difficult to appreciate. Approaches to change in work structure depend upon competent analysis and careful introduction. But it is possible. Matrix organisation structures, for example, which encourage managers to use their skills wher-

176

ever they are relevant, without too much regard for position and power are difficult to implement and manage, but they have been introduced to good effect within both the public and private sector.[1] In the private sector, changes in the procedures for getting work done have in the main been aimed at the shop-floor level – the many modified versions of 'job enrichment' and self managed work groups spring to mind. But the principle is the same and can be implemented at any level. This principle is based on the observation that behaviour is symptomatic of the circumstances in which it takes place. Change the circumstances and individual behaviour will change.

All three types of Management Development mentioned might be going on at the same time, and with the involvement of all managers. Management Development is a major responsibility of any manager. It is not the exclusive preserve of the trainer. It places heavy demands on the manager. In particular, managers will need three basic attributes. Firstly, they will need the ability to analyse an organisation, or at least their part of it and to diagnose accurately the root cause of presenting problems. Secondly, they will require a basic understanding of the techniques available for bringing about change in managerial behaviour. Lastly, they will need to exercise consultative and interpersonal skills for introducing change with the minimum of conflict and the maximum degree of commitment from others. It is hoped this book generally will encourage the manager to seek ways of developing these skills further.

The Responsibility for Management Development

But who is it with the responsibility for developing and initiating these changes and what methods ought to be used to achieve them? It is important to reflect on the role of managers who have the professional responsibility for Management Development. Usually located within the broader function of the Personnel or Human Resources Department, there are good practical reasons why they cannot achieve much on their own account. Organisation development, management development and training professionals quite simply lack the authority. The writer has often sympathised with personnel professionals who from a position in the middle ranges of management have sought to move mountains. Guided by an 'inner light', nothing has seemed beyond their scrutiny. These are the managers who sooner or later lose heart. They move to other organisations, or long experience of frustration, failure and lack of organisation commitment leads them unwillingly to accept reality. They become alienated from the job and sometimes from themselves. Change will only take place when those who have the authority (i.e. line managers) are motivated to bring it about. The increasing tendency towards the integration of management effort through greater concern for corporate planning and the declining role of the Personnel Department in implementing policy – as opposed to developing it – may increase the level of managerial motivation.

A policy making characteristic important for the MD professional is political acumen. Change is achieved more easily by working through people. This requires testing the limits of tolerance and working within these parameters. Certainly there is a problem of over acceptance of organisational constraints, but even the brightest trainers waste their talent by over-confrontation. The organisation is a system which has arrived at its present state through a mixture of external and internal pressures which makes its current structures and processes seem the most rational. Denial results in resistance. Where this denial is encountered, the organisation is quite capable of bypassing the efforts of those who seek inappropriate change. Analysis of the political relevance and appropriateness of change is a strong weapon in the professional's armoury. There are other reasons why line managers should take the responsibility for Management Development beyond these tactical points. It takes us into well worn territory – the role of the Personnel Department generally. In Britain, as already in the United States, it is increasingly realised that the major responsibility for personnel administration must lie with the line manager. The term 'manager' implies managing people and their development. Managers should be encouraged not to pass staff development over to the Personnel or Human Resources Department, tempting though it may be for personnel people to seize the chance of 'empire building'! Managers' responsibility for their staff from recruitment onwards cannot be overstated. Managers who are used to being spoon-fed cannot be expected to develop responsible attitudes towards staff development. Strategically it is worth remembering what we have observed earlier: imposed management development systems (for example, some forms of appraisal) tend to be ignored or mishandled by managers who lack the commitment which comes from ownership of responsibility.

If managers are encouraged to develop their own MD priorities they will feel a greater sense of ownership. Such ownership is crucial to commitment. Without the necessary commitment there will be no action. This means that managers will express interest in different MD activities, and this will lead to a piecemeal organisational approach. So be it. The canons of ownership and commitment should override organisational concern for neatness.

Still relating to responsibility, there is one further point that should be explored with regard to the philosophy of Management Development. The more individuals have the responsibility for planning their development, the more

178

they will learn, and the more they will be committed to undertake training and other developmental experiences. Perhaps most important, the greater the involvement by individuals in planning their own learning, the greater will be the chance that the training will be transferred to the job.

Care in the introduction of even the most enlightened development system is of the essence as many organisations have found to their cost. Bureaucratic methods of introduction will result in cynicism and inactivity. 'The medium is the message.' How Management Development is introduced speaks volumes to the employee about the real purposes which lie behind the introduction of change.

Effectively Management Development based on the principles we have discussed requires careful introduction. Both the purposes of the activity and the method by which they will be realised can sensibly be planned bearing in mind the following five principles. They stem from the basic propositions explored in this chapter.

Goal Setting. Develop learning opportunities which relate to the areas in which the learner has experience. Where there is an interest and a need to explore, training will be most effective. This is especially true of managerial skills. Successful skill training requires a high level of commitment on the part of the learner.

The experience of many trainers suggests that 'problem based' training rather than more abstract generalised approaches is most effective. This seems plausible. There is in many managers a residual antipathy to the passive relationship of teacher and student reminiscent of school, in which there appears to be little direct relevance to the 'real world'. Every trainer will recall groups in which resistance to learning was clearly present. The best way to build up resistance is to 'send' managers on courses. Working on the basis of expressed training needs presupposes careful job consultation or appraisal, from which training needs emerge.

Climate. The adult manager will react better to a learning environment which demonstrates mutual respect between trainer and participant. Managers often object to being taught. A lecture for example, however accomplished the delivery, carries with it the implied message of the expert talking at the non-expert. The physical arrangement of the trainer 'up front' armed to the teeth with multicoloured viewfoils with the learners facing him/her defines a relationship which is unsuitable for building on the knowledge the learners already have.

179

Implementation. Most managers on development courses are already reasonably good at their jobs. They have had a great deal of experience. Their experiences differ. They are, as is the way with adults, quite capable of learning from each other. The learners are themselves an invaluable resource. When they express the need to know more, they are quite capable of finding answers for themselves. The word 'facilitator', although jargon, does at least express the promise of a more productive learning environment in which all the available sources of information are likely to be exploited.

Planning. How the learning goals are to be achieved merits careful thought. Each of us learns in a different way. Some are more inclined to abstract conceptualisation, whilst others learn best from 'concrete' example.[2] Training experiences which pay some attention to these differences presuppose a flexible approach, in which a number of different learning techniques may be going on at the same time, or at least within the same learning event. In every case, some discussion as to how the learning goals are to be achieved is a suitable beginning.

Evaluation. Some form of evaluation of training is important in providing necessary feedback. What useful learning or experience the learners feel they have achieved is a prime source of such feedback. This information can be used for planning further activities as well as modifying content and methods of current training efforts. The process of involving participants in the evaluation process is important in demonstrating an 'adult' climate in which trainers and participants alike are involved in a 'learning community'.

The Organisational Life Cycle

Like human beings, organisations are constantly developing. Structures and systems must keep pace, not least Management Development. What might have been appropriate development techniques for organisations at one time might not be relevant at another. The notion of a 'life cycle' is a helpful concept in determining relevance.[3]

Many organisational analysts have over the years been struck with the analogy of the biological organism and the work organisation. They have identified four or sometimes five stages in the organisational cycle and compared them to the biological cycle. Of course the analogy cannot be taken too far. Unlike the biological organism, the organisation is capable of 'growth', say for example as a result of takeover, a characteristic not given to mortals. It does seem also that the decline phase, even if prior to regeneration, is a discernable point reached by companies sooner or later. Table 8.2 defines the stages in the cycle. They have been confined to those elements of most relevance to Management Development.

Birth. Characteristic of the small entrepreneurial firm, much beloved currently by right-wing politicians. The entrepreneur has the vision and drive to start up an enterprise which is small enough for him/her to control directly. Although a high degree of risk is involved, division of labour and decision-making systems are rudimentary. The ownership of the risk has clear implications for managerial style which inclines to the authoritarian.

Growth. Assuming the business survives, growth follows. Professional managers are employed who, whilst they lack the sense of ownership, are given a relatively free hand by the owner to develop the business. Many of the managers bring with them needed specialist skills to adjust structure and procedures to meet the demands of increased size. Because they lack the personal zeal of the owner and because there is already much to lose, the level of risk-taking declines.

Maturity. This is the phase most closely associated with bureaucracy. Further increase in size leads to highly developed structures, normally based on functional differentiation. Sophisticated information processing becomes necessary to maintain growth. By now the entrepreneur has sold out and the business is run by professional, career-oriented managers, many of whom will stay with the company for a short time only. Change in the character of management is reflected in low risk-taking and a rule-oriented management style. Not all organisations easily make the necessary and continuous adjustments to the environment – changes in market, competition and so on. The very strength of the managerial style seen in the maturity phase can be a weakness. There is often a reluctance to respond to the need for rapid change. The pursuit of divisional and departmental goals may discourage the taking of an organisational view.

Decline. In such cases decline may follow. Either the company does not see the need for adjustment to the environment or is incapable of making necessary changes to the product or service. There may be a diminution of role, due to changes in political attitudes of the government, without the emergence of a realistic alternative role (e.g. Local Government). Faced with a threatening environment, organisations in the decline phase tend to become *intensely* bureaucratic. At the same time, effective power is withdrawn so that it rests with the higher echelons of management only. Decision-making processes are harnessed to the problem of survival. There is an unwillingness to expose the organisation to anything but a minimal level of risk-taking.

	Management Style	Planning and Control	Decision Making	Risk-Taking
Birth Phase	Power Highly centralised	Informal structure	Crude information processes and decision making methods	Substantial risk taking
Growth Phase	High delegation and individual freedom	Some formalisation of structure Functional basis of organisation	Initial development of formal information processes and decision making methods	Measured risk taking
Maturity Phase	High delegation and fixed goals	Formal bureaucratic structure Highly developed functional basis of organisation	Sophisticated information processing	Conservative, low risk taking
Decline Phase	Low delegation and fixed limited goals Finance led	Highly developed bureaucratic structure Mostly functional basis of organisation	Limited information for control purposes	Very limited risk taking

Table 8.2: Phases of the Organisational Life Cycle

MD Implications of the Life Cycle

The MD professional should gear his/her strategy to help develop those skills in managers which are appropriate to the growth phase of the organisation. The direction of the strategy is suggested in Table 8.3.

Failure to relate objectives to a prior analysis of the development phase is perhaps the major cause of resistance amongst line managers. Day-to-day experience is perhaps a better basis on which to test the validity of proposed developmental opportunities rather than a theoretical model of what organ-

Phase	Activities
Birth (Innovation)	No particular MD effort required. The organisation is too small to allow of MD specialisation. The entrepreneur will intuitively resist MD. He knows what he wants in others and will find appropriate colleagues. Available capital will be directed towards defraying start up costs and the development of new market opportunities. Managers will learn on the job. Development will be problem centred and self appropriated.
Growth (Expansion)	As the organisation increases in size, the need emerges to develop a suitable structure based on differentiation. More refined financial controls will be required. Opportunities for individual development are still readily available. The critical role of the entrepreneur declines. Key MD activities: ● Development of appropriate managerial structures ● Identification and development of individual professional and managerial talent ● Management succession and appraisal ● Management by Objectives ● Team-building
Maturity (Control)	Emphasis on growth is tempered by concern with monitoring achievement. This will encourage bureaucratic "sprawl" and bureaucratic skills are seen as important. Opportunities for individual growth limited to steady career development, often within one function. Identification with the organisation decreases, with consequential decline in levels of motivation. The managerial "specialist" emerges. Key MD activities: ● Interpersonal Skills Training ● Autonomous managerial work groups ● Management by Objectives ● Counselling and Coaching ● Appraisal ● Committee (rather than Team) Skills Development
Decline (Survival)	The organisation becomes "finance led". This will have significant impact on organisational culture and management style, which will become more centralised and controlling. The level of bureaucracy will increase and middle managers will have less power. The problem of survival becomes paramount. The organisation becomes reactive to external pressure. The level of motivation declines sharply. Key MD activities: ● Political Skill Development ● Negotiation Skills Development ● Assertiveness Training ● Finance Skills Development ● External Environment Control Skills

Table 8.3: Growth Phase and Management Development Activity

isations in general should be striving towards. Nonetheless, many of the well established MD techniques stem from a time when Western society and its work organisations were in the maturity phase. Personal growth and organisational prosperity were seen as linked and equally attainable objectives. Some organisations are now in the maturity phase, but many could best be described as entering into post-maturity.

Some will perish; others will embark on the process of re-growth. Such a process requires different management structures and styles to those which were appropriate in the maturity phase. Managers will require a leaner, tougher, internal organisation climate which emphasises individualism and personal responsibility, and rewards those who demonstrably contribute to the organisation's financial stability.

It is in this context that the prime objective should be to match the MD activity to the developing needs of the organisation. Over the last few months, in discussion with senior managers of three large organisations, the writer has heard the same thing: 'The training I've had in this company has been fine for me personally, but from the organisation's point of view it's been irrelevant'.

There is a need today to build up processes and techniques which are relevant to entering a period of regrowth. The development of appropriate managerial structures and the identification and rewarding of individual and managerial talent is of paramount importance. Out of what appears to be desperation, some companies are returning to 'outward bound' methods which were in vogue at the end of the Second World War. In the writer's view, the problem of transferability of such experience to the work place remains as big a problem now as it was then. There is a long way to go in the development of adequate responses to current organisational needs.

Apart from the problem of relevance, there is the practical problem of cost. As we well know, training budgets are among the first to be cut in periods of economic pressure. In the public sector, such cuts have been particularly severe. Training initiatives which involve much more than petty cash expenditure are unlikely to survive here. It has long been argued that in times of economic depression, companies should increase their expenditure on the development of managers. They would then be in a good position to exploit market opportunities when the upwave arrived. Once the growth has begun again it is too late to begin identifying the need for increased managerial skill. This argument, though strong, has rarely proved convincing.

A feature of organisations in both the post-maturity and the regrowth phases is that the power of finance managers increases. Companies become finance led. Managers whose careers have for the most part been within the financial world are not well known for their interest and concern in the application of training to management problems. For this reason also then, training will have to demonstrate its cost-effectiveness if it is to remain a significant item in the annual budget.

184

So there are three clear principles against which we can measure the likely success of training and development in the foreseeable future:

1 The training must be relevant to company needs.

2 Ownership and commitment must be won through problem-centred training.

3 Cost-effectiveness must be demonstrated.

Let us look then at some major development techniques, bearing in mind that the user must decide for him or herself whether they are appropriate at the time.

Potentially Effective Development Techniques

Management by Objectives

It is arguable that MBO is fundamental to good management. In the late '60s and early '70s it became a fashionable technique. Frequently abused, it was later to fall into general disuse.[4] It is now more properly used as an essential element in performance review or appraisal. Its use as a technique of Management Development is likely to grow along with the need to use managerial resources more effectively.

The basic process is threefold:

1 The Managers discuss and agree with their boss the objectives of their job for a defined period (usually six months or a year). Specific goals or objectives are agreed in line with departmental objectives ('Key Results').

2 At the end of the agreed period, boss and subordinate jointly review actual performance against the agreed criteria in 1 above.

3 Strengths and weaknesses in the subordinate's performance are explored. Where appropriate, ways in which each can help the other to improve performance are reviewed. Key results are set for the next review period.

One of the major reasons for the early failure of MBO systems, apart from the obvious one that too much was expected of it, was that the technique was seen by many managers solely as a means of identifying shortfalls in performance

185

and of tying people down to specific job descriptions. MBO was originally conceived as a participative technique. Its purpose was to encourage mutual exploration of problems and the development of action plans, using the subordinate as the major resource. There should be an underlying belief that participation in objective setting leads to a higher level of commitment and therefore better results. If targets are imposed on subordinates, the latter may become competitive, using energy to justify themselves in not meeting objectives and in attempting to negotiate the least difficult key results for the next review period in order to appear better than they are on the next day of judgement.

Properly handled, as an element in effective performance review, MBO is a powerful element in any MD strategy.

Performance Review

Chapter nine deals with this MD strategy in depth. It is mentioned here mainly as a reminder that it is one of the most cost-effective techniques open to the manager who takes the development of his/her subordinate managers seriously. In recent years traditional types of appraisal have given over to the more participative methods which are not so firmly anchored to rating scales. Most managers would accept that they have a duty to review the performance of the managers responsible to them, at least annually, and that they in their turn have a right to expect such a review from their own boss.

Performance review is essentially a two-way communication process, during which boss and subordinate have an opportunity to review the latter's performance in an atmosphere which is neither competitive nor punitive. It may well be that the subordinate can suggest changes in the behaviour of the boss or in work processes and systems which are causing him problems. It is also important to bear in mind that the review provides an opportunity to explore successes as well as those behaviours which have caused the boss concern. As part of the review, targets and key results should be agreed. It is in this context that MBO has its place. It is now generally agreed that performance review should be separated from succession planning and from pay negotiation. The relationship between boss and subordinate in effective performance review is different to that normally found in negotiating relationships. The openness of the former should not be contaminated by the competitiveness of the latter. This is not to say that rewards are not important. Indeed, unless it is possible to reward desired behaviour – by salary increase; promotion; status changes and so on, there is little justification for expecting subordinates to maintain their efforts to improve performance.

There should be a clear link between performance review and salary adjustments. The emerging culture of many organisations is increasingly one which emphasises the need for a greater link between performance and reward. In the NHS for example pay is frequently related not to an incremental scale but to performance related bonuses. But since pay and performance review involve different types of relationship, they should not be combined in the same session.

In chapter five, the essential link between reward and motivation is explored more fully.

Interpersonal Skills Development

Managers who plan and develop departments or organisations should recognise the varied leadership requirements of different positions. In particular, a crucial aspect of a manager's responsibility is the development of appropriate management styles in his/her subordinates. Whether subordinates do develop them will depend greatly on the way they themselves are managed. Leadership skills can be learned. A major implication of situational theories of leadership is that managers will need to have the sensitivity to recognise what style is appropriate and when, and to have the flexibility to adjust accordingly. Readers should consult chapters five and six for a more detailed discussion of contingency in this context.

Many training programmes are available which are designed to develop the interpersonal skills of managers. Such programmes are normally experience based. That is, the participants have the opportunity to learn for themselves what impact they have on others and by experimentation to increase the repertoire of possible responses to differing situations.

The training materials developed by Hersey and Blanchard for example, are based on the identification of an individual's management style, with the use of personality profiles. Exercises, 'games' and role-playing may be used to offer the participant an opportunity to experiment with alternative forms of behaviour.[5]

Since individual managers spend most of their time working in small groups, it is not surprising that team development has become an important aspect of interpersonal skills training.[6] Progammes are readily available which help managers look at the behaviours which are necessary in effective teams, and to analyse their own preferred ways of behaving. Often with the help of a 'consultant', established work groups can learn to examine their strengths and weaknesses both in terms of how they work (clear purposes and objectives, efficient use of time and so on) and how the team members relate (listening skills, conflict management and leadership styles for example). Good team work is an important factor in obtaining and maintaining the commitment of individual managers to the achievement of individual and group goals. It is not always appropriate however. It is increasingly argued that managers, especially those who work in an organisation at the post-maturity phase of the life cycle, need to develop a greater degree of assertiveness (this is not the same as aggressiveness) and to become better negotiators. Help in the handling of change and conflict is more important than the development of team skills. Several external courses are now available which focus upon these issues.

Coaching

Coaching is a process of systematically increasing the ability and experience of subordinates by giving them planned tasks, coupled with continuing appraisal. The obvious source of coaching is the subordinate's line manager. MD professionals may well have a useful role to play in the development of coaching skills in line managers, but the activity itself can only be done within the context of the manager's job.

Coaching as an effective technique rests on six basic principles:

● It is experience on the job which teaches most.

● The ways jobs are structured influences the amount of learning which takes place.

● The example of the coach influences the attitudes, behaviour and development of subordinates.

● If subordinates participate in the setting of their learning targets they will be more committed to their attainment.

● Learning, in part, depends on knowing effort has met with success.

● Coaching is a continuing process.

Coaching involves minimally three basic activities: delegation, counselling and appraisal. It is in delegation that the boss can most clearly exercise his ability as a coach. Effective delegation involves the setting of objectives;

terms of reference and boundaries of authority and responsibility. Standards must be set and performance assessed, preferably in a quantifiable form. The action should always be in the hands of the subordinate. The skill of coaching depends on limited intervention, so that subordinates do not make too many mistakes and lose confidence on the one hand, and so that they do not come to depend on their boss on the other. The boss should encourage self-analysis of performance, but should be prepared as a normal element in appraisal to monitor performance against agreed success criteria.

There are two great dangers in delegation. The first is that the tasks delegated are themselves unlikely to provide much learning. Delegation of trivia will alienate rather than motivate subordinates. The second danger is that the boss will not use the experience as a training technique (i.e. follow it up with appraisal) but simply as a way of getting work done.

Project Learning

Often referred to as 'action learning', it is said by some to be the most important development in approaches to training in the last decade. The basic principles of action learning are that managers learn by doing real work, rather than being taught in the classroom, and that they learn from each other, rather than from management teachers. The role of the teacher is to provide conditions in which managers may learn with and from each other. Managers normally work in small groups of perhaps four or five, meeting at frequent intervals over an extended period of time, perhaps six months or more. Each manager brings to the group a work problem which they personally experience and which they are committed to resolving. There should be few limits as to what constitutes a suitable problem, but it must satisfy the criterion of ownership and be complex enough to require the shared energy of the group in exploring its dimensions and helping the manager find workable solutions. Factual problems, or problems not intimately related to the manager's job, are not suitable. It is important that the members appreciate that as much learning for the individual members of the group can come from helping each other as from receiving help with their own problems.

Much attention has been given to groups made up of senior managers from a wide variety of different organisations. It is likely, however, that projects dealing with familiar problems in a familiar setting will be the most common. Whether a stranger group or an insider group, what is more important is that the members have equality of status, otherwise the process of developing effective working relationships will be difficult.

189

The essence of action learning groups is that the learning process is self-managed and that members share the responsibility for the learning of others as well as themselves. It might be appropriate to have an 'adviser' in the group – from inside the company or an external consultant – whose function is to help develop effective working processes, rather than to get involved in substantive issues.

As with other forms of learning, individuals should have the support of their boss who, though not a member of the group, maintains interest in progress and in any specific outcome which may affect the working of their department.

Distance Learning

Sometimes referred to as 'open' learning, distance learning may be defined as learning at a time and place to suit the learner. Some companies are reluctant to release staff to attend even a one week training course, so distance learning is an important and relevant initiative in training design.

Basically, distance learning depends on the development of learning packages which can either be bought from an institution such as a University (e.g. the Open University Business School, set up in 1983) or a management training centre. They can also be developed 'in house'. They may involve the use of written material only, or a combination of written and audio visual material. Computer-based programmes linked via a modem to a centre have a great potential, alas as yet barely discovered.

However operated, any package should contain three elements:

1 Information in the form of lecture; guided and provided reading; case study exercises; video films and 'instruments' for self-appraisal.

2 Tutoring and counselling help, either face to face or via the telephone or through a computer link.

3 Self-help groups of learners engaged on the same programme.

The essence of distance learning is that it is student rather than teacher managed. It meets the basic requirements for effective training suggested in this chapter, as well as having the advantage of avoiding block release from work. It helps also to cope with the fears many managers have of going back to the classroom. Such learning is also relatively cheap, since most of the material can be used many times. It is sometimes imagined that distance learning is broad in scope. Whilst it is true that a manager may use this type of learning to obtain a degree in management studies, for example, there is nothing in the technique which prevents an application to more specific learning needs such as the personnel selection interview, or basic financial skills for managers.

Companies will need to do more than simply buy some distance learning packages. The subordinate's manager should be involved in the training, to ensure that it forms part of a coherent development strategy. His or her inter-eset in progress will be an important element in the learner's motivation. It is also important that the boss provides opportunities for the subordinate to use the skill and knowledge he has learned. Research appears to indicate that face to face contact, either with a manager or tutor or at least with a small group of fellow learners, is an important element in maintaining motivation.

Conclusion

The term 'Management Development' is generally employed to describe the use of any technique to develop managers. It includes, therefore, both education and training, together with planned 'on the job' development experience and self-development by reading and study.

In this chapter, the point has been made that there is a good deal more to MD than sending people on courses. The success of MD efforts depends largely upon using techniques which are appropriate to the organisation's growth stage and upon involving the learner in the planning and management of his or her own learning.

We have argued that the responsibility for MD must rest with the line manager. It is his or her responsibility to develop subordinates and he or she is most likely to be able to provide the most effective development opportunities. Early in the chapter we touched upon the role of the Personnel or Human Resources Department. It was argued that, except on rare occasions when personnel people may be expected to have the relevant knowledge (e.g. Industrial Relations legislation), the Personnel Department should not play a training role in MD activities themselves. This is not to say that personnel people do not have a role at all. They have a crucial role of encouraging managers to engage in effective development; in ensuring that finances and other resources are available; in the monitoring of training activities for cost-effectiveness and perhaps most important, in encouraging top management to develop a clear and positive policy with regard to MD generally, which they then ensure is carried out. In the writer's view the relative ineffectiveness of many MD specialists and trainers can be accounted for by their eagerness to 'run courses' rather than to develop policies and systems for training which line managers will accept and implement.

Such a view has been expressed by many personnel administrators over the years. It appears that in Britain line management itself is becoming aware of the need to take greater ownership of MD strategy. This should allow human resource specialists to concentrate on what they should be good at: the development of *policy* and the monitoring of its implementation. The *processes* by which the policy is implemented should become the province of line management.

References

1   Refer to Chapter 12. For a more detailed account read: S Davis and P Lawrence, *Matrix*, Addison Wesley, Wokingham, 1977.

2   The reader should consult: D Wolfe and D Kolb, 'Career Development, Personal Growth and Experiential Learning,' in Kolb, Rubin and McIntyre (Eds.), *Organisational Psychology: A Book of Readings*, Prentice Hall, New Jersey, 1979 (3rd Ed.).

3   J Kimberley and R Miles, *The Organisational Life Cycle*, Jossey Bass, San Francisco, 1980.

4   For a discussion of the problems inherent in MB, read: C Molander, *Management by Objectives in Perspective,* Journal of Management Studies, Vol. 9, No. 1, February, 1972.

5   P Hersey and K Blanchard, *Management of Organisational Behaviour: Utilising Human Resources,* Prentice-Hall, Englewood Cliffs, New Jersey, 1977.

6   Read: I Bradford, *Group Development*, University Associates, California, (2nd Ed.), 1978.

Suggested Reading

For a thorough account of Management Development generally, read: C Molander, *Management Development: Key Concepts for Managers and Trainers,* Chartwell-Bratt, Bromley, 1986.

For a detailed directory of methods, consult: A Huczynski, *Encyclopedia of Management Development Methods,* Gower, Aldershot, 1983.

Questions

1   What is meant by a 'systematic approach to Management Development'? Outline the essential elements of such an approach.

2   Under what conditions do managers learn best?

3   Distinguish between the responsibility of the line manager and the human resource specialist for the planning and implementation of MD activities.

Chapter 9

Performance Appraisal

Gerry Randell

Introduction

Performance appraisal is the process when individuals' work is observed, assessed, recorded, reported and discussed with the purpose of, somehow, improving the quality or quantity of work done, and maintaining or increasing the satisfaction the individual obtains from doing it. This somewhat simple definition obscures the enormous complexity of the process and the controversy that surrounds it. Surveys of how organisations go about reviewing or appraising performance at work, such as that carried out by Long at the Institute of Personnel Management in 1986,[1] show just how widespread and varied performance appraisal procedures are in British industry. Of the 306 organisations surveyed 82% had some kind of performance appraisal scheme. Their stated primary purpose was to improve performance through setting objectives and identifying training needs. Just 40% of the organisations gave the assessment of salary increases as one of the main purposes of performance appraisal, and 40% of the documentation analysed contained no reference to the identification or release of management potential. So this survey, like its predecessors, as described in the historical review by Randell,[2] indicates that there is no uniform agreement on the content or practice of performance appraisal.

What can be agreed is that performance appraisal is a key component of Human Resource Management, as it is from this process that the data are generated for any systematic development of individuals; their training, their reward, their career development, their promotion, their dismissal and even their early retirement. In addition, it is the source of information for plans and decisions to be made about the structure and management of the organisation as a whole. It is therefore of the utmost importance to an organisation.

The key issues that will be considered in this chapter are the relationships between the main purposes of performance appraisal, which can be grouped as follows: immediate performance improvement, performance related payment, the identification of potential for other jobs, and the validation of management procedures. The most controversial of these issues is relating financial reward directly to assessments of work performance. Even though the surveys indicate that the proportion of performance appraisal schemes that include some element of linked payment or merit rating has remained static at about 40%, what can be currently observed, particularly in the private sector, is a growing swing towards performance related pay systems.

The Present Situation

Some kind of performance appraisal goes on in all organisations. It can be seen to range from informal chats where a manager makes a few 'helpful' comments about a member of staff's work, through discussing how well plans and objectives have been met and setting new ones, to filling in an elaborate form about a person's performance and potential, often using various kinds of rating scales about the person's knowledge, skills and attitudes. These ratings are then fed into some kind of merit-rating and management development schemes which determine an individual's pay and rate of promotion. Examples of all these approaches can be seen throughout British work organisations and little agreement exists about what would be the best approach to this important area of Human Resource Management.

When the conceptual, theoretical and practical implications of performance appraisal systems are analysed the enormous complexity surrounding the process emerges. It is these difficulties that cause organisations to struggle with the problems of devising an appropriate scheme of staff development. From an analysis of the literature, research and observational studies of current practices in various organisations throughout the world, some general conclusions can be drawn. To impose some order on to the diversity of the difficulties the analysis and conclusions will be grouped into the Conceptual, Theoretical and Practical problem areas. However, it is stressed that, in practice, all these problem areas will be brought to bear simultaneously on a particular staff appraisal system.

Conceptual Problems

The overall purpose of any staff appraisal scheme should be to make an organisation more effective through developing its human resources. In other words, staff development. Organisations can take many approaches to managing their staff and the need exists to evaluate, control, develop and predict the behaviour of staff through assembling information of their past, present and predicted future performance at their jobs. By any standards this is a mighty undertaking, something that is not likely to be achieved through a single system and at one 'sitting' between a manager and a member of staff. Of the four needs, i.e. the evaluation, control, development and prediction of work performance, only one – performance development – can directly add to the performance of staff at their existing jobs. The others, important as they are, can only increase the chances of better performance; they do not necessarily bring it about.

As a performance appraisal scheme produces information collected from employees about how the organisation should handle their capacity and motivation to work, it can be regarded as an aspect of Organisation Development. Further, this information-based, rather than belief-based, decision making about organisational change should lead to decisions being made that have the commitment of the participants, rather than just tacit compliance. If, therefore, it is the policy of the organisation to build up a more committed staff then performance appraisal should be regarded as a way of achieving it. This is where performance appraisal also contributes to the corporate plan of the organisation, by providing precise information to direct planning and change within the organisation in the ways it treats its staff. This aspect of Human Resource Management is further elaborated in Chapters 12 and 13.

The meaning of the phrase 'staff development' also needs to be explored. Encouraging staff to 'work harder' and to gain more 'job satisfaction' are worthwhile intentions, but imprecise aims. In the final analysis, staff development should achieve both adding to people's capacity and to their inclination to carry out their current job. If this does not happen then any staff development procedure is a failure.

Managers are expected to get a return from and, hopefully, improve upon the resources they are designated to manage. If they are responsible for the manufacturing, marketing or money resources of the organisation they are forced to actively manage them. The nature of such resources is such that if they leave them alone the machines will corrode, the markets will be invaded and the money will be devalued; managers are therefore forced to apply considerable effort to guard and develop these resources. Modern management is also expected to do this through decision making on the basis of data rather than myth and belief. The opposite pressure applies to the management of people. If this resource is left alone it will grow by learning to respond to the experiences gained from the environment. It may not grow in the directions hoped for by the organisation but if the culture is basically benevolent and concerned, much of the growth will benefit the organisation. Consequently organisations are inclined to take a passive approach to person management and let nature take its course. If the policy decision is made to actively involve managers in the development of the organisation's human resources, then what is achieved must be more than what would have been gained by leaving people to develop themselves. This point is the basis for much of what is known as the dysfunctional outcomes of staff appraisal procedures, where this gain over nature is not obtained. Much can be done to help managers to manage more effectively. They can be given various support systems or laid down management procedures to operate, such as a merit rating scheme. Training can be given that attempts to add to their information collecting and using skill, their feelings of self-confidence or to give them a more flexible management style. The policy decision has to be made as to which should come first, either training managers in the skills of staff development or developing a system. The decision puts training first when an active approach is taken, and it implies that the training must provide managers with significant learning experiences and be directed at changing their behaviour in managing their staff. A passive approach to performance appraisal puts developing systems and procedures first. The training that follows is usually concerned with operating the system effectively through getting consistency in rating and form filling, and subsequently directing staff to conform more to the desirable traits determined by the designers of the system. It is this mechanistic, rather naive, approach to performance appraisal that is the basis of most of the criticism of the concept. It is therefore the meaning of the term *appraisal* itself that is the most taxing of the concepts for managers to handle. To many writers, and managers, the term appraisal automatically implies some kind of quantitative assessment. Some find it difficult, if not impossible, to accept that qualitative appraisal is an equally justifiable approach to performance analysis, particularly when there is not a performance related pay system to feed. It is the place of *evaluation* or *measurement* in a performance appraisal scheme that is therefore the most controversial issue.

It is often forgotten that the concept of *mensuration* starts with the observation of the presence or absence of something, defined as measurement at the *nominal* level, a level powerful enough to provide the whole basis of mathematical computing. So, too, can the precise observation of the presence or absence of something in an individual's performance at work form the basis of an effective performance appraisal scheme. However, if some kind of quantitative assessment is required to feed other aspects of the human resource management programme, such as merit rating or selection and training validation exercises, then it will be necessary to develop more advanced levels of measurement, such as employee rankings, i.e. *ordinal* level, or ordered rating scales, and even attempts at *interval* level measures through a points allocation scheme. Other textbooks, for example Carroll and Schneier,[3] abound with examples of such procedures and scales. Unfortunately, most miss the point that in any scheme of performance appraisal whose primary aim, as it should be, is the development of people's performance in their existing job, it is unnecessary, undesirable and probably dangerous to attempt to incorporate quantitative assessment as a formal part of such development based schemes.

It cannot be stressed enough that the exact measurement of human behaviour at work is fraught with considerable technical and ethical problems. Asking line managers to do something that most full-time behavioural science researchers would find extremely demanding to do is just creating unnecessary difficulties. As the objective of performance analysis is to improve performance, going through an evaluation or measurement stage to achieve this is neither necessary nor desirable. Even adjective check lists that attempt to focus observations onto kinds of behaviour which are valued by the organisation can be misleading and misunderstood. The alternative strategy to quantitative evaluation is qualitative (nominal) assessment. This is achieved by asking managers to observe and diagnose that which the individual and the organisation need to do differently *next* which would add to their performance at their tasks. The kinds of questions that can be asked of managers are of the kind, 'what should the appraisee know or be helped to learn next that would help performance in the job?''; and, 'what should the manager and/or organisation try to do next that would maintain the appraisee's motivation in the job?' The observation could then form a record and a source of pressure to bring about the agreed plan for achieving the desired change in the appraisee, the manager and the organisation. In the final analysis, this is all that effective performance appraisal need be.

Theoretical Problems

Behind the whole process of performance appraisal are various theoretical assumptions about the nature of the work, people, organisations, and even life itself. It is not the purpose of this chapter to survey all the relevant philosophical, economic and ethical issues. They are obviously of fundamental importance, but beyond the scope of this book. Nevertheless, they must at least be touched upon so that practitioners in this field are aware of the complexity of the problem. This point builds upon the issues of motivation and job satisfaction that were described in Chapter 5. The basis for the complexity is that work is an interaction between people and organisations, and the point of this interaction is known as Management. To start to understand just what goes on to make this interaction produce desirable outcomes, both to people and employing organisations, the notions about effective organisations, developing individuals, skilful management and the determinants of work performance need to be clarified.

So what is an effective organisation? Is it one that has a high return on investment? Or is it one that gives a responsible service to society? Or can it be judged by the quality of working life it provides its members? Or shall this large question-begging statement be replaced by a simple view, such as an organisation that learns, i.e. is adaptive, flexible, useful and growing? Chapters 12 and 13 in this book also touch on this view as it is one of the key concepts of Human Resource Management.

What, then, are developing individuals? Are they people who are continually adding to their capacity to do their job and experiencing growth in their motivation to do it? But just how do people learn, step-by-step or through flashes of insight? Can they be told to do such things or are they more readily obtained through a learning experience? What can be said with certainty is that people need precise information about what they should be learning for effective learning to take place. Giving a general exhortation to 'pull themselves together' and 'go off and work harder' is of little use. Similarly organisations need precise information about people's needs before they can add to the level of motivation. These observations raise the whole subject of learning and motivational theory which underpins most staff appraisal and development activity. Although there is as yet insufficient general theory to prescribe what organisations should do, there is enough to indicate that which is appropriate to apply to the problem of designing staff appraisal schemes.

What, then, are skilful managers? Are they those who are able to observe, check, get, give, share and use information about human behaviour at work; to achieve development both in the organisations for whom they work and the individuals who work for them? And to do this in a supportive way that aids understanding and tolerance of the difficulties involved in changing behaviour. This raises complex theoretical problems about the nature of human skills and implies that person management is a skill that, like any other skill, can only be acquired through practice and feedback. To learn a skill a person must first want to become skilful. A skill cannot be taught, it can only be learned. This is complicated for those skills where some kind of practice has already taken place, because then there is an 'unfreezing' problem, where a learner is helped to understand just how much more there is to learn. It is important at this stage not to undermine a practitioner's self-esteem. So managers must be helped to realise that it is no criticism of them personally to say that every manager has a lot to learn about how to manage their staff.

As Wright and Taylor[4] cogently display, it is just these interpersonal skills of gathering information, influencing behaviour and handling emotion that turn a manager into a leader. They argue that the attempt by organisations to increase the amount of that most elusive of all managerial attributes, 'leadership', within the organisation, could well start with training managers in performance appraisal skills.

What, then, are the determinants of work performance? How much of individuals' work arises from what is 'inside' them, e.g. their abilities or attitudes; or 'inside' the organisation, e.g. the tools that they have been given, or the way they are managed? Disentangling the causes of work performance, then allocating causal contribution to each determinant is one of the great theoretical and methodological problems of organisation psychology. It is a long way off being solved and, this being so, gives another reason why naive attempts at measuring what may appear to be causal factors, through simplistic rating scales, should not be lightly undertaken. In the final theoretical analysis, no matter what the determinants are of work performance, there is always something, whether it is a change in the individual or a change in the work environment that can be done that would improve an individual's performance on a job. It is the diagnosis of this that is the essential objective of any performance analysis and which should be the focus of any staff development scheme.

Practical Problems

The task now remains to consider how to establish an effective performance appraisal scheme. Although the ideas presented above are simple, putting them into practice will not be easy. The first step is to accept the enormity of the problem and like any enormous problem the only way to handle it is to break it down in to its component parts. It is often seen in practice that staff appraisal schemes are so comprehensive and attempt to achieve so much that they must have been designed to be carried out by paragons of managerial skill! Such schemes are administratively attractive but as they are to be used by ordinary line managers, who more often than not do not possess the range of the designer's technical and management competence, they are probably doomed to failure. There is also the ethical point that it is grossly unfair on people at work to evaluate their performance before attempts are made to help them to develop it. Further, it is incorrect to assume a direct relationship between performance at one level of work with potential for another. The most common practical error seen in the design of staff appraisal schemes is the attempt to achieve performance development, merit rating and potential identification all in one procedure. The most common theoretical error is the assumption that a merit rating policy, e.g. giving more reward for more work necessarily improves the quality of individuals' work or their satisfaction. It could just be that they work harder at getting rated better to the detriment of the true effectiveness of their work or motivation. Consequently, it must be a carefully considered policy decision by an organisation to link pay directly with performance through some kind of merit rating scheme. However, there are many other ways that managers can reward their staff and discrimination, precision and skill are required to manage a reward review system.

What this analysis has shown is that there is no generally agreed content or structure for a performance appraisal scheme. However, what can be asserted (see Randell et al,[5] and Cummings and Schwab[6]) is that to be thorough and effective a performance appraisal scheme must be broken down into the constituent parts, according to the particular purpose of that part of Personnel Management, and then each part operated separately. The four main groups of purposes are as follows:

Performance Review

There is little doubt that an effective performance review system which results in commitment to changes in individual, managerial and organisational behaviour is the cornerstone of any staff appraisal system. There is also little doubt that assembling information about the performance of staff for the purpose of improving it is both the responsibility and duty of all line managers. Only they have direct access to the main determinants of behaviour at work.

An approach to making the performance review more systematic, that is often advocated by many organisations, is through setting targets or some kind of objective. So-called 'management-by-objectives' has very wide support as a way of controlling and assessing the performance of people at their jobs. Unfortunately, when this technique is applied to performance appraisal, it can have many adverse effects. The main one is diverting the discussion away from any precise issues of individual behaviour. This is especially noticeable when there is effort to agree quantitative targets rather than behavioural change. Then there is the problem of allowing for chance extraneous factors in the judgements made by managers that could affect the achievement of targets.

The severest constraint on performance reviews is the ability of managers to carry them out. It is easy to design forms and relatively easy to fill them out. But to control subjectivity and to cope with the complexity of observing and changing human behaviour requires a great deal of skill and effort. Getting managers to obtain and apply these crucial aspects of interpersonal expertise is an enormous task. It should start by getting managers to realise that staff appraisal is not about assessments or ratings, although these may have to come later on in the process. In the first instance, all it is about is diagnosing what an individual needs to know next that could add to their capacity for their existing job, i.e. a development step. Also, to diagnose what the manager should try to do next that would help the individual's motivation in that job, i.e. 'motivation growth'. Unless these two fundamental purposes are understood by managers and achieved through a staff appraisal system, the whole process is a waste of time and effort.

The support system, or paperwork required for a performance review procedure need only be quite simple. In theory a blank sheet of paper should suffice. But, in practice, some pre-printed form that signals organisational sanction and support for performance reviewing would be useful for sending information, or such things as training needs, through to the appropriate departments. How well a form is completed is also a useful indicator of the effectiveness of the appraisal and can impose pressure on managers to use the process properly. Whether or not there is a need for automatic 'sending in the forms', i.e. 'staff reporting', is a debatable issue and can form an interesting aspect of organisational politics! There is little doubt that the key advice in designing a performance review system is to 'keep it simple', both in content and practice. The crucial determinant of its success is the commitment of the participants to its principles and process. Therefore, any system or paperwork procedure must be seen as a support rather than a threat.

Reward Review

A 'fair' and acceptable reward system is an essential requirement of any organisation. The process whereby people are observed, have their performance assessed, are given the opportunity to discuss their assessment, and what that means in terms of their payment, is that part of performance appraisal known as reward review. Chapter 4 reviews the issues surrounding wages and salaries and sets out the differences between assessing the worth of jobs, job evaluation, paying differential rewards for performances and merit rating. As Chapter 4 shows, the whole area of relative rewards is shrouded with cultural, historical and legislative factors. There is an important difference between job evaluation and merit-rating. Job evaluation is all about assessing the worth of a job a person is doing. As Chapter 4 explains, there is the implication of something absolute, fixed over time and separate from individual behaviour about job evaluation. Whereas merit-rating is all about relative worth of one individual's performance with another, it is variable over time, and is very much concerned with individual ability and effort. Consequently, organisations can design the two procedures separately. However, in practice, it is not so easy to make a firm distinction, particularly when both systems are expected to make use of the same performance appraisal data. An additional complication, which is most marked in those companies without a clear job grading structure within a job evaluation scheme, is when individuals perform so well that the organisation loads more work, and perhaps responsibility, on to them over the review period and now the staff expect financial recognition for performance in what is in effect a new job. It is this overlap area between job evaluation and merit-rating which is the most demanding aspect of managing an organisation's wages and salaries procedures, particularly on the skill of the manager, and the morale of the staff. So, getting the job evaluation procedures appropriate is an essential part of organisation management, whereas setting up a merit-rating scheme is not essential for developing an effective organisation.

However, where the policy of the organisation is to vary financial reward according to relative achievement or ability, information is required to feed this system. Consequently, the person responsible for the payment and perquisite procedures requires information that discriminates between individual performance so that these decisions can be made. The key issue here is devising and operating an appropriate scale, or scales, that allow for meaningful and acceptable discriminations between work performances to be made.

The history of rating scales of work performance is a long one. The two main approaches to this assessment problem are either to develop more dimensions of work performance and more elaborate scales for measuring them, or to stick to a single dimension rating scale of overall worth and then to institute procedures and training to control the subjectivity involved in its use.

The arguments in favour of a multi-dimensional approach are that they can cover a wide range of work outcomes, which can be given previously agreed relative weights, so the whole procedure appears more fair, comprehensive, thorough and even 'scientific'. Latham and Wexley[7] give a full account of this approach and provide useful guidelines for 'making the system work'.

The main argument in favour of the unidimensional approach is that the human brain cannot be beaten as an instrument for observing, assembling and analysing a wide range of imprecise, often conflicting, information and for quickly coming to a decision based upon it. The problem is to get the owner of the instrument to use these impressive facilities properly! The observation can be made here that university staff have used a 6 point unidimensional assessment scale for generations of students: First, Upper Second, Lower Second, Third, Pass and Fail. It appears to work, even though mistakes from time to time may get made, but in the highly disciplined academic environment they are thought to be rare. This unidimensional approach can be seen operating in many British companies who have deliberately ensured, over a long period of time, that the scale is used in a disciplined way by managers. It is this point that is often forgotten by designers of appraisal schemes. It is easy to design a rating scale of work performance, usually by a committee, issue it, and expect managers to use it. But without a history of experience, understanding, care and commitment, the categories on the scale will be interpreted differently by the managers. Phrases like, 'I only allow 1's to work for me', or 'staff are not as good as they used to be – all I ever get are 3's'. will soon indicate rampant subjectivity. The human brain is not only a marvellous instrument for using information, it is also superb at misusing it. So, if a straightforward approach to quantitative assessment for a reward review is required, then the first step is to define a unidimensional scale, probably with 5 or 6 categories, described as operationally as possible, perhaps in the first instance with predetermined indications of what proportion of a department's staff should fall within each category. Then to put a great deal of effort into getting managers to control their biases and prejudices when using it. The effort should be more towards attitudinal training rather than skills training, as rating exercises only help managers to be more skilful in manipulating and misusing the scales for their own ends. The key objective in this training is to bring about 'disciplined subjectivity' in the use of the scale, and this can take a long time.

Even with a great deal of care and technical expertise the use of quantitative assessment methods for discriminating between work performance and determining pay will cause an organisation a large amount of trouble and take up a great deal of managerial time. The question will be raised as to whether or not it is worth it, particularly if it appears to be causing more alienation and conflict than motivation and commitment in the people so appraised.

The alternative strategy to a reward review based on quantitative assessment and differential worth to the organisation is that based on qualitative assessment and the differential needs of individuals. It is here that the topic of performance appraisal overlaps most with the material in Chapter 5 on Motivation. It can be argued that it is effort and commitment to work that should also be rewarded by an organisation, not just achievement. The able will probably get their rewards through more interesting work to do, the accolades of their colleagues, and even promotion. But how about the group of employees of limited capacity and opportunity to achieve? Where should they come in some mechanistic evaluation based performance appraisal scheme? It is for this group that more qualitative approaches to reward reviewing are appropriate. Motivation and job satisfaction arise from having needs met, within a framework of an individual's expectations. This process is complicated by people frequently not really knowing what their real needs are, or having very unrealistic expectations about their fulfilment. If a manager can skilfully judge, albeit still subjectively, that an individual is working to the limits of his capacity, then diagnose what the organisation can reasonably do to meet that individual's more important immediate needs then this is, arguably, the most significant contribution to motivation a manager can make. It is trite to say that all an individual works for is money. On the contrary, what research into motivation has shown is that meeting an individual's next need is the most powerful and satisfying of all motivators. Of course, for some this will be money, but for most it will not. The more personal, proximate and precise that organisational act can be, the more effective the management of that individual's motivation. Consequently, a qualitative reward review system arises from skilfully judging the performance of a member of staff relative to his own experience and ability, then discussing needs and expectations in such a way that a diagnosis is made of what the manager should and could be doing differently next for the individual. Getting right the action plan arising from this diagnosis must be regarded as the height of interpersonal managerial decision making. It could be that not only is a qualitative approach to reward reviews more effective in bringing about increased performance and satisfaction at work, it may well be the cheapest approach to take to this crucial management issue.

Potential Review

Organisations have a continual requirement to identify and develop their future managers. Individuals want to know and understand how their career is likely to develop over time. To assemble and use information for predicting the future behaviour of people at work is probably the most technically complex and sensitive of all individual and organisational development activities. A key issue is deciding over how long a period of time are predictions to be made. If attempts are made to make predictions beyond the 'next' job or promotion then information requires to be assembled at some 'central' point to help data based decisions to be made by a Management Development Adviser. This is now frequently done by means of some kind of 'assessment centre'. These are occasions when a member of staff is given a battery of tests, exercises, questionnaires and interviews aimed at eliciting his capacity and inclination for higher level jobs, and the possible directions for his career. Fletcher and Williams[8] review the main issues involved and show how such activity abounds with technical and administrative pitfalls.

Like reward review procedures, potential review systems do not necessarily add directly to the performance of staff in their existing jobs. The existence of such systems may 'keep staff at it', but they may also encourage looking too much at the future, so letting the present go by default. Obviously line managers are often asked by members of staff to express an opinion about their careers and potential and, as a result of such discussions, information may be generated of use to the potential review process. Whether or not a line manager should conduct the formal review of his staff's potential and possible career path is a difficult organisational decision to make.

The crucial theoretical problem here is just what of a person's capacities, inclinations, needs and experiences are predictive of higher level managerial behaviour. The technical problem is then assessing them. On top of all this is the problem of raising expectations in those people who are led to believe they have potential, and maintaining motivation in those who are given the impression they do not. This is a veritable quagmire of organisational management.

The main practical issues in any potential review procedure are deciding who should enter it and then how the outcomes should be handled. The role of the line manager is critical. As a result of appraising staff performance the manager is best placed to form a judgement on whether or not an individual should be considered for another, possibly higher level job, and then to 'issue the ticket to ride' the potential review procedure, although the 'system' should not prevent individuals issuing their own tickets. Observations from the performance review are usefully fed into the potential review process, both qualitative and quantitative where available, preferably on a specially designed form rather than just photocopies of the performance review and reward review documents. This may sound like extra paperwork, but potential reviewing does not apply to all the staff all the time. Entering the potential review procedure should be regarded as a 'special ride', and not automatically appraised on an annual basis. This is such an important sensitive area of Human Resource Management that it has to be initiated very carefully and thoroughly by a line manager. The 'central' assessment, evaluation, and decision making process can then be followed by, hopefully, highly competent 'assessors' so that the next task for the line manager is handling the re-entry back to day-to-day departmental work. For a 'high flier' this should not be too difficult; for the 'work-horse' this may be exceedingly delicate, and will again stretch the interpersonal management skills of a line manager to the limits. Consequently, all the paperwork and demands on a line manager should be, once again, aimed at giving help and support in this difficult managerial task.

Asking, in the words of Douglas McGregor,[9] a line manager to 'play god' can be destructive to an otherwise effective day-to-day relationship. A human resource management procedure should enhance managerial relationships, not detract from them.

Organisation Review

A further aspect of performance appraisal which is frequently overlooked is the need to discover how well the organisation's management procedures are working. It is often said that an experienced observer can tell more about an organisation and a manager by studying the staff appraisal system and completed forms than from any other information about organisational activity. This observation gives the clue to how to assemble information that enables objective decisions to be made about the effectiveness of organisational procedures, such as selection and training schemes. Such information can be derived from existing staff appraisal schemes but it is probably better obtained through special 'follow-up' reports of individuals' performance. This is the field of validation and is usually the province of independent or external researchers. Some organisations are setting up internal consultancy and personnel research groups which are seen as independent enough to carry out the analysis of what may be very sensitive data. The key problem here is that of organisational politics. Many senior managers would appear to resent efforts to investigate whether or not they are managing their staff effectively. When they do they would not necessarily give their full cooperation for such data to be accumulated and analysed.

It is for organisation review that the most advanced kinds of rating scales could be usefully developed. The material of this chapter so far may have given the impression of antagonism towards the measurement of work performance. This antagonism is only directed towards unnecessary and inept performance measures. In the field of organisation review the requirement to use all types and levels of measurement is paramount. The more precise and higher the level of measurement achieved the more advanced the statistics that can be used. Also this area of personnel research can be used as a proving ground for performance measures that are needed in other areas, particularly reward and potential reviews. If they do not work here the only outcome will be that a few statistics would have been underestimated. If incorrect measures are used in staff development, then a large number of alienated performances will be the outcome. The availability of staff and resources to devise performance measures and to undertake follow-up studies within an organisation provides the opportunity not only to accumulate data on the effectiveness of personnel practices, but also to indicate how best to integrate them.

The first paperwork requirement of an organisation review procedure is sound performance measures. Research over the past twenty years, culminating in studies at Bradford, published by Bailey,[10] has shown that some kind of behaviourally anchored scale, based on empirically derived incidents and dimensions, is possibly the best available technique to use. Although exceedingly time-consuming to produce, behaviourally anchored rating scales (BARS) can provide the foundation for quantitative approaches to organisation review, and provide the source of validated measures of performance for the reward and potential reviews.

The further point can be made that the standing of Human Resource Management will be determined by the quality of organisation review statistics that are generated. At the moment 'HRM' has still to prove itself as a force in organisational management. The proof will follow the generation of high quality performance appraisal data.

The Way Ahead

There is currently a great deal of discussion about integrating personnel practices in an organisation within a strategic human resource management policy. This does not mean that all personnel practices should be run together, although bureaucratic tidiness and simplistic application of theory may be seen to imply this. On the contrary, effective Human Resource Management means getting all the bits of practice as technically sound, administratively convenient and socially acceptable as possible, and as skilfully run as practicable. This means putting effort into controlling the possible contamination of each part by keeping separate the conflicting purposes and data. Then energy can be put into ensuring that the separate parts of personnel activity are integrated into a systematic whole. This is perhaps the key issue in Human Resource Management, obtaining integration at the 'macro' level without impeding the effective operation of the parts.

The above observations and the history and analysis of performance appraisal given in this chapter should provide sufficient evidence to encourage the separation, in practice, of performance, reward, potential and organisation reviews. It is a key recommendation of this chapter that the achievement of effective performance appraisal is too important to risk the dangers involved in contaminating the information of decision making by attempting to merge the four separate groups of purposes into a single, monolithic performance appraisal scheme.

When the separation is so planned, each of the procedures can be developed

208

as an independent exercise, but sharing information where it is relevant. As the process of Performance Review is the only one of the four that can directly add to the development of an individual and an organisation, then this is the one which provides the information base for worthwhile staff appraisal schemes. If an organisation really wants itself to be developed in this way, the following then need to be undertaken, probably in parallel, and possibly starting in this order:

a Policy

The first thing that needs to be done is to spread the key concepts, as set out above, of performance appraisal around the organisation, preferably starting at the top, so as to get managerial commitment, rather than compliance, to any systems or procedures that may be developed. In Figure 9, the main conceptual differences between effective and a passive approach to performance appraisal are set out in summary form and this may help the approach advocated in this chapter to be understood. This is particularly important when there has previously been staff appraisal schemes that have fallen into disrepute. It is then essential to publicise the ways in which the new procedure will differ from the failures.

As a start, a 'Board Seminar' should be held, where the senior managers of the organisation share their views about performance appraisal and are helped to understand the concepts and practical implications of what could be effective performance development, as summarised in Figure 9. If it is then agreed that this approach is appropriate for the organisation, the policy decision to apply time and resources to achieving it can then be made, and responsibilities allocated to bring it about within an appropriate time-scale.

Whether or not performance should be linked directly with pay is a very serious policy decision for an organisation. There are philosophical, economic and practical arguments both ways. The decision should be based more on information about the current condition of the organisation, and in what direction it should go, than just on the philosophy and opinions of the most influential members of senior management. To get this decision right is a crucial issue in the Human Resource Management of any organisation.

b Training

Concepts without the ability to apply them are barren. Perhaps one of the major weaknesses of management training is the tendency to teach infor-

Effective Staff Appraisal

Is concerned with:

BEHAVIOUR	rather than	PERSONALITY
INFORMATION	rather than	BELIEF
CHANGE	rather than	EVALUATION
PRECISION	rather than	GENERALITIES
COMMITMENT	rather than	COMPLIANCE
SUPPORT	rather than	DIRECTION
SKILLS	rather than	FORMS

It uses

DEVELOPMENT STEPS — that which individuals need to know *next* that would add to their capacity to perform their job

and MOTIVATION MAINTENANCE — that which an organisation needs to know *next* to add to an individual's inclination to perform their job.

These are achieved by learning experiences gained through a 'Performance Review'.

Figure 9: Summary of the Differences Between an Effective and a Passive Approach to Staff Appraisal

mation and let the skills go by default. Unfortunately, skills can only be acquired by people who want to learn them so there is sometimes a major problem in 'unfreezing' managers from their personal view that they already have sufficient interpersonal skills to carry out performance appraisal effectively. The fact is that half of all managers are below average in their level of skill to interact purposefully with their staff, and numerous surveys and research studies indicate that the average itself is rather low.

The 'unfreezing' process to encourage managers to acquire the skills of performance appraisal can be achieved in various ways, but there are two main principles that could be applied. The first is the design and content of the skills training; the second is the sequence and timing of such training. Experiences in undertaking this work have shown that training courses in staff appraisal skills must be at least of two days' duration. The first day should aim to get across the main concepts and the notion that appraising staff is a skill, nothing more, nor less. Then the practical work on the first day should demonstrate just how much of the skill there is to learn, and then display to each and every member of the course that precise aspect of their own performance that needs to be changed to increase their own level of skill.

The second day builds upon the first, giving supervised practice in the insights gained on the first day and, additionally, developing in the participants the ability for observation, self-analysis and self-tutoring. Such precision and experiences in learning can only be achieved through the use of skilled tutors. The availability and efforts of tutors is the key to the acquisition of skill in trainees, for it is essential that the practical work undertaken on the course is accompanied by exact and acceptable guidance about the trainees' performance, i.e. feedback. Without skilled tutoring the learning can not only be inefficient, it can also be dangerous to the further acquisition of the skills of staff appraisal within trainees who are either given a false feeling of confidence, or doubt that they could ever appraise adequately. Taylor and Wright[11] set out the issues in training tutors and show how important this is.

To create acceptance and commitment to the need for acquisition and growth of performance appraisal skills, such training should start at the 'operating' top of an organisation and preferably be concentrated within divisions of the organisation rather than spread across levels. In this way a climate of understanding and a will to be skilful can be quickly achieved within working units, so that the skills are subsequently practised in a supportive environment. They will then be likely to grow rather than wither and so become an established part of managerial behaviour.

c   Support Systems

As has been noted before in this chapter, the main use for printed staff appraisal forms is the overt organisational sanction they give to the expenditure
of time and effort on the process. The design of the forms and other paperwork
in staff appraisal procedures is often seen as the end result of staff development schemes rather than a means of achieving increased performance of
both individuals and organisations. The design of such systems is enormously
complicated when they attempt to achieve Performance, Reward and Potential Reviews on a single form, even though the combination may appear
administratively attractive. Consequently, as the above principles have
explicitly stated, separate provision should be made to meet the needs of any
merit rating, job evaluation and promotion systems, and then efforts first
concentrated upon ensuring that the performance review procedure is given
the full commitment of all those involved in it.

Once training arrangements have been made and introduced for the necessary
skills to be developed in the organisation, the need for pre-printed forms can
be directed towards providing guidelines and support for the exercise of
performance appraisal skills, and to meet the secondary organisational need
for a control procedure to ensure that staff development has taken place. It
cannot be stressed enough that forms should be designed to meet the needs
of the line managers to be skilful rather than seen as material for a records
department.

An important remaining issue is what to call the performance appraisal
scheme. The word 'appraisal' has so many emotive associations that it should
probably be replaced by a more neutral term. The Civil Service has moved
towards emphasising the job rather than the person and call their system Job
Appraisal Review (JAR). The term gaining favour with the Bradford influenced organisations is Work Review and Action Plan (WRAP). Some organisations are trying to move away completely from the old connotations of
appraisal and are using terms like 'counselling' and 'coaching' to describe
their performance review procedure. Some ingenuity is required within each
organisation to get the description of both the whole and the parts of a performance appraisal appropriate to the expectations of the people involved in
it.

d   Development

No human resource management procedure should ever remain static and, in
the light of practice and experience, it should be improved. Once the level of

performance appraisal skill in managers has been increased then the support procedures could be changed in accordance with the growth of this skill so that even more effective performance development is achieved. If personnel policy decrees that a fast pace of development takes place, then refresher and advanced training courses need to be implemented. Problems will also arise with changes in the expectations of the individuals making up the organisation, and with the rate of growth of the organisation itself. These factors may lead to desirable changes in the performance appraisal procedure. Therefore, the scheme will need to be monitored and changed in accordance with information about its effects and effectiveness.

Conclusion

This chapter has ranged widely over the many issues surrounding the concept of performance appraisal. It has not put forward a set of proposals that would enable an instant performance appraisal scheme to be installed. Instead, it has laid down the principles that should guide the design and implementation of a scheme in accordance with the present state of the organisation. It is this 'contingency approach' that is the central conclusion of this chapter. The main factor influencing what approach to take to staff appraisal is whether or not there has been an attempt at a system before. If there has not, then the task is easier than if there is a long history of unpopular attempts to run a staff appraisal scheme.

Many managerial colleagues will have their own views about the meaning, purpose and practice of performance appraisal. Some of them are difficult to shift and it may be unrealistic to suppose that a truly effective staff development scheme will be able to be achieved easily. The fundamental principles about the appraisal and development of an organisation's human resources that should guide the design and implementation of any scheme can be summarised as follows:

1   Performance appraisal should be 'development led' rather than 'assessment led'. This means that managers should appraise their staff for the purpose of diagnosing what they should be doing differently next that would add to their performance in their existing job; and to discover what the organisation should be doing differently for them that would add to their inclination to apply their capacity to their job. In the light of fairness and natural justice this diagnosis and action plan should precede any assessment of a person's relative worth to an organisation, and their potential for higher level work.

2   Performance appraisal should be 'skills led' rather than 'forms led'. This means that early on in the process of introduction of a new or revised staff appraisal scheme a start should be made to ensure that managers have the interpersonal skills necessary to interact purposefully and effectively with their staff.

3   Performance appraisal should be 'line-management centred' rather than 'personnel centred'. This means that it should be designed and accepted as a procedure for helping line managers to develop their own staff better, rather than being a part of the personnel department's attempt to develop work and power for themselves. Clearly a delicate balance has to be established between the line manager's need for help and guidance in developing their own staff and the Personnel Department's need for information about employees. Getting this balance is one of the essential features of Human Resource Management.

References

1   P Long, *Performance Appraisal Revisited*, Institute of Personnel Management, London, 1986.

2   G A Randell, 'Employee Appraisal', in *Personnel Management in Britain*, K Sisson (Ed.) Blackwell, Oxford, 1989.

3   S J Carroll and C E Schneier, *Performance Appraisal and Review Systems*, Scott Foresman, Glenview, Illinois, 1982.

4   P L Wright and D S Taylor, *Improving Leadership Performance*, Prentice Hall, Englewood Cliffs, N.J., 1984.

5   G Randell, P Packard and J Slater, *Staff Appraisal – A First Step to Effective Leadership*, Institute of Personnel Management, London, 1984.

6   L L Cummings and D P Schwab, *Performance in Organizations*, Scott Foresman, Glenview, Illinois, 1973.

7   G P Latham and K N Wexley, *Increasing Productivity through Performance Appraisal*, Addison-Wesley, Reading, Mass. 1981.

8   C Fletcher and R Williams, *Performance Appraisal and Career Development*, Hutchinson, London, 1985.

9   D McGregor, 'An Uneasy Look at Performance Appraisal', *Harvard Business Review, 35*, 89-95, 1957.

10 C T Bailey, *The Measurement of Job Performance*, Gower, Aldershot, 1983.

11 D S Taylor and P L Wright, *Developing Interpersonal Skills Through Tutored Practice*, Prentice Hall, Englewood Cliffs, N.J., 1988.

Suggested Reading

Of the above books the two that could be most usefully read next are Cummings and Schwab, *Performance in Organizations*, and Fletcher and Williams, *Performance Appraisal and Career Development*.

Questions

1   Compare and contrast a development led with an assessment led performance appraisal scheme.

2   What principles should be followed in the design of 'paperwork' for a staff appraisal scheme?

3   Discuss the skills required by a manager to influence behaviour at work.

Chapter 10

Employment Law

Mark Hall

Introduction

The past twenty years have seen a significant increase in the legal regulation of employment and industrial relations, such that the law now exerts a major influence on the relationship between employer and employee and on the role of the personnel manager. Legal developments in the 1970s were widely seen as making a substantial contribution to the rise in the number, status and influence of personnel specialists in British industry.[1] While the wider economic and industrial environment of the 1980s may have served to downgrade 'industrial relations' as a key management concern, the continued rapid rate of change and the increasing complexity of employment law mean that legal considerations remain of considerable importance in the development of management policies.

Employment law has over the same period been a crucial political and electoral issue and, while the overall trend has been one of increased legal regulation, the nature of the reforms that have been initiated has reflected the political complexion of the Government of the day. Thus, the legislation introduced by th 1974-79 Labour Government as part of the 'Social Contract' with the trade union movement was intended to strengthen workers' statutory employment rights and support union organisation and collective bargaining. Similarly, as Government policy and 'human resource management' have tended increasingly to emphasise flexibility and deal with employees as individuals rather than as groups, the legalisation of the 1980s has diminished employment protection measures and inhibited trade union organisation and activity.

Against such a background, this chapter aims to provide a basic introduction to key issues and developments in British employment law. It is in two parts. The first gives an overview of recent changes in the law affecting employment and industrial relations matters, and identifies the main strategies pursued by Governments which have shaped the development of employment law. The second part of the chapter goes on to outline current legal provisions on a number of important aspects of employment, and to assess their impact, particularly on management practice.

The Changing Legal Framework

In Britain, the voluntary regulation of employment (by means of collective bargaining between employers and unions or by means of employers acting unilaterally) has traditionally been more important than legal regulation. Indeed, for much of the twentieth century, a general policy of non-intervention by the law in industrial relations was applied. For the most part, terms and conditions of employment and industrial relations procedures were matters for voluntary self-regulation by employers and unions. 'Voluntarism' – as this approach has been termed – was supported by both sides of industry. Unions saw the main role of legislation as preventing hostile intervention by the courts in industrial disputes on the basis of the common law (i.e. judge-developed law as opposed to statute law passed by Parliament). Employers were keen to avoid legislation which constrained their freedom to manage.

The era of voluntarism had its roots in the 1870s when important steps were taken towards the legislation of basic trade union activities. However, it was not until the Trade Disputes Act 1906 that the legal framework which was the cornerstone of the voluntary system was completed. The 1906 Act ruled out most legal action against trade unions (as opposed to officials or members) and granted the organisers of industrial action statutory protection or 'immunity' against liability at common law for civil wrongs, including that of inducing a breach of employment contracts, providing they acted 'in contemplation or furtherance of a trade dispute'. This statutory mechanism was intended to preclude the operation of the common law in industrial disputes. The immunities thus underpinned the voluntary system of industrial relations.[2] Other key aspects of the voluntary system included the absence of any legal obligation on employers to bargain with unions and the fact that collective agreements were not legally enforceable between employers and unions.

However, although industrial relations remained essentially voluntary in character, this did not imply the complete absence of employment legislation other than the statutory immunities. A number of measures were enacted from the late nineteenth century onwards to encourage and support voluntary collective bargaining, including the provision of conciliation and arbitration machinery and the establishment of wages councils to regulate minimum wages in industries where collective bargaining was virtually non-existent. Elementary protective legislation on health and safety and on the payment of wages dated from earlier in the nineteenth century. (Moreover, the voluntary system was replaced by special wartime measures during both world wars, and the Trade Disputes and Trade Unions Act 1927, passed in the wake of the General Strike and repealed in 1946, contained restrictions on trade union activity which clearly fell outside the tradition of voluntarism.) Yet compared with other industrial countries the crucial and distinguishing characteristic of Britain employment law was its limited role.

The 1960s

In 1965, the Trade Disputes Act was passed to restore the intended effect of the trade dispute immunity after the courts had developed a new common law civil liability the previous year undermining the lawfulness of industrial action. However, by this time, the efficacy of the voluntary system of industrial relations was being challenged. The first steps in what was to become a more general trend towards the legal regulation of employment and industrial relations matters were the Contracts of Employment Act 1963, which concerned minimum periods of notice and written particulars of terms and conditions of employment, and the Redundancy Payments Act 1965, which provided for age- and service-related redundancy compensation. More fundamentally, there was growing political pressure for a more general review of industrial relations and employment law, resulting in the establishment of the Royal Commission on Trade Unions and Employers' Associations (the 'Donovan Commission') in 1965. This pressure reflected increasing concern about the inflationary impact of unregulated collective bargaining in the context of the prevailing post-war policies of full employment and economic growth. One response was the use of incomes policy to influence directly the outcome of collective bargaining. However, greater legal intervention was also advocated from some quarters to restrict industrial action (and therefore limit unions' bargaining power) in order to influence indirectly the level of pay settlements. There were, in addition, other concerns about particular aspects of industrial relations including the growth of unofficial and unconstitutional strikes and the incidence of restrictive practices.

When it reported in 1968, the Donovan Commission's main recommendations focused on the reform of the structure of collective bargaining and were generally, if not entirely, consistent with the notion of voluntarism. Indeed, the Donovan Commission argued against 'destroying the British tradition of keeping industrial relations out of the courts.'[3] The legal enforceability of collective agreements was rejected, at least until the defects in collective bargaining identified by Donovan had been remedied. The retention of the system of immunities in respect of industrial action was supported, though clarification was urged and there were divisions within the Commission about the scope of the immunities. A number of changes in the law were, however, proposed. These included the introduction of legislation to enable complaints of unfair dismissal, and a procedure for investigating complaints that employers refused to recognise trade unions.

The Labour Government's subsequent White Paper 'In Place of Strife', published in January 1969, reflected the Donovan Commission's recommendations but also contained a number of additional proposals. These included measures for resolving inter-union disputes and for a statutory 'conciliation pause' in unconstitutional strikes (i.e. those in breach of procedure) which were enforceable by the imposition of fines. A bill intended to implement these two provisions (but not the others in the White Paper which were to be enacted later) was strongly opposed by the trade unions and was dropped by the Government in return for a 'solemn and binding' undertaking by the TUC to take action on inter-union disputes and unconstitutional strikes. The eventual Industrial Relations Bill, excluding any 'penal clauses', fell with the 1970 general election at which the Conservatives won power.

The Industrial Relations Act

The Industrial Relations Act 1971, introduced by the new Conservative Government, was an ambitious attempt at the comprehensive legal regulation of industrial relations and thus represented a notable departure from the tradition of voluntarism. Heavily influenced by American legislation, the 1971 Act reflected the Government's view – contrary to that of Donovan – that the law could be a key instrument in the reform of industrial relations. The National Industrial Relations Court (NIRC) was established, and unions' common law liabilities and the traditional immunities were replaced by new restrictions on industrial action, breach of which made the organisers of the action liable to be sued for 'unfair industrial practices'. These restrictions were also linked to a provision on the registration of trade unions, under which unions derived certain benefits but also had to meet a number of stringent requirements as to the contents of their rules. 'Closed shop' arrangements were tightly regulated and those involving unregistered unions were not permitted. Collective agreements were to be legally enforceable unless they contained a clause to the contrary. A new legal procedure was instituted for deciding on appropriate bargaining units and sole bargaining agents. There was also a procedure whereby the Government could enforce a 'cooling-off' period followed by a strike ballot in cases of major national stoppages.

These were just some of the more controversial aspects of the Industrial Relations Act. It also introduced certain provisions recommended by Donovan including protection against unfair dismissal. As a result of its restrictive provisions, however, it was strongly opposed by the TUC which instructed its affiliates not to register under the Act. The operation of the Act led to a number of clashes betweeen unions and the NIRC and in particular to the dramatic escalation of two industrial disputes – in the docks in 1972 and in the engineering industry in 1973-4. In the first of these, legal action under the Act concerning unlawful picketing and blacking led, among other things, to the imprisonment of the 'Pentonville Five' and their subsequent release on the basis of a House of Lords decision taken in the face of widespread sympathetic strike action. In the second case a national strike, called by the Amalgamated Union of Engineering Workers over the NIRC's decision to sequestrate the union's assets, was averted when the NIRC accepted an offer from a group of anonymous donors to pay the outstanding fines and compensation incurred by the union during a recognition dispute. These and a number of other confrontations associated with the Industrial Relations Act had the effect of seriously undermining the legislation's credibility, and it was repealed by the Labour Government elected in February 1974.

The 'Social Contract' Legislation

The Trade Union and Labour Relations Act 1974 reverted to the traditional system of immunities which the 1971 Act had replaced, and restored the law on trade disputes, the 'closed shop' and the legal status of trade unions broadly to what it was before 1971. It was not however until after the October 1974 election, when the hitherto minority Labour Government achieved a majority in the House of Commons, that it was possible, in the Trade Union and Labour Relations (Amendment) Act 1976, to widen the scope of the trade dispute immunity to cover new judge-made civil liabilities (those of inducing breach of and interference with commercial contracts) developed in the second half of the 1960s. The 1976 Act also restricted the statutory protection against dismissal for non-unionists in a 'closed shop' to those who objected to union membership on grounds of religious belief.

The second phase of the 'Social Contract' employment law programme was the Employment Protection Act 1975. This restructured much of the institutional framework of the industrial relations and employment law system as well as introducing new legal rights both for individual employees and for trade unions. The 1975 Act put the Advisory, Conciliation and Arbitration

220

Service (ACAS) on a statutory footing, and established the Central Arbitration Committee (CAC) primarily to carry out a range of statutory arbitration functions. The Certification Officer was given responsibility for overseeing the then minimal statutory requirements affecting internal trade union administration. A range of new individual rights was contained in the 1975 Act supplementing the unfair dismissal provisions first introduced by the 1971 Act and re-enacted by the 1974 Act. (Many of these new rights, though individual in form, were intended to safeguard and promote trade union membership and activity and therefore had important collective implications.) The individual rights were later brought together in the Employment Protection (Consolidation) Act 1978 – and are outlined below in the section on current legal provisions.

Perhaps the most important innovation of the 1975 Act, however, lay in its new legal rights exercisable by trade unions. Sections 11-16 of the Act contained a statutory recognition procedure whereby unions seeking recognition from employers could refer the issue to ACAS for conciliation, enquiry and recommendation, and to the CAC for arbitration as a remedy for an employer's non-compliance with an ACAS recommendation. Schedule 11 of the Act gave unions the unilateral right to go to arbitration by the CAC where an employer was undercutting the recognised level of pay for a particular trade or industry (as under the earlier Terms and Conditions of Employment Act 1959) or, in the absence of a recognised rate, the 'general level' for comparable workers in the district. The Act also obliged employers to disclose information for collective bargaining purposes to recognised unions, and to consult them in advance about proposed redundancies.

The third phase of the 'Social Contract' reforms was to have been legislation to promote industrial democracy, but despite the report of the Bullock Committee of Inquiry in 1977 and a White Paper the following year, the fierce controversy over the issue of 'workers on the board' meant that the Labour Government did not legislate in this area before leaving office in 1979.

The 1980s

Since the 1979 election, successive Conservative Governments have implemented a 'step by step' approach to redrawing British employment law. A series of Acts of Parliament – most notably the Employment Acts of 1980, 1982 and 1988 and the Trade Union Act 1984 – has brought about a transformation of the legal environment within which relations between employers, employees and unions are conducted.

Five essential strands can be identified in this legislative programme. First, the Government has curtailed the scope of existing individual employment rights, in particular by adjusting the qualifying period and procedural rules relating to unfair dismissal and by narrowing maternity rights for working women. The Employment Bill due to become law during 1989 continues this theme of 'deregulation' – of relieving employers, particularly small employers, of legal obligations which the Government views as unjustifiable 'burdens on business' which act as a deterrent to the employment of more people, but which unions see as essential minimum standards ensuring the fair treatment of workers. Secondly, the Government has dismantled most of the statutory support for collective bargaining. The statutory union recognition procedure in the Employment Protection Act 1975 has been repealed, along with Schedule 11 of the 1975 Act and other similar measures enabling unions to trigger arbitration unilaterally where employers are undercutting the relevant recognised or general level of pay and conditions. Another aspect of the same policy has been the restriction (by the Wages Act 1986) of the role of wages councils in setting minimum rates of pay applicable in industries where adequate collective bargaining does not take place.

Thirdly, the Government has made repeated changes to the law surrounding the 'closed shop'. With the passage of the Employment Act 1988, dismissal of an employee on grounds of non-membership of a union became automatically unfair and the closed shop became, in effect, legally unenforceable. Commercial arrangements and industrial action to ensure that work is done only by unionised labour have also been made unlawful.

Fourthly, extensive legal restrictions have been placed on industrial action. The statutory immunities from judge-made liabilities have been presented by the Government as unique 'privileges' putting trade unions 'above the law' and have been narrowed significantly. Industrial action authorised by unions without a secret ballot, picketing other than at the pickets' own workplace, strikes deemed to be politically-motivated and most secondary industrial action have been made unlawful, exposing unions and union officials to injunctions and damages.

Fifthly, the measures in the Trade Union Act 1984 and the Employment Act 1988 to 'give trade unions back to their members' and 'safeguard the rights of members in relation to their unions' represent the most detailed statutory regulation of internal union affairs yet attempted, based on a highly individualistic model of the rights and obligations associated with trade union membership. The law now requires, among other things, fully postal and independently-supervised five-yearly membership ballots for the election of union presidents, general secretaries and executive committees, and provides a range of statutory rights for individual union members enforceable against their union with the assistance of the new 'Commissioner for the Rights of Trade Union Members'.

Underlying Strategies

The various and increasingly divergent employment law measures pursued by different Governments over the past twenty years have been seen by academic commentators as representing two broad strategies – those of 'reform' and 'restriction'. The strategy of reform was associated with the Donovan Commission's recommendations. These emphasised the importance of the reform of industrial relations in order to reduce inflationary wage bargaining, strikes and inefficient working practices – an approach which was parallel to but separate from the emphasis on incomes policy prevailing at the time – while retaining an essentially voluntary system of collective bargaining. However, the law was to have an important if limited role in achieving reform, and measures designed to restrict industrial conflict as part of a wider reformist programme were not totally ruled out. The strategy of restriction, on the other hand, sees legal intervention and sanctions as the main instrument of industrial relations policy. 'Its hallmark', according to one commentator, is 'the use of the law to restrict trade union power, particularly a union's ability to engage in industrial action and to maintain the infrastructure of collective bargaining . . . The object is to free the employer from the constraints of union power, to which "free market" analysis ascribes the blame for inflation, strikes, inefficiency, and unemployment . . . While the logic of the market points to the legal regulation of unions, it requires that the burden of state intervention is lifted from employers.'[4]

Aspects of both strategies can be seen in the Labour Government's 1969 White Paper 'In Place of Strife' and also in the Industrial Relations Act 1971. In both these cases, the inclusion of restrictive provisions overshadowed and in practice undermined their other, reformist intentions. The legislation of the 'Social Contract' era represented a developed form of the strategy of reform, reflecting many of the Donovan principles, particularly in respect of the role of ACAS, but the legislation was 'sufficiently extensive to jeopardise the reform strategy's aim of keeping industrial relations out of the courts.'[5] The 1980s legislation exemplifies the 'pure' strategy of restriction, the 'central thrust' of which is 'to constrain trade unions within a complex web of legal liabilities.'[6] Although there are similarities between aspects of the 1971 Act and some current provisions, a sharp distinction has been drawn between the underlying policies of the two legislative programmes, one reason being that the present Government is 'the first . . . since the war to pursue a policy of industrial relations law which is integrally geared to its overall [free market] economic policies'.[7]

Juridification

It has also been argued that, whichever variant of the strategies of reform or restriction has been pursued over the past two decades, each has contributed towards the underlying trend of the 'juridification' of the employment relationship whereby, in general terms, 'the law exerts an increasingly important influence on the conduct of personnel management, collective bargaining and dispute tactics'.[8] This is most obviously the case in those areas such as dismissal and equal opportunities where employees' individual legal rights have directly affected personnel practice. Similarly the law appears to be having an increasing impact on the conduct of industrial disputes. It remains the case that to a very large extent the key area of employees' pay and other terms and conditions is subject to voluntary regulation by means of collective bargaining thus, arguably, limiting the process of juridification. Notwithstanding this, however, the influence on collective bargaining of legal measures such as the equal pay legislation also seems likely to grow.

Nor has the trend been broken in the 1980s. Despite its emphasis on 'deregulation', the present Government has left largely intact the basic system of individual employment rights which is seen as an important source of the juridification process. At the same time, the UK has been forced by virtue of its membership of the European Communities to introduce important new regulatory measures in the employment sphere, including the Transfer of Undertakings (Protection of Employment) Regulations 1981, the Equal Pay (Amendment) Regulations 1983, the Sex Discrimination Act 1986, and aspects of the Employment Bill due to become law in 1989. However, the present Government has blocked the adoption by the EEC of several draft directives, including those on parental leave and leave for family reasons and on part-time and temporary work, which would have required new employment legislation in this country.

Future Prospects

The run-up to the completion of the Single European Market in 1992 has generated considerable uncertainty over the scope for increased EEC influence on British employment law and industrial relations. The introduction of 'qualified majority voting' by the EEC Council, designed to bypass individual member states' veto on issues relating to the internal market, does not apply to, among other things, measures 'relating to the rights and interests of employed persons.'[9] Moreover, the original programme for completing the internal market said very little about the further harmonisation or approximation of employment law in member states. However, concern has been expressed that continued disparities between the requirements imposed by domestic employment legislation in different member states will distort the functioning of the internal market, and that the failure to develop the so-called 'social dimension' of the Single European Market could result in 'social dumping' – that is, the possibility that employers will establish or relocate their operations in member states where labour market conditions and legislation are more to their advantage, to the detriment of the member states with more stringent employment law standards. European trade unions are therefore pressing for a European charter of basic employment rights and for legislation on employee participation in company decisions, among a range of other measures. Such an approach runs directly counter to the deregulation philosophy of the British Government and is generally opposed by European employers' organisations. The outcome of this debate within the EEC will have considerable implications for future British employment law.

Irrespective of whether the 1992 exercise leads to further EEC employment legislation or accentuates the trend towards deregulation, the present Government has indicated its intention to continue with its 'step by step' approach to reshaping the domestic legal framework. At the time of writing, the Government is considering the total abolition of the wages council system on the grounds that it 'inhibits flexibility', and the introduction of legislation to give individuals a statutory right not to be refused employment because of non-membership of a union, to outlaw 'secondary' industrial action altogether, and to enable the Commissioner for the Rights of Trade Union Members to assist union members in court proceedings over a union's failure to observe the requirements of its rulebook.[10]

Current Legal Provisions

This part of the chapter highlights the main legal provisions (as they stood at April 1989) which have the most practical significance for personnel managers. Thus, although measures affecting trade unions' internal affairs have been a central feature of recent legislation, only those aspects of trade union law which are of direct relevance to management-employee relationships are referred to here. It will also be appreciated that current employment law is extensive, detailed and often highly complex, and that what follows is intended to be a practical, non-legalistic outline of key points of the law and consequently is far from comprehensive.

Individual Employment Law

In addition to the rights of employees under their contracts of employment, a range of statutory rights are conferred by legislation.

Contractual Rights. Until the legislation of the 1960s and 1970s, the legal regulation of the individual employment relationship was by means of the common law rules associated with the contract of employment. All employees have a contract of employment, though it is not always clear just what in the eyes of the law has been agreed between an employee and his or her employer. A contract of employment can include not only expressly agreed terms written down in a letter of appointment or agreed orally at an interview, but also collective agreements between management and unions, works rules, custom and practice, and terms implied by common law (e.g. that employees will obey reasonable orders given by the employer and that the employer pays the agreed wages when they fall due). Moreover, formally no changes can be made to the employment contract unless agreed by both parties to it although quite often, of course, employees have little choice but to accept management's proposals for changed conditions. As far as dismissal is concerned, before the introduction of the law of unfair dismissal in 1971, the only means of challenging a dismissal on common law/contractual grounds was suing for wrongful dismissal. Unless the employee has broken a major term of the contract (say, through an act of 'gross misconduct'), dismissal without due notice would in the eyes of the common law be wrongful dismissal.

Today, however, the statutory rights of individual employees enacted in the 1960s and 1970s are in practical terms of much greater importance in regulating the employment relationship than common law rules. Of these, it is the legal protection against unfair dismissal that has had by far the biggest impact on personnel practice.

Unfair Dismissal. The law on unfair dismissal, first introduced in the Industrial Relations Act 1971, is now contained in sections 54-80 of the Employment Protection (Consolidation) Act 1978 (as amended). The law provides that 'every employee shall have the right not to be unfairly dismissed' though certain occupations (e.g. the police) are in fact excluded. The right to claim unfair dismissal is also subject to qualifying periods of employment. To qualify, employees who work for over sixteen hours a week must have done so continuously for two years or more. Those working between eight and sixteen hours per week qualify for legal protection if they have five years' continuous service. (There is no qualifying period for protection against dismissal on grounds of union membership or non-membership, trade union activities, race or sex.) Complaints of unfair dismissal must be made

226

within three months of the effective date of termination. All complaints are notified to ACAS, which will attempt to reach a conciliated settlement between the parties. Where this fails, cases proceed to an industrial tribunal hearing. Where a dismissal is found to be unfair, the remedies available to industrial tribunals are reinstatement, re-engagement or compensation, with the latter being by far the most frequent remedy.

In defending a complaint of unfair dismissal employers must first show that the reason for dismissal is among those listed as potentially fair by section 57 of the 1978 Act (i.e. reasons relating to competence and performance, conduct, redundancy, contravention of statute, or 'some other substantial reason'). The tribunal will then determine whether the dismissal was fair or unfair by deciding whether the employer acted reasonably or unreasonably in treating that reason as sufficient for dismissal. This underlines the importance of employers adhering closely to relevant internal procedures and following the ACAS Code of Practice on Disciplinary Practice and Procedures in Employment or the 1972 Industrial Relations Code of Practice. (However, dismissal for certain 'inadmissible' reasons – trade union membership or non-membership, trade union activities, race or sex – is automatically unfair.)

In addition, under the Transfer of Undertakings (Protection of Employment) Regulations 1981, employees have the right not to be dismissed on the transfer of an undertaking to a new employer except for certain reasons.

Other Statutory Rights. As well as the unfair dismissal provisions, a range of other individual employment rights is contained in the Employment Protection (Consolidation) Act 1978. The areas covered include:

- **maternity** (maternity pay and the right to return to work following maternity leave);

- **time off** (for trade union duties and activities, public duties, ante-natal care, and to look for work or make arrangements for training);

- **terms of employment** (written statement of terms of employment, itemised pay statement, minimum period of notice, and written statement of reasons for dismissal);

- **financial matters** (guaranteed pay during lay-offs, remuneration on suspension on medical grounds, redundancy payments, and payment of certain debts owed by an insolvent employer); and

- **trade union membership and activities** (protection against 'action short of dismissal' to penalise trade union membership and activities or non-membership).

Complaints that these statutory rights have been infringed may be made to an industrial tribunal, subject in many cases to the applicant having been employed for the relevant qualifying period.

Individual employment rights are also provided by the anti-discrimination statutes. Under the Equal Pay Act 1970 (as amended by the Equal Pay (Amendment) Regulations 1983), employees have the right to receive the same pay and other terms of employment as an employee of the opposite sex working for the same or an associated employer if engaged on like work, work rated as equivalent under job evaluation, or work of equal value. Under the Sex Discrimination Act 1975 (as amended), employees have the right not to be discriminated against – directly or indirectly – in employment, training and related areas on grounds of sex or marriage, or victimised for pursuing their rights under the Act. The Race Relations Act 1976 provides parallel protections against discrimination on grounds of colour, race, nationality or ethnic or national origins. The law on sex and race discrimination is also backed up by two 'semi-legal' Codes of Practice designed to promote equal opportunities in employment, issued by the Equal Opportunities Commission (EOC) and the Commission for Racial Equality (CRE) respectively, which can be taken into account in relevant industrial tribunal cases.

Impact

The impact of the employment protection legislation and related statutory rights is a matter of some debate. As noted earlier, the legislation has been seen by the Government and employers' bodies as placing unacceptable 'burdens on business' and consequently inhibiting employment. However, research evidence has over a number of years suggested that the unfair dismissal legislation has actually had a highly marginal impact on employers' recruitment decisions.[11] Similarly, legislative changes made during the 1980s to lighten the perceived 'burden' have also had an insignificant impact.[12]

The main effect of the unfair dismissal legislation has been to encourage the introduction, formalisation or reform of (often jointly agreed) disciplinary and dismissal procedures and, to a lesser extent, the improvement of selection and recruitment procedures.[13] That this has happened primarily in large and medium-sized companies is reflected in the fact that most unfair dismissal claims tend to arise in small (and usually non-union) companies.[14]

228

Some 85 per cent of all compaints of the infringement of employees' statutory rights concern unfair dismissal. About four-fifths of unfair dismissal claims do not reach the stage of an industrial tribunal hearing. In 1987, 63 per cent of all cases were settled at the conciliation stage by ACAS, and a further 16 per cent were withdrawn.[15] The bulk of conciliated settlements involve compensation, with the proportion of settlements involving reinstatement or re-engagement being small. Around one-third of the cases which do reach the tribunal stage are upheld. The median award of compensation in 1986-87 was £1,394. Reinstatement or re-engagement was awarded in only 1.1 per cent of cases proceeding to a hearing in 1986-87.[16] Thus, claimants' success rate in unfair dismissal cases is low, as is the general level of compensation, with the remedy of re-employment being extremely rarely utilised. This has been reflected in growing criticism of the law of unfair dismissal – and the industrial tribunal system more generally – by trade unions and some legal commentators. Concern has also been expressed about excessive legalism in tribunal hearings, and adverse developments in case law.

As far as the impact of other aspects of individual employment law is concerned, statutory redundancy payments are widely seen as having facilitated redundancies by weakening union resistance to job losses. The anti-discrimination provisions, and the activities of the EOC and CRE, appear to be encouraging the adoption of detailed equal opportunities policies at least by some larger employers, though discriminatory employment practices still remain widespread. The implications of the equal pay for work of equal value regulations for established pay structures are profound but the provisions have yet to have a real impact, at least in part because of the complex and convoluted procedures involved. Various options for making equal pay law more effective have been put forward by the EOC.[17]

Collective Employment Law

This section is concerned with those aspects of the law which directly affect the relationship between employers and unions, including collective bargaining and industrial conflict.

Rights of Recognised Unions Although there are no legal provisions obliging or inducing employers to recognise and bargain with unions representing their employees (the statutory recognition procedure in the Employment Protection Act 1975 having been repealed in 1980), where employers *do* recognise unions, the unions concerned may invoke a number of collective rights.

Sections 17-21 of the 1975 Act contain provisions designed to encourage employers to disclose information to recognised unions for collective bargaining purposes. The duty of disclosure is backed up by an ACAS Code of Practice on Disclosure of Information. Complaints by unions of non-disclosure can be made to the Central Arbitration Committee, which can make declarations that the employer concerned is in default, and ultimately may arbitrate on a union's claim for improved terms and conditions, bargaining over which has been impeded through lack of information.

Section 99 of the 1975 Act requires employers to consult recognised unions about proposed redundancies, and certain minimum consultation periods are laid down. Where such consultation does not take place, unions may complain to an industrial tribunal which may make a 'protective award' requiring the employer to keep up the remuneration of the employees concerned for a 'protected period' related to the minimum consultation periods.

Section 2 of the Employment Act 1980 gives recognised unions the right to complain to an industrial tribunal if employers refuse to allow their premises to be used for the purpose of carrying out secret ballots where this is required by the union. If the tribunal finds the union's complaint justified it can order the employer to pay compensation to the union. Certain minimal information and consultation duties are also imposed on employers involved in business transfers under the Transfer of Undertakings (Protection of Employment) Regulations 1981. Recognised unions may make a complaint of failure to comply to an industrial tribunal which is empowered to award compensation of up to two weeks' pay to the workers concerned.

Industrial Conflict. Under section 13 of the Trade Union and Labour Relations Act 1974, as amended, the organisers of industrial action are given immunity from liability for inducing or threatening to induce breach of a contract or interference with its performance where they are 'acting in contemplation or furtherance of a trade dispute'. The meaning of 'trade dispute' is contained in section 29 of the 1974 Act, as amended, and is defined as 'a dispute between workers and their employer which relates wholly or mainly' to a range of issues including pay and conditions, dismissal, allocation of work, discipline, union membership and facilities, and negotiating rights and machinery. Immunity is also dependent on meeting the terms of section 10 of the 1984 Trade Union Act. This removes from trade unions and the officials involved their immunity against civil liability for industrial action the union authorises or endorses without having gained majority support for the action in a ballot of the members concerned not more than four weeks before the commencement of the action or (where the union endorses previously unofficial action) before the endorsement. (Moreover, as a result of amendments by the Employment Act 1988, separate ballots may be required at each workplace in some circumstances.)[18]

The immunity for industrial action provided by section 13 of the 1974 Act does not apply to picketing other than at the pickets' own place of work (section 15 of the 1974 Act, as amended). 'Secondary' industrial action – i.e. action by workers whose employer is not a party to the trade dispute – is also unlawful where it interferes with commercial contracts, except in certain tightly defined circumstances (section 17 of the Employment Act 1980).

In cases of unlawful industrial action, it is open to employers to take legal action against individual organisers and, since the Employment Act 1982, trade unions themselves where they have 'authorised or endorsed' unlawful industrial action under section 15 of the 1982 Act. Section 16 of the 1982 Act lays down limits on the damages that may be awarded against unions, depending on the size of their membership. Legal action against unions or union officials in such circumstances normally takes the form of seeking an injunction (court order) requiring named organisations and individuals to cease organising the industrial action complained of. (Non-compliance with an injunction is a contempt of court which can lead to the imposition of sanctions including fines and the sequestration of union property.) The obtaining of an injunction is technically an interim measure prior to a full trial of the action for damages, but normally an employer's objective is primarily to stop the industrial action, in which case the claim for damages is unlikely to be pursued.

In addition to employers' right of recourse to the courts, section 1 of the Employment Act 1988 enables an individual member of a union to obtain a court order requiring the union to stop industrial action it has authorised or endorsed without having held a secret ballot beforehand.

Impact

The statutory provisions concerning obligatory information disclosure to, and consultation with, recognised unions, have generally proved to be of limited value to unions. In particular, the permitted exceptions to the duty of information disclosure under sections 17-21 of the 1975 Act have in practice limited the number of union successes in the disclosure area. Employers' duties in respect of redundancies and business transfers require consultation, not negotiation, and are effectively only procedural in character. Moreover, the sanctions against employers for failure to adhere to the legal requirements are minimal. As a consequence, little effective use has been made by unions of this type of provision.

In contrast, employers have made significant use of the legal opportunities open to them as a result of the major changes made in the 1980s to the law regulating industrial conflict. In several major industrial disputes during the 1980s, extensive use of the law has had a major and possibly decisive impact. Examples include the 1983 dispute between Messenger Newspapers and the National Graphical Association, the 1984-5 mining dispute, the 1986 dispute between News International and the print unions, and the 1988 dispute between P&O Ferries and the National Union of Seamen, all of which resulted in the sequestration of union assets. More generally the law is being used by employers during disputes with considerably higher frequency than during the 1970s (despite the widespread belief initially that, as during the Industrial Relations Act period, employers would abstain from invoking the law because to do so might inflame the dispute as well as causing long-term damage to industrial relations). One study identified 114 injunction cases over the period from September 1980 to April 1987. Of these, 28 cases related to picketing, 27 to secondary action and 47 to pre-strike ballots.[19]

However, there is little doubt that recourse to the courts by employers occurs in only a small proportion of disputes in which the potential for legal action exists. (For example, the available figures for pre-strike ballots amount to only a fraction of the overall number of industrial disputes.) What does appear to be the case, though, is that employers are willing, in the current legal climate, to consider legal action – and certainly the threat of legal action – as a potentially worthwhile tactic in disputes. It remains the case, however, that little interest has generally been shown by employers in going beyond the injunction stage and pursuing claims for damages against unions. Moreover, only a small number of employers, for example News International and P&O, have set out to use the law strategically to undermine effective industrial action during disputes, including pursuing contempt proceedings against the unions concerned. It remains to be seen how the new right of individual union members under the 1988 Act to restrain industrial action authorised by their union without a ballot will interact with employers' existing, generally pragmatic approach to launching legal actions against unions.

As far as the union response is concerned, there are indications that unions have become more cautious in the tactics they adopt during disputes. Moreover, because of the greater risk of court action being taken against their unions, union leaders have tended to strengthen central union control over how and when strikes should be called and who should be empowered to authorise industrial action.

Conclusion

After a period of relative stability between the passing of the Trade Disputes Act 1906 and the 1960s, British employment law has undergone a series of rapid and far-reaching changes which have undermined the traditional pattern of voluntarism. Although conflicting legal strategies have been pursued by Labour and Conservative Governments, both have encouraged the trend towards the legal regulation of industrial relations. The 1980s, however, have seen a decisive shift in policy towards the restriction of trade union activity and deregulation in respect of employers' legal obligations in the area of individual employees' rights and collective bargaining. The present Government's legislative programme thus lends support to the emphasis on 'flexibility' which is central to the theories of the 'human resource management' school of thought, and which implies the marginalisation of trade unions and traditional collective industrial relations.

Much of Britain's employment law is highly complex, and has become more so over the 1980s as, instead of the 'big-bang' approach of the Industrial Relations Act 1971, the present Government has adopted the approach of making repeated amendments to the existing legal framework. While this may have made the legal changes more difficult for trade unions to oppose effectively, it will have caused considerable difficulty for managers, union officials and employees seeking to understand and respond to the laws which can vitally affect their working lives. Moreover, the area of employment law remains politically highly controversial, the implicit consensus which underpinned the era of voluntarism having irretrievably broken down. The main opposition parties have each put forward proposals for extensive employment law reforms. Nor has the present Government shown any sign of letting up in its 'step by step' legislative programme. Thus, irrespective of any change in Government (and irrespective of EEC employment law developments), the rapid and complex development of the legal regulation of employment is set to continue for the foreseeable future.

References

1   W Brown (ed.), *The Changing Contours of British Industrial Relations*, Oxford: Blackwell (1981), p. 33.

2   For accounts of the history and development of the law relating to industrial disputes, see Green Paper, *Trade Union Immunities*, Cmnd 8128, London: HMSO (1981), Ch 2; and Lord Wedderburn, 'The New Policies in Industrial Relations Law' in P Fosh and C Littler (eds.), *Industrial*

Relations and the Law in the 1980s, Aldershot: Gower (1985).

3 Royal Commission on Trade Unions and Employers Associations, *Report*, Cmnd 3623, London: HMSO (1968), p. 47.

4 R Lewis, 'The Role of the Law in Employment Relations' in R Lewis (ed.), *Labour Law in Britain*, Oxford: Blackwell (1986), p. 35.

5 Lewis, *op. cit.,* p. 32.

6 Lewis, *op. cit.,* p. 31.

7 Wedderburn, *op. cit.,* p. 36.

8 R Lewis, 'Reforming Labour Law: Choices and Constraints', *Employee Relations,* Vol 9, No 4 (1987), p. 30.

9 B Hepple, 'The Crisis in EEC Labour Law', *Industrial Law Journal,* Vol 16, No 2 (1987), pp 83-4.

10 *Wages Councils: 1988 Consultation Document,* London: Department of Employment (1988); and Green Paper, *Removing Barriers to Employment,* Cm 655, London: HMSO (1989).

11 W W Daniel and E Stilgoe, *The Impact of Employment Protection Laws,* London: Policy Studies Institute (1978); R Clifton and C Tatton-Brown, *Impact of Employment Legislation on Small Firms,* Research Paper No 6, London: Department of Employment (1979); and S Evans, J Goodman and L Hargreaves, *Unfair Dismissal Law and Employment Practice in the 1980s,* Research Paper No. 53, London: Department of Employment (1985).

12 Evans *et al, op. cit.,* p. 71.

13 L Dickens, M Jones, B Weekes and M Hart, *Dismissed: A Study of Unfair Dismissal and the Industrial Tribunal System,* Oxford: Blackwell (1985), p. 258.

14 M Stevens, 'Unfair Dismissal Cases in 1985-86 – Characteristics of Parties', *Employment Gazette* (December 1988), p. 651.

15 Advisory, Conciliation and Arbitration Service, *Annual Report 1987,* London: HMSO (1988), p. 81.

16 'Industrial Tribunal Statistics', *Employment Gazette* (October 1985), p. 498.

17 Equal Opportunities Commission, *Equal Pay . . . Making it Work,* Manchester: EOC (1989).

18 For an account of this highly complicated provision see J Bowers and S Auerbach, *A Guide to the Employment Act 1988,* London: Blackstone (1988), pp 13-18.

19 S Evans, 'The Use of Injunctions in Industrial Disputes', *British Journal of Industrial Relations,* Vol XXIII, No 1 (March 1985), and 'The Use of Injunctions in Industrial Disputes: May 1984 – April 1987', *British Journal of Industrial Relations,* Vol XXV, No 3 (November 1987).

Suggested Reading

B A Hepple and S Fredman, *Labour Law and Industrial Relations in Britain,* Kluwer (1986).

R Lewis (ed.), *Labour Law in Britain,* Blackwell (1986)

Lord Wedderburn, *The Worker and the Law,* 3rd ed., Penguin (1986).

Questions

1 What were the key features of the tradition of 'voluntarism' in British industrial relations?

2 In which areas of employment has there been the most notable increase in legal regulation in the past three decades, and with what impact?

3 Does employment protection legislation place too great a burden on employers, particularly small firms?

Chapter 11

Industrial Relations

Mark Hall and Andrew Pendleton

Introduction

Industrial relations is one of the most important and complex aspects of the management of employee performance. It refers to the institutions and procedures in which employers, managers, unions and workers deal with aspirations and grievances, the process of bargaining and communication within these, and the general character of the relationships between these individuals and groups. Management goals in industrial relations focus on two main outcomes. The first is the efficient and productive use of labour: the second is overall control of labour utilisation. Where insufficient attention is paid by management to industrial relations it is likely that these objectives will not be fully met.

The dominant approach to industrial relations management in Britain has traditionally tended to be pragmatic rather than strategic and pro-active. Comparison with the pattern of industrial relations in competitor nations suggests that this approach may be an important reason why labour productivity in Britain is significantly lower than in, say, the USA and Japan. In these circumstances, Human Resource Management, with its emphasis on strategic linkages between business goals and employee management, has been widely seen as having much to offer.

However, 'full-blooded' HRM, where management-employee relationships are put on an individualistic rather than collective basis, would seem to be of limited applicability in the British context. The reason for this is that labour management in large firms in most sectors is about managing with unions. During the 1980s there appear to have been few attempts to de-recognise unions in companies where they are already established, though union recognition in new enterprises is also rare. Some organisations, not least in the public sector, have taken steps to weaken union organisation, though the general picture is one of institutional stability. Perceptions of declining union bargaining influence are difficult to quantify and generally reflect a possibly temporary shift in the balance of power rather than a fundamental change inthe prevailing pattern of industrial relations. Moreover, the proportion of the labour force whose pay is determined by negotiation with unions has actually increased.

It would therefore be wrong for managers to conclude from unfavourable circumstances for unions in the 1980s that industrial relations is no longer an important area of management. As most aspects of the system have not fundamentally changed, the choices and issues facing managers in the 1990s will not be dramatically different from those in the 1970s and 1980s. Moreover, where novel approaches to managing human resources have been successfully adopted, as by some of the Japanese companies in Britain, this has been the result of considerable attention to industrial relations issues. The purpose of this chapter, therefore, is to provide a practical, introductory account of some of the main features of industrial relations in Britain. It is divided into two parts. The first looks at the nature of collective bargaining between employers and trade unions and goes on to outline the wider aspects of industrial relations in the context of the key developments and reforms which took place in the 1960s and 1970s. Against that background, the second part is devoted to discussing the changes and continuities in industrial relations discernible in the 1980s.

The Pattern of British Industrial Relations

Collective Bargaining

In this section the focus is primarily the institutions and processes of collective bargaining between managements and workforce representatives. The starting point of the analysis presented here is that the relationships between members of organisations are not necessarily harmonious. Organisations are composed of a variety of interest groups, all of which may have distinct and competing objectives. If institutions and procedures for resolving these conflicting goals are either non-existent or inappropriate, then outcomes may be seriously unsatisfactory for some groups. This in turn may lead to absenteeism, high labour wastage, low productivity, and industrial disputes. Such are the symptoms of poor industrial relations.

To explore these issues it is useful to examine industrial relations in the private manufacturing sector since the early 1960s. Although, at the end of the 1980s, this sector accounts only for some 25% of the employed labour force, manufacturing remains especially important to the long-term economic health of the nation. This sector also provides a particularly graphic illustration of the industrial relations problems that may arise where industrial relations structures are inappropriate.

In the mid-1960s industrial relations came to be viewed as one of the most pressing problems of the British economy. In that decade mounting concern over the productivity and performance of British companies coincided with the apparently growing assertiveness of trade unions in pay bargaining. For many the problem was (and has been since) over-mighty trade unions: cut them down to size and economic performance would swiftly improve. Analysis of industrial relations at the time indicated, however, that the problem was far more complicated than this. What was taking place was the breakdown of the institutional framework of industrial relations that had been in place to varying degrees from the early part of the twentieth century.

This framework has been described as an *externalised* system of industrial relations.[1] The distinguishing feature was that bargaining over pay and conditions took place not within the firm between worker representatives and managers but outside, between district or national union officials and officials of employers' associations. Bargaining could thus be said to be multi-employer bargaining. For employers, reliance on these associations for industrial relations management had a number of advantages. Initially they provided a common front against union recognition strategies. Once union strength was such that employers accepted that their employees could legitimately become union members, bargaining outside the firm served to keep union organisation away from the workplace itself, thereby leaving employers with a free hand in labour utilisation.[2]

Other benefits to employers in belonging to employers' associations included the provision of advice on labour management issues, representation of constituents to outside bodies (such as Government), and in some industries the provision of a disputes procedure into which individual and collective grievances could be fed.[3] The importance of these derived in part from the embryonic state of management hierarchies at the time. Until the 1960s, management specialisation and skills were weakly developed in most British companies.[4] As a result, there simply was not the capacity in most firms to manage these aspects of industrial relations internally.

The district-wide or industry-wide regulation of wage rates found in this external system also provided mutual benefits to employers and unions. From the employers' perspective, this pattern of regulation tended to preclude potentially damaging labour market competition. For unions, it met the objective of standardising wage rates and separating the achievement of wage rates in a given workplace from the balance of power in that location. There was one further aspect of the system which appealed to both employer and unions: collective bargaining was unencumbered by legal regulation. In this *voluntaristic* system of industrial relations, agreements had no legal force (and still do not) and operated for a timespan agreed by the parties to them rather than according to any legal guidelines. Industrial relations was essentially a private matter between employers and unions.

By the 1960s, however, this approach to industrial relations appeared to be breaking down. One important indicator of this was the prevalence of short, often unofficial (i.e. unsanctioned by the union) and unconstitutional (i.e. in breach of agreed procedures) strikes. Coupled with this, many firms felt they were losing control over their labour costs and their utilisation of employees. The fundamental problem seemed to be that an uncontrolled *internal* system of industrial relations was emerging alongside the external system. During the sustained post-war boom shop stewards within companies had assumed a growing role in the process of labour deployment. They had sought to protect the interests of their immediate work groups by insistence on demarcation lines and other job controls ('restrictive practices') and by seeking payments to supplement nationally-agreed wage rates. This type of shop-floor bargaining by work groups led to competitive sectional wage settlements and chaotic pay structures, as well as to the growth of unofficial and unconstitutional strikes. It also led to concern about spiralling labour costs and industrial relations passing out of management's control.

The most sustained official analysis of what had gone wrong was presented by the Royal Commission on Trades Unions and Employers' Associations in 1968 (the 'Donovan Report').[5] The main argument of the Donovan Report was that what it called the 'formal' system – that of externalised industry-wide collective bargaining – had come to be supplemented by an 'informal' system in which shop stewards and production managers and supervisors played the primary roles. The problem with the informal industrial relations system was that it took place outside formal institutions and was ungoverned by formal procedures. There were thus few explicit guidelines on how to conduct industrial relations properly. The Commission believed that a return to the old system was unrealistic: instead, the solution proposed was that the informal system should be put onto a proper constitutional footing. If managers were prepared to accept that unions had a legitimate role in bargaining within the workplace they could, to use Flanders' phrase, 'regain control by sharing it'.[6]

Though the graphic distinction between formal and informal systems of industrial relations was highly influential, the Report's empirical validity did not go unchallenged. There is little evidence that parallel patterns of industrial relations had developed in either the public sector or private services. Many of the public corporations possessed well-established formal procedures and institutions at workplace as well as national level, and collective bargaining was underdeveloped or non-existent in much of the private services sector. Within manufacturing the formal, external pattern was still intact in many industries (such as textiles). In some industries, such as petro-chemicals, the dangers of the informal pattern had been recognised sometime before the Commission reported, and steps taken to put plant-level industrial relations onto a proper procedural footing. The Donovan analysis, as was pointed out at the time, seems to have applied mainly to engineering.[7]

Nevertheless, the internal procedural formalisation urged by Donovan took place in most industries during the 1970s. By the end of the 1970s a core framework had been created which was to last throughout the 1980s. Several aspects are worth mentioning here. First, the adoption of written procedures to deal with grievances, discipline and pay and conditions accelerated. Research has shown that 80% of manufacturing establishments possessed formal procedures of this sort at the end of the 1970s compared with around 50% in 1972.[8] Second, managements in the public and private sectors encouraged 'responsible' union representation by supporting union and shop steward organisation. Managements frequently undertook to promote union membership and to deduct union membership dues from employees' pay at source. The role and duties of shop stewards in the operation of the procedures referred to above were explicitly defined. It was hoped that by formally incorporating shop stewards into aspects of workplace administration, they could be encouraged to take a more considered approach to the representation of employee interests.

Third, many firms in manufacturing created formal bargaining institutions internally, so that the main locus of pay bargaining could be transferred to establishment or company level. This involved both decentralisation of bargaining from industry-wide institutions and centralisation away from the level of the work group. Data for 1980 shows that manual workers' pay was primarily determined by bargaining at establishment or company level in 56% of workplaces. In 41% of cases pay was primarily determined externally.[9]

The effects of procedural formalisation and internalisation have been several. First, the incidence of small-scale, short, unofficial strikes was greatly reduced. However, some have argued that the process of formalisation itself led to industrial relations problems since the creation of new procedures restricted managerial flexibility and provided shop stewards with additional bargaining tools.[10] Second, the role of employers' associations has generally declined as increasingly firms have created their own internal pay structures. This is not to argue that these associations have become irrelevant. In industries such as engineering they bargain on hours of work, holidays and base pay rates (which still have a significant influence in determining the actual pay of lower paid workers), as well as providing important advisory services to their member firms. But generally speaking, the main trend in the 1970s was steady progress towards the internalisation of labour management and industrial relations.

Wider Industrial Relations Developments

So far this chapter has focused on the changing structure of collective bargaining between employers and unions. However, alongside the moves during the 1960s to promote the voluntary reform of collective bargaining, there was considerable pressure for Governments to play a more generally interventionist role in industrial relations matters, as opposed to the traditional approach of British Governments which was broadly to rely on voluntary self-regulation by employers and unions.

Incomes Policy. Incomes policies – a 'device designed to restrain directly the growth of money incomes so that they do not rise faster than the growth of real output' – were frequently adopted during the 1960s and 1970s because they offered the prospect of pursuing simultaneously full employment, economic growth and price stability.[11] The incomes policies pursued by the 1964-70 Labour Government were by no means the first attempts at Government intervention in pay bargaining in the post-war period. A voluntary incomes policy was operated between 1948 and 1950 by the then Labour Government with TUC support, and the Conservative Governments of 1951-64 made various non-statutory attempts to restrain the rate of growth of earnings. Under the 1964-70 Labour Government, however, there was a sustained series of incomes policies in operation, including statutory controls. The various norms set out for pay increases during this period – and the pay freeze of July-December 1966 – 'totally transformed the context of collective bargaining in Britain. Wage negotiators, who in the 1950s had acted alone and in private, now had to organise their private negotiations conscious first of all of the relationship of what they did to what the government required'.[12] (One consequence of these incomes policies after 1966 was to encourage the spread of 'productivity bargaining' – and in turn the spread of plant-level bargaining. Agreements designed to bring about productivity increases were the main basis for legitimate settlements above the pay norms, leading in effect to the 'buying out' of job controls or 'restrictive practices' operated by organised work groups.)

Although initially pursuing no incomes policy in respect of the private sector, the Conservative Government of 1970-74 attempted through its 'n-1' policy to reduce by 1% the level of successive pay settlements in the public sector. After the success of the 1972 miners' strike, however, and with wage rates rising rapidly, the Government dropped its opposition to general incomes policies and introduced its statutory Counter Inflation Policy – a six months' pay freeze followed by two phases of wage restraint. Subsequently the Labour Government of 1974-79 resorted to a voluntary incomes policy in response to the economic crisis of mid-1975 (when, by way of illustration, the NUR rejected a 28 per cent arbitration award). Phases I and II of the policy (a flat rate increase of £6 followed by a 5% limit) were agreed with the TUC. Phase III was not, but the 10% maximum was not overtly opposed by the unions. In 1987, however, the Government was unable even to secure union acquiescence for a fourth year of wage restraint. A 5% maximum limit on pay increases unilaterally imposed by the Government was the prelude to the so-called 'winter of discontent' in 1978-79.

While the overall experience of incomes policies is difficult to evaluate, their impact on wage inflation generally appears to have been limited (with the exception of 1975-77) and shortlived, and 'largely offset by a rebound effect once the policy comes to an end'.[13] Moreover, the wages explosions which have marked the demise of successive incomes policies have on each occasion been accompanied by upsurges in industrial action (particularly by public sector workers), and it is to the changing pattern of strike activity that we now turn.

Industrial Action. It is often assumed that Britain is a particularly strike-prone country but, in fact, it has consistently occupied a broadly middle-ranking position in the 'league-table' of industrialised nations in terms of working days lost through industrial disputes. In the 1960s the annual number of strikes fluctuated in the range between 2000 and 3000 per year, though with an upsurge in 1970 to almost 4000 – the highest number of strikes ever recorded. These statistics, however, obscure a sustained upward trend in the number of strikes outside coal mining (coal accounting for 59% of all strikes in 1960 but only 4% in 1970). During the 1970s, the number of strikes again fluctuated in the 2000-3000 range, though at a slightly higher average level than in the 1960s.[14] From 1980, however, there has been a significant downward trend. The main factors affecting trends in the number of strikes are usually identified as the changing structure of collective bargaining, the

242

incidence of incomes policies, inflation and unemployment, though the influence of such factors can of course be conflicting.

It has been suggested that, during the 1960s:

> 'the rise of shopfloor bargaining power gave workers the organisational resources to engage in large numbers of strikes. The volume of workplace bargaining, together with pressures on workers' real wages associated with inflation . . . provided ample opportunities for the use of this power. Relatively low levels of unemployment meant that the use of bargaining power was less constrained than it was later. The main constraint was provided by incomes policies between 1966 and 1968, but their overall effect seems to have been slight, while their breakdown during 1969 and 1970 gave the upward trend in the number of strikes a powerful push.'

During the 1970s:

> 'post-Donovan reform may have tended to reduce the number of strikes, although the evidence here is not strong . . . Although the pressures of inflation became greater than they were during the 1960s rising unemployment and a succession of incomes policies tended to counteract these pressures. Hence the number of strikes fluctuated according to the precise state of the labour market and the form of incomes policy being employed. There was no general upward or downward trend until the end of the decade when rapidly rising unemployment was associated with a steep fall in the number of strikes.'[15]

The other key indices for measuring strike trends are the numbers of workers involved and the number of work days lost through strikes. There was a major upsurge in these figures in the late 1960s and the early 1970s and again in the late 1970s, associated with the re-emergence of the large national strike, primarily in the public sector in response to the impact of incomes policy and other pressures.

The Public Sector. While the main focus of political concern about industrial relations in the 1960s was the nature and impact of workplace collective bargaining in manufacturing, 'by 1980 it had become commonplace to consider the major source of instability . . . as lying in the relationships between governments and public sector trade unions.'[16] Until the 1960s, a combination of factors such as formal, highly centralised collective bargaining arrangements, pay comparability with the private sector, reliance on arbitration, and the generally favourable post-war political and economic climate for

243

public sector expansion meant that most of the public sector (the main exception being the coal industry) was characterised by peaceful and stable industrial relations. In the latter part of the 1960s and the 1970s, however, growing pressures on public expenditure and the impact on public sector pay of successive incomes policies transformed the traditional pattern of public sector industrial relations.

Under the 1960s incomes policies, not only were pay norms more rigorously applied in the public sector than in the private sector, but there was also considerably less scope for productivity bargaining, at least in respect of non-manual workers and the public services. This had the effect of creating anomalies and disturbing customary pay relativities, a process which was then aggravated by the incoming Conservative Government's 'n-1' policy and its subsequent general incomes policy. The result was a wave of industrial action by public employees in the 1969-74 period, often for the first time in the case of teachers, hospital staff, civil servants and other such groups. A similar round of widespread public sector industrial action occurred during the 'winter of discontent' in 1979, again the result of the strict enforcement in the public sector of the Government pay limits of 1977-78 and 1978-79 at a time when such limits were widely broken by private sector settlements.

Union Growth. Another key feature of British industrial relations during the 1970s was the substantial growth in trade union membership. After a period of relative stability from 1949 to 1968, when union membership was around the 9-10 million mark, net union membership grew by over three million between 1969 and 1979, and union density (i.e. the proportion of the working population – including the unemployed – who are union members) increased from 44% to 55.4%.[17] This growth has been explained at the aggregate level primarily in terms of economic factors, employers' attitudes, and Government policy. The threat to workers' living standards posed by rapid price rises and the credit unions may be given for securing pay increases are seen as providing 'a good deal of the explanation for the contrasting experience of union growth between 1949-68 and 1968-79'.[18] The rise in unemployment during the 1970s was insufficient to offset other factors promoting union growth. Workers' decisions about union membership are also significantly influenced by employers' attitudes: 'the greater the degree of union recognition the more likely workers are to join unions and remain in them'.[19] This, in turn, is affected by Government policy, particularly whether its legislation and other Government action helps or hinders trade union recognition, directly or indirectly. During the 1970s, the climate in terms of both employer attitudes and Government policy was relatively favourable. As far as inter-industry differences in unionisation are concerned, a key determinant appears to be establishment size.

Government Strategy. In the post-war period, Governments of both parties were committed to the active management of the economy through state intervention to ensure full employment and economic growth, and employers' organisations and unions were involved to a significant extent by successive Governments in the development of public policy. There was a particularly close relationship between unions and the 1945-51 Labour Government, and the subsequent Conservative Governments of 1951-64 pursued a generally conciliatory policy towards the unions. Arrangements for involving the two sides of industry in the process of national decision-making included extensive direct consultation by Government departments as well as the use of tripartite advisory committees and agencies. All post-war Governments were concerned about the impact of collective bargaining on their attempts to manage the economy and about other aspects of industrial relations (strikes, restrictive practices etc.). 'It was not until the mid-1960s, however, that concern over these different, though related, issues became fused and "trade union power" became a major issue'.[20] Prior to this, 'the State [had] stayed out of industrial relations: holding the ring . . . but not actively pursuing any industrial relations reform'.[21] Since the mid-1960s, however, successive Governments have intervened extensively in industrial relations.

In doing so they have followed one of two broad strategies. The first approach, frequently termed 'corporatist', has been an increased emphasis on tripartism in the formulation of national economic and social policy, with union influence on broad policy developments providing the context for agreement on wage restraint. Such an approach was pursued by both Conservative and Labour Governments in the 1960s and 1970s, with the 'Social Contract' of the 1974-79 Labour Government being the most developed form of this strategy. The second approach is an anti-corporatist one of neo-liberalism – involving a reliance on market forces, the rejection of incomes policy, the minimisation of trade union involvement in policy making, and the legal restriction of trade union power. This approach was abortively tried in the early years of the 1970-74 Conservative Government, but has been pursued by the present Conservative Government throughout the 1980s.

Industrial Relations in the 1980s

Some commentators have argued that a new pattern of industrial relations has developed during the 1980s.[22] Key aspects of this 'new industrial relations' are seen as the loss of trade union influence, the decline in the incidence of industrial action and the diminished salience of collective bargaining. However, while it is apparent that the economic and industrial conditions of the 1980s have had the effect of generally strengthening the position of employers in relation to organised labour, claims of more fundamental changes in the nature of industrial relations or in workers' attitudes have met with greater scepticism.

The Effects of 'Thatcherism'

In many ways, the direction and tone of industrial relations in the 1980s have been set by the Government. The election of the Conservative Government in 1979 reversed the general post-war trend of Government intervention in the economy and brought about a major change in the industrial relations environment. Emphasising control of the money supply and public spending, the Government pursued a severely deflationary economic policy which exacerbated the scale of the recession between 1979 and 1982. This represented 'a complete break with the traditions of Keynesian macroeconomic management of the post-war years'. As well as abandoning the commitment to full employment, the Government 'eschewed incomes policies, believing that a sufficiently strict monetary regime would force both capital and labour to adjust expectations and later their bargaining behaviour',[23] the consequences of not doing so being reduced output and employment. The major wave of redundancies and closures, particularly in manufacturing, which took place between 1980 and 1983, and the rapidly growing levels of unemployment over the same period, provided the context for the changes which have taken place in industrial relations in the 1980s.

A related aspect of Government policy has been its determination to reduce the size and role of the public sector. The public sector is the most highly unionised part of the British economy, and the present Government's approach to the public sector has been intended, at least in part, to undermine the position of the public sector unions. The Government has been strongly critical of the 'inefficient' public sector and has attempted to introduce 'private sector' commercial values into the management of public sector concerns. This has led to increasingly tight financial controls, restrictions on borrowing, the rejection of pay comparability and an emphasis on efficiency, competitiveness and profitability at the expense of 'social' objectives. These developments have been accompanied by the weakening of the statutory monopolies of some public corporations, the privatisation of many public enterprises and aspects of the public services, moves to decentralise management structures and collective bargaining, and Government attempts to encourage a less consensual style of industrial relations management in the public sector.

A further feature of the present Government's approach to public sector industrial relations has been its determination to sit out major industrial disputes often involving protracted industrial action by key public sector groups. The largest and most significant industrial disputes of the 1980s have taken place in the public sector, including disputes affecting the steel and coal industries, the civil service and schools, and have often resulted in defeat for the unions concerned.

The Government's extensive and continuous changes to the legal framework of employment and industrial relations (discussed in Chapter 10) have also reflected its aim of curbing trade union bargaining power in order to 'improve the operation of the labour market'. Restrictive legal measures have been accompanied at the national, political level by steps to limit union involvement in the development and implementation of Government policy – intended as an explicit rejection of the 'corporatist' approach adopted by Governments during the 1970s. While the present Government has not totally abandoned the basic procedural relationships which the TUC has with Government departments and public bodies, it has declined to engage in genuine consultation with the trade union movement on policy matters. In other words, far from having a negotiating relationship with the Government of the day – which is the TUC's objective – during the 1980s it has been largely excluded from the corridors of power where it has traditionally sought to initiate and influence public policy developments.

Management Policies

The main management goals in industrial relations are efficiency and control over labour utilisation. Faced with difficult market conditions in the 1980s, to what extent have managers sought new ways of achieving these outcomes?

'Macho-Management'. One view suggests that a new breed of tough 'macho-managers' has attempted to dismantle important elements of the industrial relations system inherited at the start of the 1980s. Evidence of 'macho-management' may be sought in managements' approach to shop stewards, unions and collective bargaining. There does appear to have been some 'roll-back' of the activities of shop stewards, at least in the early part of the decade. Some facilities granted earlier, including time-off for union duties, have been restricted or withdrawn by some employers and the proportion of manufacturing workplaces with full-time shop stewards declined by some 17% between 1980 and 1984.[24] However, these changes do not represent a dismantling of the workplace system of industrial relations constructed over the previous decade: rather they are a tightening-up of the system, reflecting the imperative of cost containment in the 1980s.

Collective Bargaining. If British employers had followed the lead of their American counterparts we would expect to find evidence of comprehensive de-unionisation strategies during the 1980s. Survey evidence from the private manufacturing sector does indeed show a decline in the number of workplaces where pay is determined by collective bargaining between management and unions.[25] But a closer examination of a sample of firms who had de-recognised unions for pay bargaining purposes found that only one out of thirty six had achieved complete de-unionisation.[26] Employer disinterest in de-unionisation is not altogether surprising. To pursue such a strategy is potentially disruptive and costly, whilst the gains are by no means obvious. There can be efficiency advantages in dealing with some issues, such as pay rates, collectively. Notwithstanding developments in private manufacturing, overall the proportion of workplaces in which pay is determined by collective bargaining has increased during the 1980s.[27]

By and large managements appear to have sought to narrow the range of issues over which they are prepared to negotiate rather than to withdraw from collective bargaining altogether. In particular, they have aspired to reduce the influence of worker representatives over work organisation. Faced with acute competitive pressures, removal of constraints on labour deployment has been especially important for managers. That joint regulation of work organisation in much of private manufacturing has been informal in nature has meant that many employers could achieve this without threatening the basis of the existing industrial relations system. It has been a different story in the public sector, particularly the public corporations, where work organisation had traditionally been formally regulated to a considerable degree. Management proposals to introduce new working practices in steel, coal, postal services and the railways were widely interpreted as a repudiation by management of the traditional approach to industrial relations.

A further break with tradition came with the moves of public sector organisations to decentralise elements of pay bargaining (from national level) towards the end of the decade. These reflect the policy of the Thatcher Government that wage rates should be tailored to sub-national labour markets. In the private sector, there have been no major shifts in bargaining levels overall. The trend towards internalisation has continued, albeit modestly, whilst within companies there has been a certain degree of centralisation from plant to company or divisional level bargaining.[28] British Leyland, for instance, shifted pay bargaining from plant to company level in the early 1980s. Equally, some major firms, such as Lucas, have decentralised pay bargaining to plant level.

Participation. The implementation of Human Resource Management

248

would imply moves towards a more individualistic approach to employee communications, consultation and participation. There is indeed some evidence that many firms have sought to communicate directly with their employees without going through the medium of union representatives. However, the incidence of joint consultation involving union representatives seems to have been more or less static.[29] There does appear to have been significant growth in forms of participation that involve employees directly, such as quality circles (where groups of workers discuss production problems) and team briefing (where first-line supervisors regularly brief their subordinates on company affairs). However, the evidence suggests that these new institutions work best when unions are involved in their operation from the outset.[30] Employees appear to doubt the credibility of managements' commitment to participation when managers attempt to exclude unions from these innovations.

Flexibility. Greater flexibility has also figured large in many managers' thinking in the 1980s. 'Functional flexibility', where employees are trained to perform a variety of tasks, thereby facilitating moves between product markets, and 'numerical flexibility', where employee numbers can be adjusted swiftly to overall levels of product demand, have been widely advocated. One study suggests that around 90% of large firms have attempted to increase flexibility in the 1980s.[31] However, the significance of these findings may be questioned. In many cases it seems that barriers to flexibility, such as demarcation lines, have been weakened but that the resources devoted to training have been insufficient to achieve genuine multi-skilling. Critics of the 'flexible firm' model have argued that moves towards flexibility have been primarily ad hoc cost-cutting rather than the embodiment of a new approach to labour management.[32]

'Japanisation'. Flexibility is viewed as an integral component, however, of Japanese approaches to industrial relations. Great interest has been shown in the 'new-style' agreements reached primarily by Japanese companies in Britain, such as Sanyo, Toshiba and Nissan, with British unions. These agreements typically consist of a number of inter-related elements: single-union recognition; single status; a commitment to job flexibility; a strong emphasis on training and retraining; a consultative management style; and a reliance on arbitration procedures (frequently 'pendulum' arbitration) to preclude industrial action. Such agreements are 'novel not in their individual components, all of which have long been used from time to time, but because they form integrated packages of measures which, taken together, are designed to reinforce pressures for consensus'.[33] Arguably the most crucial feature, however, is their strategic and comprehensive approach to industrial relations. This contrasts with both the conservatism displayed by many British firms during the 1980s and their reluctance to deal with industrial relations issues at the strategic level.

Impact on Trade Unions

One result of the present Government's restrictive trade union legislation and its rejection of unions as participants in the national decision-making process has been to sharpen political divisions within the TUC about union strategy. Considerable debate has centred on whether the TUC should sanction the non-compliance by unions with court orders issued under the new legislation, and whether unions should be free to accept the public funds available under the Employment Act 1980 for the holding of postal ballots. Relations with the Government have also been a controversial issue. The TUC has continued to assert the right to influence and be involved in the development of national policy. At the same time, however, there is a strong body of trade union opinion that argues that the lack of consensus on fundamental issues makes the TUC involvement with the Government pointless.

The Government's attempts to challenge the representativeness of the TUC have been reinforced by the fall in the level of trade union membership. Since 1979, trade union membership in Britain has fallen by some 3 million. The recession in the early 1980s accounted for much of this dramatic decline, with major job losses occurring particularly among highly unionised manual workers in large-scale manufacturing industry. However, although the number in employment in Britain has been growing since the end of 1982, current labour market trends have continued to have an adverse impact on union membership levels, as employment shifts towards traditionally less well-organised sectors and occupations, and towards part-time and self-employment. Unions have had little success in securing recognition in newly-established plants. Unions' traditional difficulties in organising small firms, foreign-owned plants and the private services sector have intensified and the TUC has acknowledged that unions are finding it 'generally difficult to recruit and bargain in the fastest growing parts of the economy'.[34] Lower levels of inflation than in the 1970s and hostility to trade unionism on the part of the Government are also likely to have contributed to unions' organising problems. Union density has dropped significantly over the 1980s – to 41.6 per cent by the end of 1986.[35]

Against this background, a TUC review currently taking place is focusing on how unions can widen their membership base and recruit more effectively. Plans have been developed for improving the services to members offered by unions, improving unions' public relations, and targeting special recruitment

250

initiatives on groups of workers (such as women and young people) and on localities in which membership is low. These proposals reflect the perception of a number of major unions that, in view of the serious decline in membership, and the limited effectiveness of the TUC's policy-making and representational roles during a sustained period of hostile Conservative government, a higher priority must be given by the TUC to organisational matters. On the other hand, such matters have traditionally been seen by individual unions as their own preserve, and this accounts for the relatively limited nature of the proposed new TUC initiatives. Indeed, a more interventionist proposal of a TUC organising fund to finance specific recruitment campaigns attracted insufficient support.

The fall in trade union membership in the 1980s and employers' resistance to union recognition has stimulated heightened competition between unions for new members and new agreements with employers. This in turn has led to an increase in jurisdictional disputes between unions (which it is the TUC's responsibility to settle) particularly over single-union agreements. Much of British industry is, for historical reasons, characterised by multi-unionism. Single-union agreements which cut across other unions' established interests are not permitted by the TUC's rules governing inter-union competition, and a number of such agreements have been cancelled by the unions concerned on the TUC's instructions.

The new-style single-union/no-strike agreements have become the focus not only of unions' conflicting organisational ambitions but also of ideological differences between unions. Left-led unions are unhappy with the new-style agreements' limitations on the right to strike and on traditional trade union methods. For some unions on the right, however, such agreements are a crucial part of the fundamental reappraisal of trade union strategy they consider necessary in the light of prevailing social and industrial attitudes. While many British unions have an essentially pragmatic approach to the question of single-union/no-strike agreements, this has not prevented a damaging dispute from developing within the TUC. In September 1988, the Electrical, Electronic, Telecommunications and Plumbing Trades Unions (EETPU) – the principal advocate and main beneficiary of the new-style agreements – was expelled from the TUC for refusing to withdraw from two such agreements signed in contravention of the TUC's inter-union rules. This development represents one of the most serious splits in the TUC's history and is likely to inhibit the TUC's efforts to reverse the decline in its influence.

A further reflection of the decline in union membership and structural changes within industry is the significant increase in union merger activity currently taking place. In addition to a steady stream of transfers of engagements from small declining unions to larger ones, a spate of 'strategic' amalgamations between major unions is occurring for a variety of industrial and political reasons. Recent mergers of this latter type include that between the Association of Scientific, Technical and Managerial Staffs (ASTMS) and the technical, administrative and supervisory workers (TASS) to form the Manufacturing Science and Finance union (MSF), the merger between the General, Municipal, Boilermakers and Allied Trades Union (GMBATU) and the Association of Professional, Executive, Clerical and Computer Staffs (APEX) to form the 'GMB', and the merger between the Society of Civil and Public Servants (SCPS) and the Civil Service Union (CSU) to form the National Union of Civil and Public Servants (NUCPS). A number of other such mergers are currently under discussion though the expected merger between the Amalgamated Engineering Union (AEU) and the EETPU now seems in doubt following a decision of the AEU's national committee. While reducing the overall number of unions, and easing inter-union difficulties in some sectors, this process is tending to reinforce rather than eliminate inter-union competition over recruitment and representation in the key area of manufacturing, and to accentuate political divisions between major unions.

The impact of developments during the 1980s on unions' bargaining strength has been a matter of considerable debate. The growth in unemployment is widely assumed to undermine union bargaining power. However, different indicators seem contradictory. During the 1980s, strike activity has fallen substantially. The trend in the number of strikes per year has been sharply downwards, dipping below 1000 in 1985. The number of working days lost has also generally declined during the 1980s, with the exception of the years affected by the 1984-85 mining dispute. At the same time the average increase in earnings has been above the retail prices index virtually throughout the 1980s. As regards the stability of union organisation, we have already seen that few managements have so far sought to withdraw recognition from unions, and established collective bargaining structures and procedures have generally survived the 1980s intact. Yet it appears that adherence to such arrangements has not in general prevented employers from securing substantial job cuts, changes in working practices, and increased productivity and flexibility. Moreover there is reported to have been a widespread reduction in the scope of non-pay issues regulated by collective bargaining. Notwithstanding the apparent inconsistency of the available evidence, there are also problems in inferring union strength or weakness from data on such issues as strikes and wage movements,[36] so while few people would argue that unions have grown stronger during the 1980s, the extent to which their bargaining power has been affected is far from clear.

Conclusion

In retrospect the 1980s presented many managements with the opportunity to transform their approach to industrial relations. High levels of unemployment and the loss of confidence amongst many unions could have facilitated the significant shift from collective representation to the individualistic relationships between employees and managers which is associated with Human Resource Management. However, the industrial relations framework which evolved in the 1960s and 1970s is more or less intact at the end of the 1980s. Whilst the difficult trading conditions for much of the 1980s dictated that fewer concessions be made to workforce representatives, the great majority of managements showed little serious inclination to de-unionise their organisations. Many have introduced HRM-style changes in employee management, such as performance-related pay and individualistic systems of participation and communications, but in essence these have been grafted onto existing industrial relations frameworks. Arguably the greatest hostility to unions and 'traditional' industrial relations and union activity has been found in the public sector. However, it is questionable whether public sector managements have achieved any significant permanent reduction in union strength whilst they may have dissipated that level of employee consent and commitment necessary to re-construct an effective pattern of industrial relations.

Overall it is fair to conclude that the tradition of pragmatism in industrial relations management has been maintained during the 1980s. Relatively few managements have adopted a strategic and comprehensive approach to industrial relations. However, there are indications that this may change in the 1990s. Severe shortages of qualified labour are forecast and already this is forcing employers to devise new strategies for recruitment, training, remuneration, representation and participation. After a decade in which many managers believed that employee aspirations and industrial relations were of limited importance, it is now becoming clear that organisations need to devote considerable attention to securing harmonious and efficient labour-management relationships if they are to attract and retain the labour forces they need.

References

1   See H Gospel, 'Comprehensive Patterns of Labor-Management Relations: Great Britain, the U.S. and Japan', *Business and Economic History,* Vol. XV (1986).

2   See K Sisson, 'Employers' Associations', in G S Bain (ed.) *Industrial Relations in Britain,* Oxford: Blackwell (1983), p. 121.

3   Sisson, *op. cit.,* pp 125-32.

4   Gospel, *op. cit.,* pp 120-1.

5   Royal Commission on Trade Unions and Employers' Associations, *Report,* Cmnd 3623, London: HMSO (1968).

6   A Flanders, *Collective Bargaining: Prescription for Change,* London: Faber (1967), p. 32.

7   H A Turner, 'The Royal Commission's Research Papers', *British Journal of Industrial Relations,* Vol. VI, No. 3 (1968)

8   W A Brown (ed.), *The Changing Contours of British Industrial Relations,* Oxford: Blackwell (1981), pp 42-7.

9   N Milward and M Stevens, *British Workplace Industrial Relations 1980-1984,* Aldershot: Gower (1986), p. 232.

10 See E Batstone, 'What have Personnel Managers Done for Industrial Relations?', *Personnel Management,* (June 1980), and H A Turner, G Roberts and D Roberts, *Management Characteristics and Labour Conflict: A Study of Managerial Organizations, Attitudes and Industrial Relations,* Cambridge: Cambridge University Press (1977).

11 R J Davies, 'Incomes and Anti-Inflation Policy' in Bain *op. cit.,* p. 419.

12 D Coates, *The Crisis of Labour: Industrial Relations and the State in Contemporary Britain,* Oxford: Philip Allan (1989), p. 50.

13 R J Davies, *op. cit.,* p. 443.

14 P K Edwards, 'The Pattern of Collective Industrial Action' in Bain *op. cit.,* pp 211-212.

15 Edwards, *op. cit.,* pp 218-219.

16 D Winchester, 'Industrial Relations in the Public Sector' in Bain *op. cit.,* p. 155.

17 G S Bain and R Price, 'Union Growth: Dimensions, Determinants and Destiny' in Bain *op. cit.*, pp 5-6.

18 Bain and Price, *op. cit.*, p. 16.

19 Bain and Price, *op. cit.*, p. 18.

20 D Barnes and E Reid, *Governments and Trade Unions: The British Experience 1964-79*, London: Heinemann (1980), p. ix.

21 Coates, *op. cit.*, p. 19.

22 For a useful discussion of the evidence, see J Kelly and R Richardson, 'Annual Review Article 1988', *British Journal of Industrial Relations*, Vol. XXVII, No. 1 (March 1989).

23 J MacInnes, *Thatcherism at Work*, Milton Keynes: Open University Press (1987), p. 51 and p. 58.

24 Milward and Stevens, *op. cit.*, p. 80.

25 Milward and Stevens, *op. cit.*, pp 229-233.

26 T Claydon, 'Union Derecognition in Britain in the 1980s', *British Journal of Industrial Relations*, Vol. XXVII, No. 2, (July 1989).

27 Milward and Stevens, *op. cit.*, pp 225-228.

28 Milward and Stevens, *op. cit.*, p. 226.

29 Milward and Stevens, *op. cit.*, p. 139.

30 R Collard and B Dale, 'Quality Circles: Why They Break Down and Why They Hold Up', *Personnel Management* (September 1985).

31 Institute of Manpower Studies, *Changing Working Patterns: How Companies Achieve Flexibility to Meet New Needs*, London: NEDO (1986).

32 A Pollert, 'The "Flexible Firm": Fixation or Fact?', *Work, Employment and Society*, Vol. II, No. 2 (1988).

33 Advisory, Conciliation and Arbitration Service, *Annual Report 1986*, London: ACAS (1987), p. 21.

34 Trades Union Congress, *Meeting the Challenge: First Report of the TUC Special Review Body,* London: TUC (1988), p. 5.

35 R Hyman, *The Political Economy of Industrial Relations,* London: Macmillan (1989), p. 232.

36 For discussions of these problems, see M Terry, 'How Do We Know If Shop Stewards Are Getting Weaker?', *British Journal of Industrial Relations,* Vol. XXIV, No. 2 (July 1986), and J Kelly, 'Trade Unions through the Recession 1980-1984', *British Journal of Industrial Relations,* Vol. XXV, No. 2 (July 1987).

Suggested Reading

In addition to Bain's *Industrial Relations in Britain* (cited frequently during the chapter), the following are useful textbooks on industrial relations:

M Salamon, *Industrial Relations: Theory and Practice,* London: Prentice-Hall International (1987).

D Farnham and J Pimlott, *Understanding Industrial Relations* (3rd ed.), London: Cassell (1986).

J Goodman, *Employment Relations in Industrial Society,* Oxford: Philip Allan (1984).

Although in print for some ten years, H A Clegg, *The Changing System of Industrial Relations in Great Britain,* Oxford: Blackwell (1979) is still a valuable reference book on British industrial relations.

For a review of managerial priorities in industrial relations during the 1980s, see C Brewster and S Connock, *Industrial Relations: Cost-effective Strategies,* London: Hutchinson (1985).

Questions

1 Why did employers embark on the rationalisation of industrial relations in the 1960s and 1970s?

2 To what extent have managerial approaches to industrial relations changed during the 1980s?

3 Have shop stewards and workplace trade union organisation been weakened during the 1980s? What are the prospects for the future?

Chapter 12

Organisational Design

Andrew Pendleton

Introduction

The design of an organisation is its configuration of tasks and the relationships between organisation members performing them. It is rarely the outcome of a grand master plan. More usually it is the end-product of a multiplicity of small-scale, often ad hoc, decisions made by a variety of managers. Their main concern is usually to 'get the job done' more effectively in their part of the organisation rather than to adhere to an overall blueprint for the design of the organisation. In the same way attempts to re-design organisation structures are generally limited in scope. Most involve small-scale re-allocation of duties between a small number of jobs or marginal revisions to departmental boundaries.

In the harsh climate of the 1980s, however, top managers in many large organisations – both public and private – have embarked upon fundamental re-designs of their organisations. Their motives have been varied: to cut overhead costs, increase staff motivation and commitment, make decision-making more responsive to customer wants and to improve staff productivity. Accounts of these reconstructions in the management press indicate that the following changes are common: clearer separation of 'strategic' and 'operational' decision-making between head office and operating divisions respectively, decentralisation of decision-making and responsibility from middle to ground-level managers, transfer of executive authority from staff or support departments (such as personnel) to line managers. Organisations where such changes have been introduced are commonly described as becoming 'leaner and fitter' as a result.

What will be provided in this chapter is an account of the main principles in organisation design and how re-designs should be conducted. The perspective guiding the chapter is that organisations are essentially collections of people, all with tasks or sets of tasks which make some contribution to organisational objectives. There are two important dimensions to this 'social system'. The first is the formal division of labour – who does what task, and who decides how and when it should be done. We can call this the *formal structure* of the organisation. The second is the behaviour of members of the organisation and the relationships between them. There are a range of important issues here. Are the relationships between superordinates and subordinates cooperative or conflictual? Do employees carry out the instructions of their bosses, and in the manner intended? Consideration of these directs our attention to the *processual* aspect of organisational design and performance. The connections between structure and process are complex. Structure will have a powerful causal impact on social processes but the latter will also be influenced by, inter alia, employees' lifestyle aspirations.[1] The issue of organisation design presents enormous challenges to human resources managers, not least because those initiating the process are often reluctant to invole these managers in the key decisions. Human resources managers therefore need to assert the value of their participation in organisation design from the outset. Since the human resources professional will generally have a deeper understanding of organisation behaviour than most of their colleagues he or she is potentially well-equipped to influence social processes as well as create formal structures. To do so, however, they must be able to overcome other managers' scepticism or simplistic conceptions of the relevance of social processes to organisational performance.

The Design of Individual Jobs

As a first step to analysing organisation design it will be useful to consider the design of individual jobs. There are two reasons for this. The first is that they form the 'building blocks' of the organisation – they are fractions of the organisation's total work tasks which can be performed (more or less) by each person. The second is that re-design of the organisation, be it a small-scale revision or a large-scale transformation, will require revision to existing jobs either in terms of tasks performed or decision-making powers.

To analyse job design two basic dimensions can be used, 'task width' and 'task height'. *Task width* refers to the range of identifiable tasks which constitute a particular job. Manual production jobs, which generally involve a small range of tasks, can be said to be narrow in width, whereas managerial jobs seem somewhat wider. In general, the narrower the task range, the more repetitive the job is likely to be. A good illustration of this is assembly line work. In the extreme case, the worker performs a single identical task, such as fitting car components, repeatedly.

Task Height refers to the degree of decision-making involved in carrying out the required task(s). Those jobs which require little decision-making can be said to be 'low' in height. To use the example of the assembly line again, a simple repetitive task will make little demands on the decision-making capabilities of the employee performing it. As a worker quoted in a study of Ford's Halewood (UK) plant puts it,

> *'It's the most boring job in the world. It's the same thing over and over again. There's no change in it, it wears you out. There's no need to think. Ford class you more as a machine than men'*.[2]

As this example suggests, task width and task height tend to be positively correlated. The greater the range of tasks, the greater the degree of decision-making that seems to be required. At the very least the employee will have to decide which tasks to perform at any given time. Conversely, those jobs that are narrow and repetitive seem to require little decision-making.

This relationship and the basic dimensions of analysis are illustrated in Figure 12.1.

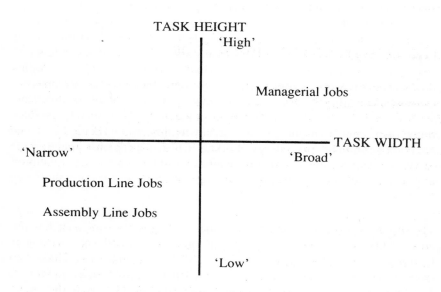

Figure 12.1: Task Height/Width Quadrant

Although jobs differ widely in the range and height of tasks, most can be placed into the two broad categories shown. It is rather difficult to think of jobs that are narrow in width yet involve substantial decision-making (Stock Market dealers may be an example of this type). Even more difficult to conceive of are jobs that embrace a wide variety of tasks yet require little decision-making. Of course, the division into narrow/wide and low/high jobs found in this schema is somewhat arbitrary, and it is not easy to stipulate the precise point of separation between, for instance, narrow and wide jobs. Nevertheless, it is a useful analytical tool for classifying and comparing jobs.

There is a further observation which can be made about these categories which is of considerable significance for job design. That is, that those performing jobs that can be located in the bottom left quadrant tend to experience low levels of job satisfaction. By contrast jobs found in the top right quadrant generally provide high levels of satisfaction to those performing them. It is not difficult to discern the relationship between the two dimensions and the intrinsic rewards of jobs. Employees doing jobs that lack variety will in many cases find them tedious. In addition, he or she may be unable to perceive the rationale for them since the contribution of the task to the final product or service may not be obvious. These problems may be compounded by a generalised sense of powerlessness resulting from an inability to take on-the-job decisions.

Low levels of job satisfaction often manifest themselves in poor motivation, a lack of commitment and shoddy standards of work. These in turn can lead to conflict between members of the organisation. The dynamics of this process can be summarised as follows. Employees whose jobs are unrewarding do not generally work as effectively as they might. Incentive pay schemes can counterbalance this to some extent by keeping output at requisite levels but such workers are rarely committed to producing a high quality product. Supervisors and managers often respond to this by enforcing rules and applying disciplinary procedures. Workers in turn react against what they see as unjustified pressure from management by further reducing the quality of their performance or by go-slows, sabotage and strikes. It is but a short step to chronically poor industrial relations.

The structure of work tasks then seems to have a strong bearing on behaviour and relationships at work. For this reason some have argued that it is possible to modify behaviour and relationships by attention to job design. Rather than responding to the symptoms of dissatisfaction in the manner described above, the cause itself should be treated. In this way superior levels of performance can be achieved. This solution found favour in the 1970s when growing competition in product markets and difficulties in recruiting labour to perform tedious jobs led to a greater emphasis on commitment, quality and contentment. A loose-knot body of academics and enlightened managers advocated what came to be known as Quality of Working Life (QWL) programmes.

Quality of Working Life programmes generally comprise a number of changes to job design.

Job enlargement – here the range of tasks each worker performs is widened so as to produce greater variety.

Job rotation – introduced greater variety by enabling employees to rotate around various jobs in the plant or office.

Job enrichment – expands the decision-making element of jobs with the intention of making them more meaningful to those performing them.

Incremental changes can be made in any of these three ways but QWL programmes are notable not simply for usually embracing all three but also for underpinning them with a philosophy of employee participation and co-operative management-worker relationships. In the more comprehensive attempts at job re-design much of the responsibility for task decisions is passed from supervisors and managers to teams of workers known as *autonomous* or *semi-autonomous work groups*.

The most celebrated case of a QWL programme in action is that at Volvo's plant in Kalmar, Sweden where the rigid and minute division of labour of the assembly line was replaced by work teams with collective responsibility for entire assembly operations. The benefits that appear to result from this sort of change include higher and better quality output in the long term, lower absenteeism and labour turnover, and a reduced requirement for supervision. But, as John Child has emphasised, claims that job re-design leads to better company performance need to be treated with caution because adequate data is often unavailable, it is difficult to isolate the causal importance of job design from other factors, and because the full range of costs are often overlooked.[3]

There is a certain amount of evidence that improvements to the quality of working life often fail to live up to expectations. Often this can be attributed to job designers' conception of job re-design as a simple revision to formal task structures, and a failure to take account of the full range of social processes operating within the workplace. Child cites the case of a washing machine factory where the production operatives disliked a programme of job

261

enlargement because the increased task range slowed down their speed of work thereby reducing the time they could socialise with each other away from their work stations.[4] A widespread problem too is supervisor resistance since the transfer of decision-making powers to production workers seems to make their role in the production process less important or even redundant.

A fundamental problem with attempts at job re-design is that managers neither understand nor are committed to the underlying principles of the scheme. For these reasons QWL is often viewed as a set of discrete changes to the structure of work tasks rather than one, albeit important, element of a more participative approach to work organisation. Thus, managers will often continue using hierarchical approaches in other aspects of the relationship with production workers, such as in unilaterally deciding promotions. This conflict of approaches frequently engenders cynicism – if managers are still doing some things the old way they can hardly be really committed to the new. And this is often in fact the case. When, for example, pressure to meet delivery dates becomes intense, managers may revert to the traditional pattern of giving instructions rather than relying on the knowledge and abilities of the workforce to devise a satisfactory solution. It is no exaggeration to state that a QWL scheme can be wrecked in minutes in these circumstances. Workers quickly sense that managers do not believe in it.

The human resources manager should attempt to forestall these problems by instigating a comprehensive programme of communication to gain acceptance at all levels of the organisation that job re-design is about participative and co-operative relationships rather than just re-assembly of work tasks. And where production workers are not competent to take production decisions, he or she should encourage training programmes to rectify this. At the heart of the human resources professional's approach is the knowledge that job re-design involves change to both formal structures and social processes.

Dimensions of Organisation Structure

i Centralisation and Specialisation

Individual jobs can be viewed as the 'building blocks' of the organisation. In conceptual terms, the total work of the organisation can be broken down – the division of labour – to achieve tasks or sets of tasks that can be performed by individual employees. But having established the division of labour, these tasks then need to be 're-assembled' and coordinated to achieve the desired outputs. There are, of course, a myriad ways of doing this. However, as with individual jobs, there appear to be two fundamental design principles when

262

considering organisational structure. These are the 'height' of the organisation in terms of the levels of the jobs and its 'breadth' – the number of jobs at any one level.

Starting with the vertical dimension the most important question facing the organisational designer is how many levels should there be in the management hierarchy? In a very small organisation two may be sufficient – the chief executive and his or her subordinates. As organisations grow in size it is likely, all things being equal, that the number of levels will increase. Otherwise the chief executive would have to supervise directly an impossibly large number of employees. By inserting intermediary levels into the hierarchy it is possible to achieve a more manageable 'span of control'.

Those organisations with a large number of management levels are often referred to as 'tall', whilst those with few are known as 'flat'. Generally speaking, there is a tendency for decision-making to be centralised in those organisations that can be characterised as tall. Conversely adoption of a flat structure forces a certain degree of decentralisation if the upper reaches are not to become overloaded. Flatter organisational structures are currently more fashionable since the relative centralisation of decision-making in tall organisations is thought to detract from motivation and performance in the lower reaches (i.e. they are remote from where decisions are taken), whilst the large number of management levels are believed to inhibit communication between the top and bottom. In the past tall hierarchies were thought necessary in large organisations because of the volume of work tasks – such as information processing – combined with the problems of adequately supervising subordinates where there is a broad span of control. Automation of routine tasks using micro-electronic technology has done much to facilitate flatter organisation structures.[5]

The span of control can be thought of as the horizontal counterpart of the levels in the hierarchy. It refers to how many subordinates each manager oversees or has authority over. Classical management theory – developed by Urwick and Fayol – suggested that there is an optimal figure to the span of control of between 3 and 6.[6] The reasoning behind this is that there are practical limits to the number of people any one manager can effectively supervise. Nowadays it is widely believed that the optimal number is determined by the nature of the supervisory relationship. Where the superordinate manager is prepared to delegate substantial elements of decision-making, there is no necessary objection to a broader span of control.

The desired span of control has an important bearing on a key element of horizontal structure. How far should tasks be grouped together into specialist

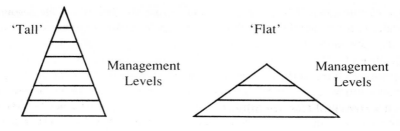

Figure 12.2: Hierarchy in Organisations

departments? Should all the discrete elements of personnel work for example – manpower planning, recruitment and selection, training, industrial relations to name but a few – be organised as separate departments or in one personnel department? Or should they even be conducted in a separate personnel department at all?

Needless to say, there are no easy answers to these questions. In general, the organisation designer would need to consider both the relative volume of work in these areas and the importance attached to them. They would also need to weigh up the advantages and disadvantages of specialisation. The advantages include the following: concentration of staff pursuing similar tasks in one department tends to facilitate the construction and maintenance of specialist expertise. A related advantage is that the grouping of activities in this way enables a career ladder to be provided within the area. Both these factors tend to encourage job satisfaction.

Equally, there are a number of potential problems with specialisation. Once personnel tasks are grouped into a personnel department(s) it may prove more difficult to coordinate them with, say, production because each department will develop its own priorities. Indeed one powerful disadvantage is that the construction of specialist expertise encourages an 'esprit de corps' which puts the interests of the department before those of the organisation as a whole.

So far we have discussed the key structural dimensions of centralisation and specialisation. It is these which are shown formally in the organisation chart. However, to outline the formal structure is not enough to understand how organisations actually operate. As the foregoing discussion has indicated, certain patterns of *behaviour* seem to be associated with varying degrees of specialisation and centralisation. We now need to consider the behavioural

264

aspect more fully. The key issue facing the designer here is how to get the required behaviour from employees. In other words, how to ensure that employees do what they are meant to do and in conjunction with others in the organisation. These imperatives are those of control and coordination.

ii Control and Coordination

In the rest of the section we will outline the various ways control and coordination of employee behaviour can be sought. It needs to be emphasised at the outset that this is problematic. In part it can be viewed as a technical problem – employees do not necessarily know what is expected of them. But there is a deeper problem that workers' interests may not be congruent with those of the organisation. The task of management here is to encourage behaviour which is conducive to the achievement of organisational goals. In designing the organisation, therefore, the human resources manager should develop appropriate patterns of control and coordination as well as constructing a formal structure. Four basic approaches to this problem of control and coordination can be discerned.

Personal whim. Here the head of the organisation plays an important directive role, issuing instructions as circumstances demand. This 'autocratic' or entrepreneurial style of control and coordination is commonly found in small organisations in the early stages of development. Once organisations have moved beyond this stage, however, this becomes inappropriate. There is the danger that the leader will become 'overloaded' with supervisory tasks, whilst employees for their part may come to resent this autocratic style of management. Furthermore, once organisations have moved into a phase of stable growth it is possible to standardise procedures. Unfortunately, many young organisations fail to develop structures and methods consistent with their stage of development. The problems they encounter are familiar: poor staff-leader relationships, ad hoc responses to customer requirements, and stifled creative talents.

Rules. This approach to control and coordination is characterised by specification and standardisation. What should be done is specified by rules and standardised to all situations of a similar type. Rules can cover the whole range of the organisation's activities: 'all visitors must report to reception'; 'staff should not leave their work-station without the supervisor's permission'; 'all cash inflows should be individually recorded'. This emphasis on rule-governed behaviour is found in most medium and large-sized organisations. Without rules many employees would not know what to do; nor would they perform tasks which they objected to.

265

The key question is how far should organisational behaviour be governed by rules? Too great an emphasis on rules can be counter-productive. It can stifle individual initiative, and can encourage employees to devote more attention to following the rules than achieving organisational objectives (a process known as 'goal displacement').[7] Organisations in which behaviour is strongly circumscribed by rules are often described as 'bureaucratic' (though in organisation theory all organisations making use of rules are described as bureaucracies) or 'mechanistic'.[8]

Consent and Commitment. The negative consequences of relying on rules to achieve control and coordination has led some commentators to argue that it is preferable to generate commitment to the organisation in their place. The foremost exponents of this view are Peters and Waterman in their book *In Search of Excellence*.[9] As they see it, if an employee is highly committed to the goals and values of the organisation, they will in most cases do what is required of them without instruction. If anything their work performance is likely to be better than in the traditional bureaucratic organisation because freedom from constraints leads to greater motivation. Mistakes will undoubtedly occur from time to time but this price is worth paying for the sake of greater motivation and innovation. This approach seems particularly suitable for young organisations where committed enthusiasm and innovation are especially important. There may well be problems, however, in maintaining this degree of enthusiasm in the long term. Furthermore, as organisations grow, the task of coordination becomes more complex. It seems wiser to entrust at least some of this to standard rules rather than relying on chance. There is as yet no firm evidence that 'removing the rules' generates superior company performance in the long term.

Internal Contract. An approach to control and coordination which is becoming fashionable attempts to push the disciplines of the market and contracts into the organisation. In place of rules to govern inter-departmental relationships, contracts are struck between departments for the supply of goods and services. Notional payments are made on receipt of these. Failure to deliver can result in payment being withheld or purchasing power being taken elsewhere (potentially even outside the organisation). The rationale is that rules merely encourage satisfactory or punish unsatisfactory behaviour: the objective here is to stimulate maximising behaviour. Time will tell how successful this approach can be. The organisation designer should be aware, however, of problems that could arise. These include the pursuit of sub-goals by departments at the expense of those of the organisation as a whole. There is also little here to boost the *real* commitment of employees – once again, the emphasis is essentially on enforcement. In addition, the need to define the circumstances in which 'payments' may be withheld or contracts 'broken'

266

could ironically lead to a proliferation of rules rather than their reduction.

None of these approaches are mutually exclusive. In practice elements of all four may be found in large organisations today. The task of the organisation designer is to analyse the organisation and its objectives and to assess what the most appropriate balance would be. To do so may call on a diverse range of skills and methods. To increase reliance on rules, he or she will need to embark on a painstaking process of codifying organisational practices into rules. A good example of this is the formalisation of personnel and industrial relations practices that took place in many British organisations during the 1970s. Alternatively, if the human resources manager identifies internal contract as a useful form of control and coordination, a key task will be securing the agreement of top managers to such a radical change in the way the organisation operates. If, however, the Peters and Waterman approach is believed to be worth adopting considerable attention will need to be given to designing programmes to enhance employee commitment and to achieving cultural change in the organisation. Whatever the direction chosen, there is one very important message that emerges here. That is, that organisational design is not simply about creating or changing structures. It also involves influencing the social processes of control and coordination within the organisation.

Company Structures

Already organisations have been shown to be complex entities with varying degrees of centralisation and specialisation, and differing approaches to coordination and control. However, there are further issues which the organisation designer has to consider. Given than most large business organisations in Britain and the USA provide a range of quite varied goods and services at a range of locations, how are the relationships between head office and the constituent business units to be organised and how are decisions to be distributed between them?

Three main approaches can be identified.

Functional

The functional form of organisation is where the organisation is structured on a departmental basis. Below the chief executive can be found a set of self-contained departments such as personnel, production and finance. At each level (apart from the top) a departmental manager reports to a manager in the same department.

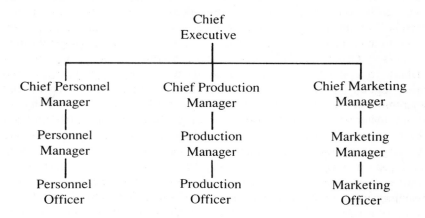

Figure 12.3: The Functional Form of Organisation

As the figure suggests, formal coordination takes place primarily at the top of the organisation. In essence, the functional form involves a high degree of specialisation, and both the advantages and disadvantages of specialisation (discussed in the previous section) apply here. In addition to the factors discussed earlier, there is a powerful tendency towards centralised decision-making in functional organisations since only the apex has formal coordinating powers. Informal coordination can take place at the lower levels but the strong departmental boundaries associated with this form render achievement of this a recurrent problem. In general, this form of organisation can be appropriate in single site organisations or in those multi-site organisations where the product and the pattern of operations are very similar and the environment comparatively stable, thereby requiring comparatively few important decisions at local level.

Divisional

Most large British and American companies, however, are organised along divisional lines. Here, hierarchical departments are replaced by sub-units based on particular products or localities. Coordination takes place at lower levels in addition to the chief executive. Rather than reporting to the personnel director for instance a personnel manager in one of the divisions would report to the divisional general manager.

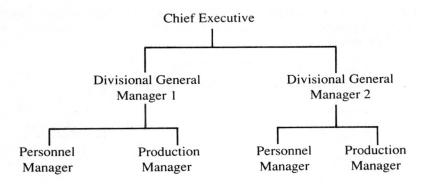

Figure 12.4: The Divisional Form of Organisation

This pattern of organisation was pioneered in the USA in the 1920s. It was not until the late 1960s that it came to be the predominant form for large companies in Britain.[10] Its primary advantage is that it facilitates the management of diversity. In principle, a company could accommodate any pattern of operations by establishing a separate sub-unit based on product-type. For instance, an insurance firm could move into sheet metal production using this structure: such a market entry would be somewhat problematic with a functional structure.

A further related advantage that is claimed for this type of organisation is that it facilitates relatively decentralised decision-making. Important decisions can be made at sub-unit level rather than head office, leaving the head office to make key strategic decisions, and permitting lower level decisions to be tailored to the particular context.

However, the clarity of roles and decision-making found in this model is not always there in practice. Research has shown that there is not always a clear separation in the types of decision made at product division and head office.[11] Both take a mixture of operating and business strategy decisions according to their importance at the time. Furthermore, context-driven diversity may be accompanied by a certain degree of standardisation throughout the organisation. If a company wants to facilitate the movement of staff between product divisions it will be desirable to have standard terms and conditions of service. To achieve standard personnel policies it will be necessary for personnel (and other) managers to respect and implement personnel policies made centrally. Thus the Personnel Manager may be obliged to heed two superiors: the Divisional General Manager and the Personnel Director at head office, even though he or she is formally accountable just to the General

269

Manager. The relationship between the Personnel Manager and the Personnel Director in this situation is often shown as a 'dotted-line' relationship on organisation charts.

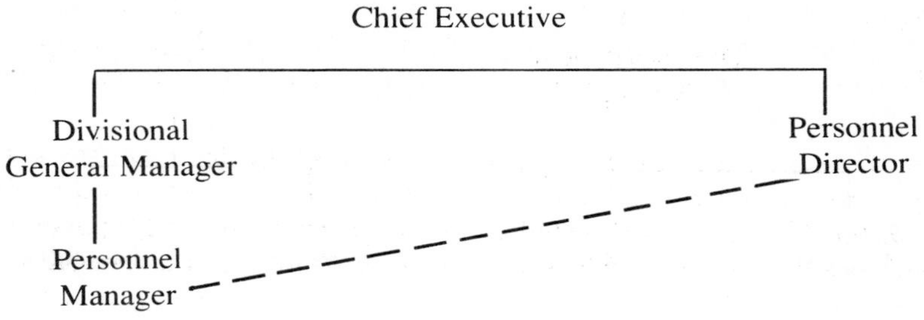

Chief Executive

Divisional
General Manager

Personnel
Director

Personnel
Manager

Figure 12.5: 'Dotted-Line Relationship'

The apparent simplicity of the formal structure shown in such charts is often belied by what actually happens in practice. The Personnel Manager may well receive conflicting messages from the two superiors. In many organisations the subordinate manager has felt greater obligation, often because of a community of professional interests, to the dotted line superior rather than to the manager to whom they formally report.

Matrix

Multiplicity of reporting relationships is the outstanding feature of our third pattern of organisation.

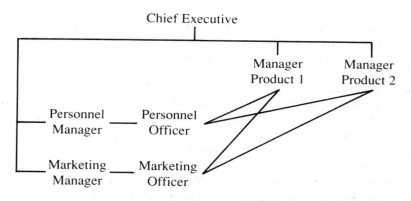

Figure 12.6: The Matrix Form of Organisation

Here a given manager reports to two or more superiors drawn from different management functions. The rationale is to achieve decentralised coordination during innovation, and is thought to be particularly suitable for project team organisation.[12] If a product development team reports to both marketing and production directors then it seems likely that marketing and production considerations can be incorporated into the development effort from the outset.

A further advantage of matrix organisation seems to be that it can break down department boundaries, thereby stimulating creative management behaviour. However, if there has been a tendency for departments to rigidly pursue their own interests in the past, it is possible that a shift to matrix organisation will do nothing to solve this. This is because departmental members will often attempt to insulate the department from what they see as potentially damaging instructions from others 'who do not understand what the department does'. As has been argued before in this chapter, reliance on simple structural solutions to complex behavioural problems can be counter-productive.

A further problem is that the lack of clarity in reporting relationships can be destructive. Project team members may be uncertain what to do when conflicting instructions or objectives are received from superiors. Contrary to the intentions of organisational designers, this could lead to intertia and caution. In addition, where conflict of this sort is experienced there is the danger that organisation designers will create additional rules to regulate those areas of potential conflict thereby further stifling creativity.

In general, matrix organisation may be appropriate for organisations or parts of organisations in the innovatory stages of the product cycle. Attempts to invigorate mature organisations by adopting the matrix form are fraught with danger as existing problems may be intensified rather than solved. Similarly, changing to a functional or divisional structure does not necessarily leave the difficulties of the previous structure behind. To avoid incorporating old problems into the new structure it is vital that organisation designers appreciate that organisational behaviour is not entirely determined by the dimensions of formal structure. To achieve the desired benefits of organisational change the designers should supplement structural reforms with programmes of Organisation Development (see Chapter 13).

Approaches to Organisation Re-Design

Organisational re-design can take many forms. It can, for instance, require a small-scale programme of job enlargement or it can involve transforming the entire company from a functional to a multi-divisional structure. In all cases, however, the organisation designer needs to take heed of the social processes within the organisation as well as its formal structure.

How should the organisational designer go about this task? To consider this we can assume that a major re-organisation is thought to be necessary. The following brief discussion attempts to highlight the main steps.

1 Formulate the company's basic goals and objectives.

2 Analyse the external environment and the organisation's response to it using SWOT analysis (Strengths, Weaknesses, Opportunities, Threats) or portfolio analysis (consideration of opportunities for growth in profitability and market share).

In these two initial stages the organisational designer is attempting to determine what the organisation is trying to do, whether its objectives are realistically attainable and whether there is a gap between desired and actual performance. If the environment is such that the organisation cannot realistically improve its performance, then market withdrawal and an accompanying re-design will be necessary. Alternatively, re-design may be necessary to re-align the organisation to new market opportunities. If, for instance, a hitherto mass market has evolved into a set of 'niche' markets, change from a functional to a multi-divisional structure could well be beneficial.

3 To discern any internal blockages to desired performance, designers will need to collect information on individual performance and behaviour. Relevant data can be gathered using job analysis (see Chapter 3), by a programme of interviews, or by using the information gathered during the staff appraisal process (see Chapter 9).

4 This data will need to be rigorously analysed to determine whether the existing design is presenting obstacles to desired performance.

5 Formulate proposals for change.

6 Communicate changes and their rationale to all organisation members. Ideally, the nature of the plans should be discussed with all those likely to be affected, directly and indirectly, by them.

7 Implementation of plans, including re-assignment of job-holders, reformulation of job duties and modification of reporting relationships. To achieve the desired behavioural changes it is vital that these structural solutions are accompanied by a full programme of training (see Chapter

7) and Organisation Development (see Chapter 13).

8   Monitoring, assessment and feedback.

Presented in this way organisation re-design seems to be a rational process which, if conducted properly, should achieve nothing but benefits for the organisation. However, it is an activity which can be beset with pitfalls. As a result re-design often fails to fulfil its promises. Sometimes the consequences are disastrous.

The most fundamental problem is that those responsible for re-designing organisations have generally received little training in the analysis of organisation and social systems, with the danger that their approach and thinking may be more influenced by 'conventional management wisdom' on how organisations function than by the results of rigorous research. Very rarely do human resources professionals take the leading role in organisation re-design. In most major re-organisations in the 1980s their involvement has been limited to the 'nuts and bolts' issues of implementation, such as handling job transfers.[13] By and large, organisation design has been the province of managers from other functions. In Britain these managers have generally been most strongly influenced by 'mechanistic' conceptions of organisation. In other words, much greater importance is attached to structural than behavioural variables. American management thought, by contrast, seems to take much greater cognisance of the latter.

The danger here is obvious. Organisation designers fail to recognise that processual changes may be needed to accompany structural reforms. Or, what is perceived to be a structural problem may in fact be one of behaviour. For instance, the failure of two departments to work satisfactorily together may be thought to be the outcome of inappropriate departmental boundaries. In this case the solution might be thought to be the transfer of parts of one department to the other. In reality, however, this failure may result from a lack of communication skills. Instead a programme of communications training could be the appropriate solution. The first problem can be said, then, to be a narrow conception of design, with the danger that the wrong questions are posed and the wrong data sought.

This is not to argue that designers are unaware of or disinterested in behavioural outcomes. Rather they often assume a simplistic relationship between structural form and behavioural results. For instance, the common juxtaposition of centralised decision-making and low motivation at the base of the organisation is often translated into a straightforward causal relationship. In this case the solution to poor motivation will be seen to be decentralisation of decision-making. However, this particular problem may be the outcome of a range of social processes such as lack of clarity in what is expected of ground level managers. To decentralise decision-making may leave the problem untouched or even intensified since what these managers really want is clarification of the rationale for their decision-making rather than an expansion of it. More attention to communication by higher level managers could well be a better course of action.

Where organisation re-design is viewed primarily as modification to formal structures, there is a danger that inadequate attention will be devoted to the consultation process (stage 6). The objective of communication may be seen as simple explanation of what structural changes are to be implemented. However, if genuine consultation does not take place, then achieving the commitment of staff members to them could well be problematic. Furthermore, they are unlikely to fully comprehend the rationale for them. In these circumstances, it cannot be guaranteed that staff will operate the new structures in the spirit intended by their designers. To minimise this problem a full programme of consultation is necessary.

Just as consultation is often truncated, so is the implementation process. If re-design is viewed in structural terms, the main task will be seen as inserting people into new formal positions, taking people out of established positions, writing new job descriptions and issuing new organisation charts. However, as job descriptions and organisations charts are only a partial guide to what is required of staff members and how their duties will relate to those of others, this is not sufficient to ensure that the new organisation operates effectively. A good illustration of this is provided by London Underground Limited prior to the Kings Cross underground fire in November 1987. In 1984 the Lifts and Escalators Division had been transferred from the Operations to the Engineering Department. Unfortunately, the new separation of responsibilities between the Division and the Operations Department was never fully clarified. This problem was intensified when the relationship between the Division and the Engineering Department was changed to one of internal contract in 1986. Once again insufficient attention was devoted to preparing employees for their new roles and the division of responsibilities was left unclear. As a result new arrangements for improving the cleaning of escalators were delayed (it was a build-up of dirt on an escalator that contributed to the magnitude of the Kings Cross fire).[14] To ensure that re-organisations do not lead to problems of these proportions, implementation of organisational change should involve a programme of training and development. That way, staff can collectively establish what they need to be doing in their new roles.

274

Conclusion

The main argument of this chapter has been that organisation design is comprised of formal structure and behavioural processes. Too often, design has concentrated on formal structure or has assumed a simple relationship between structure and behaviour. Better design will be achieved through a greater appreciation of the complex linkages between them.

In the area of organisation re-design three options seem open to human resources professionals. The first is to continue with the current practice of Personnel Management. That is, to accept the subordinate role of personnel specialists. In this role they primarily deal with the 'nuts and bolts' aspects of implementation such as issuing new job descriptions. The second, more pro-active, option is to attempt to influence those designing organisations, with the objective of raising their awareness of the complex relationships between structure and process, and of the other possible determinants of behaviour. The third option is for human resources professionals to get to the core of strategic decision-making. Here human resources managers themselves re-design organisations. To achieve this position of power is not easy given the traditional role of personnel management. To do so will require a re-conceptualisation of personnel to strategic Human Resources Management and an assertion of the close links between successful business strategy and the far-sighted management of human resources.

References

1 J Goldthorpe, D Lockwood, F Bechofer and J Platt, *The Affluent Worker: Industrial Attitudes and Behaviour*, (Cambridge University Press, 1968).

2 H Beynon, *Working for Ford,* 2nd Edition (Penguin, 1984).

3 J Child, *Organization: A Guide to Problems and Practice,* 2nd Edition (Harper and Row, 1984), p. 45.

4 *Ibid,* p. 44.

5 see D Boddy, J McCalman and D Buchanan, *The New Management Challenge: Information Systems for Improved Performance,* (Croom Helm, 1988).

6 J Child, *op. cit.*

7   P Blau, *The Dynamics of Bureaucracy* (University of Chicago Press, 1955).

8   T Burns and G Stalker, *The Management of Innovation,* (Tavistock, 1961).

9   T Peters and R Waterman, *In Search of Excellence,* (Harper and Row, 1982).

10 D Channon, *The Strategy and Structure of British Enterprise*, (Macmillan, 1973).

11 D Hickson, R Butler, D Cray, G Mallory and D Wilson, *Top Decisions: Strategic Decision-Making in Organisations,* (Blackwell, 1986).

12 see K Knight (ed.), *Matrix Management*, (Gower, 1977).

13 A Evans and A Cowling, 'Personnel's part in organisation restructuring', *Personnel Management* (October 1985).

14 D Fennel QC, *Investigation into the Kings Cross Underground Fire,* (Department of Transport, 1988, Cm 499).

Suggested Reading

For short discussions of organisation design see C Handy, *Understanding Organisations*, (Penguin, 1982).

A Kakabadse, R Ludlow and S Vinnicombe, *Working in Organisations,* (Penguin, 1988)

For a more thorough treatment see J Child, *Organization: A Guide to Problems and Practice,* 2nd Edition (Harper and Row, 1984).

Questions

1   What are the main dimensions of job and organisation structure?

2   What are the key differences between functional, divisional and matrix organisations?

3   Why does organisation re-design often fail to live up to expectations?

Chapter 13

Organisational Development

Ian McGivering

Introduction

In this chapter we discuss the nature of Organisation Development and suggest that it is mainly an attempt to counter the encroachment of bureaucracy
and to move the organisation towards an HRM culture. We describe its aims
and values and therefore its uses and some possible misuses, and then
describe the more specific areas of organisational behaviour to which the
organisation development practitioner is likely to direct attention. Finally, we
argue that although Organisation Development can be an extremely effective
way to improve an organisation's efficiency, it is not the answer to all organisational problems.

The management of change is probably one of the biggest challenges confronting the management of any enterprise. As we are frequently reminded,
organisations are confronted with the need constantly to adapt to the pressures
of an increasingly unstable environment. Changing markets and competitor
behaviour necessitate the redefinition of marketing strategies and changes in
product mix. Changes in technological knowledge lead to the modification
of production techniques. Changes in legal and social conventions require
commensurate changes in the personnel policies of the enterprise. The list of
external forces to which the organisation must adapt could be extended
almost indefinitely. Words like 'change', 'modify', 'innovate', 'adapt',
'develop', 'introduce', 'scrap', 'discard', are very much part of the day to day
language of the present day manager. Yet the intellectual recognition of the
need for behavioural flexibility is much easier to obtain than is the development of organisational procedures which embody flexible thinking and
practice.

To understand why this should be the case, it may help if we remind ourselves
of some of the salient features of organisations.

The Tendency to Bureaucracy

The word 'organisation' implies an orderly structure with activities properly coordinated by clearly understood rules and procedures. Without organisation there would be chaos. Unfortunately, however, there is a danger that organisations may continue to develop their control systems, to refine their procedures and to define individual duties and responsibilities in increasing detail. Particularly is this so as the organisation increases in size and, arguably, it is necessarily so. The negative aspect of this evolution, however, is the encroachment of bureaucracy. All organisations display some of the features of bureaucracy, and when we refer to an organisation as 'bureaucratic' we imply that it is over-organised: that in its attempt to be highly efficient it may, ironically, have created inefficiencies for itself.

What are the characteristics of an organisation that cause it to be described as bureaucratic? They are the characteristics of any organisation . . . but carried to an extreme.

- **Hierarchical structure.** The system of authority is represented by a structure of superiors and subordinates showing clearly who is responsible for whom and who is accountable to whom. Delegation is not a matter of individual manager decision but is defined by the description of individual duties and responsibilities. Upward movement in the hierarchy is influenced strongly by seniority.

- **Role definitions.** Individual duties and responsibilities are defined in detail so that all know, or can readily find out, just what is required of each. Departures from the specified behaviours are strongly discouraged, thus individual initiatives are frowned upon. Over-performance is likely to cause as much difficulty as under-performance.

- **Rules and Procedures.** Operations are very much governed by the system of procedures. Uncertainties are resolved by reference to handbooks and manuals or by the search for a precedent. If consultation with one's superior fails to identify the appropriate process, the troublesome issue may then be passed to another part of the organisation.

- **Coordination.** The necessary coordination of activities is achieved by laid down procedures complemented by formal committees. In a bureaucratic organisation, committee work is likely to absorb a great deal of time.

To these structural features may be added a number of attitudinal or behavioural characteristics:

278

- The hierarchical emphasis in the design of the structure encourages a preoccupation with one's position relative to others; that is to say, with status and the trappings of status and with the protection of the power and authority which are accorded by virtue of one's position.

- Paramountcy of the procedural rules induces a tendency to do things the right way rather than to do the right things. By following the rules, the official assures maximum protection from subsequent reproach should actions result in undesirable consequences.

- To insure the smooth and accurate working of the administrative machine, each individual part is designed to a specification as precise as possible. It is assumed that efficiency will be maximised if each person then carries out his or her role exactly as defined. This however leads to an acceptance of responsibility only for one's own narrow area of activity and not for its consequences or for problems which might arise elsewhere in the system.

- As initiative is considered to be largely dysfunctional, emphasis is placed on the avoidance of error. Dedicated, hardworking bureaucrats do exist, but for many working in the highly structured system, motivation is difficult to sustain when actions are tightly governed by predetermined sequences.

- The hierarchical design is based on the assumption that knowledge is concentrated at the top, for only at the top is there the freedom to determine organisational goals, strategy and policies and, importantly, to determine the structure and procedures to secure their attainment. The task of the other employees at whatever level is to follow the procedures relevant to their positions in the system.

- Communication flow is largely vertical, upwards and downwards through the chain of command with problems and requests for guidance passed upwards and instructions and rulings passed downwards. Necessary horizontal communication is accomplished by coordinating mechanisms.

- Relationships are formal and impersonal. In the more extreme examples members address each other by title or status rather than by name. Easy communication flow is discouraged by the formality influencing face-to-face relationships.

- Advancement is by seniority and organisational members, therefore, have a strong interest in maintaining the vertical structure that provides their career path. Similarly, as the basis of their expertise is a profound knowledge of rules, procedures and precedents there is an equally strong interest in avoiding change. A radical restructuring of the system can have very negative consequences for many of those who work within it.

These features of the more heavily bureaucratic organisation are unlikely to be encountered in any particular organisation but it is suggested that, although the description may be exaggerated, it falls short of caricature. Clearly, the more the organisation possesses bureaucratic characteristics, the less able will it be to recognise and to respond quickly to the need for internal modification and adjustment. The detailed design of a bureaucratic structure is possible only when the range of activities with which it is to deal can be predicted with a high degree of confidence. It is the unexpected that disrupts the system. The characteristics of an organisation that is prepared for change are very different from those of an organisation prepared for stability:—

● instead of an unyielding structure, we need high flexibility;

● instead of communication restricted to formal channels, we need free, fast communication;

● instead of centralised decision making, we need decision making, as far as possible, at the point of action;

● instead of equating knowledge with position, we need recognition of knowledge in the individual regardless of position or status;

● instead of conformity with the narrow confines of an individual job description, we need personal commitment to wider organisational goals;

● instead of individual responsibility for individual tasks, we need joint responsibility for results;

● instead of a concern for procedures, we need a concern for task accomplishment;

● instead of discouraging personal initiative, we need to reward personal endeavour and experimentation.

The process of moving the organisation from the more to the less bureaucratic is Organisation Development.

A Definition of Organisation Development

Organisation Development has been variously defined and the essential elements are included in that which follows:

Organisational Development (O.D.) is the application of behavioural science knowledge in a deliberate organisation-wide effort to change the functioning of the system in the direction of greater effectiveness. It is a long term effort, requiring the consistent support of top management, and frequently makes use of an external consultant.

The different elements embodied in the definition merit some deeper exploration. The use of behavioural science knowledge, with the implication that no other knowledge is involved, limits the type of change which is being contemplated. There are undoubtedly many other ways of increasing an organisation's effectiveness, but we are considering here changing the organisation's culture rather than, for example, reorganising its production processes or its product lines, although changes of a technical nature may well be seen to be necessary as the members of the organisation appraise their basic position.

The need to focus on the whole organisation, or at least on some quasi-autonomous sub-division, is a recognition of the interlocking, interdependence of the key elements within the system. A change in any one part will almost certainly require reciprocal change in other parts, and the division to be tackled must have sufficient freedom to determine its own systems and ways of behaving without interference from some superior authority.

A programme of O.D. is likely to take several years. The objective is ambitious, for it seeks not to achieve minor modifications of behaviour but a major shift in the organisation's culture. The concept of 'culture' has been the subject of much academic debate, and inevitably definitions vary, but for our own purposes we may stipulate that if a group has existed for some considerable time, the members will have acquired more or less common assumptions, attitudes, beliefs and customs. Many of these habits of thought, values and behaviour are unspoken, unexamined and therefore unchallenged, but are nevertheless powerful forces in the determination of the way in which organisational members relate to each other and to the problems they confront. The newcomer may be instructed formally or informally in the 'correct' modes of thought or action but will generally be expected to conform intuitively to 'the way we do things here'.

The culture of the organisation is a unifying factor which is largely experienced unconsciously and taken for granted. To change it is a substantial undertaking.

Persistent and patient effort by top management is essential for the success of the programme. It is quite unrealistic to suppose that widespread behavioural change can be accomplished without a clear and consistent lead from the top. Furthermore, only top management can initiate or, at the least, sanction, any necessary changes in organisational structure, appraisal systems, performance measurement, and so on, which may be necessary as the organisation reshapes itself.

As the member of management with most behavioural science awareness, the Human Resource Manager may be expected to direct the attention of senior colleagues to consider the possibility that the organisation needs a radical restructuring. It is improbable that the Personnel Department will be well placed to undertake the role of O.D. consultant for they are an integral part of the organisation to be changed and may therefore have, or be thought to have, a vested interest in possible outcomes. They may, however, have a role as the internal 'link' facilitating the activities of the independent external consultant.

This denial of an active role in the O.D. process should not, of course, be taken as negating the importance of the Human Resource Manager and, indeed, any manager as a consultant to colleagues and subordinates when coaching and counselling.

O.D. Values

It may be apparent by now that O.D. practitioners and advocates have a set of assumptions or values which depart radically from those of the traditional theorist. As social scientists, their values are humanistic. Many organisations would improve their effectiveness by becoming more bureaucratic rather than less, but not only would such a task lie outside the competence of most O.D. consultants, they would probably be loth to accept the assignment on ideological grounds. Rather would they wish to assist the organisation to modify its structure and processes more on the basis of mutual trust, integrity in relationships and the willingness and ability to confront conflict and problems constructively as they arise. It is assumed that employees at all levels wish for challenging work which carries individual or group responsibility and that they are capable of a much greater contribution to the organisation's effectiveness than is usually acknowledged or allowed. An organisational culture which emphasises commitment to task and to colleagues with a reward system reflecting personal and group contributions is a demanding environment within which to work. But to the employee, at whatever level, it is likely to be satisfying and motivational as the opportunities for personal development and the recognition of personal value replace bureaucratic irritations and managerial indifference.

The Role of the Consultant

The consultant is frequently drawn from outside the organisation. This has the advantage that he or she is not part of the organisation's political system and has no allegiance to any interested group. It is essential that the consultant be universally perceived to be neutral and independent. Coming from outside the organisation also helps the consultant to avoid preconceived ideas concerning problems and solutions.

It is consonant with the consultant's value system that prescriptive exhortation is generally avoided. Rather is the function that of a facilitator, assisting clients to a greater understanding of their problems as they experience them. The possession of theoretical knowledge and practical experience of organisational behaviour will enable issues to be suggested to clients for their consideration which they otherwise might miss. The consultant's personal behaviour should exemplify the new behaviours towards which organisation members are striving, confronting clients in a non threatening, non judgemental manner, yet not colluding in problem or conflict avoidance. The role requires behaviour as both catalyst and expert resource.

The O.D. Process

It is difficult to present a detailed model of the process of an O.D. programme for its various elements will differ as different problems are encountered and the necessary actions will, therefore, differ from one situation to another. Also, although it may be possible to identify the source of the programme, the point of its conclusion may be much less readily apparent for the process, if successful, becomes self-generating.

Firstly, there would be a presenting problem sufficiently serious to cause top management to engage in a radical rethink of the organisation's practices. In one case, ('Premier Mfg.') the organisation had experienced a succession of niggling confrontations with the Trade Unions. There had not been a major strike but the continual skirmishings about petty issues had indicated that relationships were not good. The Board then commissioned a firm of consultants to conduct an attitude survey throughout the several plants operated by the company. The subsequent report indicated that there existed a considerable reservoir of goodwill at all levels and a widely expressed desire to be more closely involved in decision making. Employees apparently wished to make a fuller contribution to the company than they felt to be currently possible. The report was simultaneously reassuring and worrying and the Board pondered its implications at length. Clearly, management were failing to make full use of an important resource. Procedures and practices were apparently inhibiting the motivation of large sections of the labour force.

Secondly, the services of a person or persons competent in the theory and practice of organisational behaviour would be secured. This assistance is frequently drawn from outside the organisation although in some of the larger firms an O.D. unit may be attached to Head Office, and can supply the necessary personnel to any of the company's locations. Even here, however, an external consultant may be hired to work closely with the Head Office nominee. In the case of Premier Mfg., the board sought the help of an experienced member of a northern business school and with his help they drew up a statement describing the organisation and the relationships within it as they wished them to be. The statement defined the objectives of the programme and the problem was then to determine the strategies necessary to move the system from its existing to its desired state.

Thirdly, data need to be collected to enable a diagnosis of the problems being experienced. This step is in itself a major intervention into the organisation's existing state for the process of data collection signals to the employees at all levels that top management are aware of the existence of problems and seem prepared to do something about them. Furthermore, to the extent that the data will be collected, at least in part, from discussions held with people individually and in representative groups, widespread participation in the process may be seen as a sign that traditional authority relationships are being modified. However, hopes on these lines should not be too high, for attitudes and expectations based on long experience are not readily changed. Premier Mfg., for example, circulated the statement of objectives among their senior managers for their discussion and comment. The board were startled to learn that the document was interpreted as an instruction requiring the senior group to change their behaviour and, given that interpretation, discussion and comment were not wholly constructive. This experience was instructive for the Board and brought home to them that their own behaviour must be seen to change – and that the change must be consistent – before they could reasonably expect others to change.

Fourthly, the data collected need to be analysed and their significance asses-

284

sed. During this stage, considerable use is likely to be made of the theoretical knowledge and specialist skills of the consultant. Accurate diagnosis of the problems is essential if subsequent action is to be effective. Practising managers tend to see problems in isolation whereas, commonly, problems are linked with a cluster of causative factors and cannot usefully be tackled singly and sequentially.

Fifthly, groups of problems need to be arranged in an order of priority and a strategy developed for their solution. At this point, it should be emphasised that not all problems will be behavioural. A basic concern with behavioural considerations, such as interpersonal communications, values, authority relationships, and so on, must not deflect attention from technical issues like production bottlenecks and inappropriate allocations of responsibility. Even problems which seem clearly to be behavioural may have their origin in technical or structural inadequacies.

Sixthly, action steps must be planned to implement the strategy and evaluation criteria agreed. Both must be planned in close collaboration with those who are going to be involved in the action.

Seventhly, as action proceeds, data should be collected and fed back to the directing group and their implications assessed. New problems and disappointments must be expected and action steps may need constant revision as the programme progresses.

It is not possible to identify any further specific stages in the conduct of the programme for the stages are recycled as the programme proceeds. As problems are tackled, new problems emerge and appropriate measures are devised to deal with them. The members of the organisation gradually acquire the attitudes and skills to cope with their situation themselves and, as this learning process advances, their dependence on the consultant decreases and the consultant's involvement will become less intensive.

O.D. Interventions

The term 'interventions' refers to the repertoire of techniques which are at the disposal of O.D. consultants and their clients. Like the medical practitioner who possesses an array of diagnostic and therapeutic methods and skills, the O.D. consultant will be familiar with and competent to use a wide range of techniques for helping the members of the client organisation. Again like the medical practitioner, the consultant must be careful not to develop so strong a preference for certain techniques that they are prescribed unnecessarily or when inappropriate.

- **Action Research** is commonly treated by writers on Organisation Development as the most basic technique. Yet it may be argued that it is much more than a technique, however basic. It is a process which is almost indistinguishable from O.D. itself and involves a step by step approach to uncover the unpredictable solution to a problem. A step is taken and data are collected and assessed, another step is taken based on the analysis of the data so far collected . . . and more data are collected. The process continues, planning-doing-assessing-planning-doing, and so on, so that understanding is steadily enhanced and the objective becomes increasingly attainable. It is a systematic way of discovering a path through unchartered territory and beset by unforeseeable hazards. It makes use of available theory and refines it by continual testing and discovery.

- **Survey Feedback** is a method of collecting data about the organisation and feeding back the results to groups throughout the system for their consideration and necessary action. It will be remembered that an attitude survey of employees at Premier Mfg. prompted their Board to initiate a programme of Organisation Development. However, such an example is less common in the UK than it is in the USA. The specific activities to which a survey might give rise will, of course, depend on the particular problems to which it draws attention. The data are most commonly collected by means of a distributed questionnaire completed anonymously and are therefore subject to the problems that are intrinsic to such a method. (See, for example, A N Oppenheim, *'Questionnaire Design and Attitude Measurement'*, Heinemann 1968.) The important feature of data feedback which distinguishes it from conventional attitude surveys is the fact that the data are fed back to the groups whose members supplied the data. It is then the task of the groups themselves to determine the significance of the data and what action to initiate.

- **Team Building** is probably the most widely known of the various interventions although it is too frequently misused. The goal of team building is to improve the effectiveness of the various teams within the organisation. Most obviously this would include that formed by a manager and a group of immediate subordinates but other teams can often be identified in project teams, working parties, coordinating committees, and so on. Attention is usually directed to the level of the team's task success, relationships between members, and the relationship between the team and its environment. More specifically, the group may be invited to focus on the role expectations the team members have of each other, the relationships between team members and, particularly, between them and the leader, their capacity to handle conflict constructively, and their decision making competence. Typically, the team leader invites the consultant to help the

286

team to improve their performance. It is vital at this stage that the leader fully understands what will be involved and has the maturity to deal with the issues that may be raised, no matter how psychologically threatening they may be. It may be desirable for the team leader, in particular, to undergo some sensitivity training (see below) before starting the team building, for although it is difficult for team members to discuss issues openly in front of their boss, it is even more difficult for the boss to deal with the issues constructively and not defensively or punitively.

Typically, the consultant will discuss the proposal to hold team building sessions with the team members, individually or collectively, in order to explain as clearly as possible what would be involved and in order for them to meet and assess each other as persons. Their willingness to trust the consultant is important for the success of the sessions. Each member may then be interviewed in turn, including the team leader, to obtain their personal views on the strengths and weaknesses of the team's functioning, what problems are experienced by or with the other team members and what, if anything, seems to inhibit the solutions to the problems. The consultant will then prepare a list of the various topics which have been raised and present them to the team for their consideration. The role from this point is likely to be that of process consultant, as we have described it below. Team Building is Organisation Development in micro, and the team will go on to improve its performance by identifying problems, discussing their implications, planning and taking action steps and assessing the results, uncovering deeper problems, and so on. It must be emphasised here that team building involves more than the creation of harmonious relationships. Sooner or later structural factors within the team's environment will require attention. The systems of performance measurement, of individual appraisal, of rewards, of authority relationships, of goal setting and role definitions may all require examination and possibly amendment. Sometimes, the team's effectiveness may be blocked by factors lying outside the team's control. Organisations frequently espouse the importance of cooperation amongst management whilst rewarding successful competition. In these circumstances managers will see their colleagues as competitors and rivals, and effective team working will be difficult to develop.

Most of the foregoing discussion has concerned team building with command groups; that is to say, groups consisting of a manager and immediate subordinates, but there are other groups whose work may be improved by consultant help. Project or special task groups can be formed of people who are strangers to each other. Often important decisions are made before the members of the group have properly settled down. A large firm of civil engineers, who make considerable use of project teams to plan and oversee major constructions from greenfield site to finished development, recognised that a project team in its first two or three meetings made decisions which committed the organisation to the extent of several million pounds. Some of these decisions were, with hindsight, not as high quality as they should have been. This sub-standard decision making was attributed in large measure to the fact that important issues were being considered before the group members were socially and psychologically in tune with each other. The firm have now adopted the practice of taking the members of the newly constituted team off company premises for a couple of days where, with the assistance of a behavioural science consultant, they engage in 'ice-breaking' activities, getting to know each other personally and identifying and agreeing the formal and informal routines which will govern their subsequent work together.

It may be necessary to introduce a word of warning here. The concept of team building has a seductive appeal but not all managerial groups are suitable for the team building treatment and there are numerous examples of managers, collectively or individually, resisting well-meaning attempts to put them through a team building programme. Only if the managers concerned are required to work closely together in pursuit of common aims is team building an appropriate activity.

Sensitivity Training is probably the most misunderstood of the various techniques available to the O.D. practitioner. Under the heading, T-group, it has been the object of much criticism (some of it justified) and the object of many 'travellers' tales'. The purpose of sensitivity training is to enhance the participant's self knowledge, to develop a greater awareness of the emotional states and reactions of self and others, and to become more aware of the effect of one's behaviour on others. The methods by which these learning objectives may be attained will vary but, common to them all, will be the group. Members of the group, with a consultant, will experience each other's behaviour and provide feedback on their personal reactions. Self analysis questionnaires may also be used and theoretical observations and interpretations may be offered by the consultant at appropriate moments. In the classic T-group there is no agenda and no formal structure of authority. With the consultant, the members attempt to study their behaviour as and when it occurs. Our own preference as a trainer is for quite a strong element of structure to be provided and to work consciously with the group to develop a culture of warm support and mutual trust. Being the subject of open appraisal can be stressful and the more vulnerable members must be protected from experiences they cannot handle. It is certainly not the case that sensitivity training necessarily involves 'character assassination', 'emotional blood letting', and savage interpersonal confrontations. The experience is likely to touch the emotions as well as the intellect and it is often difficult for the participant later to articulate with

288

confidence the amount and nature of the benefit derived. The criticism has been made that the world of the sensitivity group is so far removed from that of the normal work environment, that the transfer of learning is minimal – even that the behaviours learnt in the training group may be dysfunctional in the participant's sponsoring organisation. To an extent this is true and research has indicated that behavioural change following a sensitivity programme is greater in the social and domestic life of the participants than in their working life. The author has been told by participants on more than one occasion that he was more interested in helping them to become better human beings than better managers. It did not seem to be intended as a complaint . . . and the distinction between 'human being' and 'manager' is interesting to contemplate!

Process Consultation. As the term implies, process consultation is the activity of a consultant helping the members of an organisation, or some part of it such as a team, to become aware of, and to understand, the processes which affect them. If its definition is interpreted broadly, then O.D. consists almost entirely of various types of process consultation. However, in its narrower and therefore more useful interpretation, it refers to the assistance given by a consultant to the members of a problem solving group and is the basis of team building. With the consultant's help, the team members learn to identify, to diagnose and to deal with the various difficulties which they encounter. The team members will learn that their activities can be subsumed under two main headings – task and maintenance. Task activities are all those behaviours which directly relate to the attainment of the group's primary task such as the creation of a good quality decision or recommendation. It will be desirable to make sure that all members of the group are in agreement as to their purpose and objectives. They should move together through the various stages of the task process: identifying the problem; assembling the data necessary for its diagnosis; suggesting and exploring possible solutions; selecting the most appropriate solution; planning action steps to implement it; determining evaluation criteria; and arranging to receive and to act upon feedback data as implementation proceeds. Maintenance activities are those behaviours which relate to the manner in which the group sets about its task. How do they make decisions? Do one or two members exert an undue influence and, if so, what effect does this have on the others? Do they decide by voting and, if so, what happens to the defeated minority? How are suggestions received – constructively or destructively? Is there roughly the right amount of conflict in the group and how is it handled? To what extent do they listen to each other? Do there seem to be underlying issues which affect what is happening but which are not discussed? Are individual members making the contribution of which they are capable? How do the members feel about each other and the way they work? Data may be provided by the consultant's drawing on the observation of the group at work and helping them to interpret what has been seen. It is a matter of judgement whether observations are made in fairly general terms after the group has carried out its task or made immediately after a specific incident occurs. Data may also be gathered by questionnaire completion by each member and the results shared and discussed. Alternatively, group members may allocate a period of time following a meeting, to review their performance. Whatever means of generating data may be employed, the group must go through a three stage process: a) collect data concerning their performance, b) determine the implications of the data, c) plan to modify their behaviour in the light of the data.

Managerial Grid is a training package devised by Robert Blake and Jane Mouton. The grid itself is a graphic presentation of managerial style using two axes: vertical, *Concern for People*, and horizontal, *Concern for Production*. (Notice that the two axes approximate the concepts of Maintenance and Task discussed in the preceding section). An organisation intending to make serious use of the grid as an O.D. technique will require all, or a significant proportion, of its managers to attend the one week seminar which constitutes stage one.

After some pre-course work, in which they are expected to familiarise themselves with the basic concepts, they identify their own style of managing, using the grid positions 1.1 (getting by with minimum effort); 1.9 (emphasis on good relationships with comfortable work loads); 9.1 (emphasis on production with minimal human concern); 5.5 (compromise between conflicting demands of production and human needs); 9.9 (coordinated team effort to achieve high performance targets). The week then consists of highly structured sensitivity training with the focus on personal interaction styles. Stage two is concerned with team development in which a manager and the immediate subordinate group meet for a week to engage in team building activities. This week, too, is highly structured. Stage three examines the relationships between one department and another and offers methods for their diagnosis and improvement. Stage four requires the higher management in the organisation to develop long term corporate objectives and stages five and six are concerned with the implementation of the strategy to achieve the objectives, their consolidation and a review of the entire experience. The full grid programme is a complete O.D. process and may well be expected to last five years or more. Many organisations have used stage one for the training of individual managers and have not proceeded to further stages, presumably not wishing to undertake the substantial task of achieving genuine organisational change.

Interpersonal Conflict Resolution is the process of resolving conflict bet-

The Managerial Grid

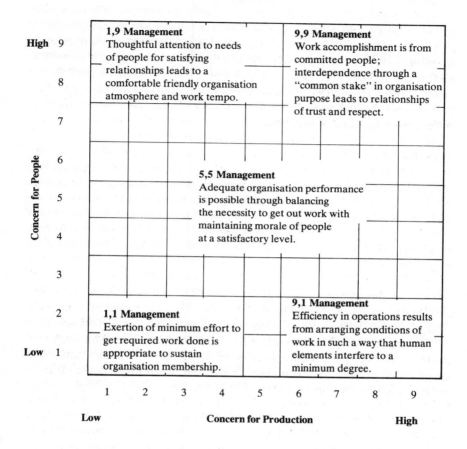

Figure 13: The Managerial Grid

ween two persons with the help of a consultant. It is a necessary precondition that both parties are aware of the existence of the conflict and that both wish to replace it with a cooperative relationship. The role of a consultant may be necessary if the conflict has developed to the point that the two contestants distrust each other so that unaided problem solving is impossible. The role of the consultant is much more than referee, although just being there is likely to have an ameliorating effect. The consultant will seek to keep the attention and the behaviour of the two conflicting parties focused on the basic structural or procedural issues which underlie their mutual hostility. So-called 'personality clashes' are usually the result of the personalisation of incompatible positions. The consultant will need a good understanding of organisational structures and processes and of the psychology of the dynamics of interpersonal conflict. This is an area in which the well-meaning amateur can make a bad situation very much worse.

Intergroup Conflict Resolution is probably one of the most difficult activities facing the O.D. consultant, although the phenomenon is endemic in organisations. Relations between different departments or sub-units are seldom as cooperative as efficiency would require and may vary from a cautious accommodation to overt hostility. High morale and helpful relationships among the members of a cohesive, productive group often go hand-in-hand with negative attitudes and therefore relationships towards the members of other groups. It is important that an accurate diagnosis be made of structural origins before conflict resolution has much hope of success. This is one of the few areas in O.D. in which an imposed solution may be effective. A restructuring of the relevant parts of the organisation may achieve the desired results although the restructuring may not find immediate favour with those restructured. Yet for most of the other possible lines of action, the constructive involvement of the protagonists will certainly be desirable. As with the resolution of interpersonal conflict, it is necessary that both groups shall want a cooperative relationship. In the case of groups, the psychology of the dynamics of conflict are compounded by the emotional support given by the members of a group to each other as they engage in negative behaviours. What may be perceived as childish or petty if performed by an individual in isolation, is likely to be approved and applauded if done on behalf of the group. This reinforcement of attitudes makes change more difficult but a number of techniques have been developed to change the groups' attitudinal sets to enable the opposing factions to meet in a joint endeavour to explore the underlying reasons for the conflict and to design procedures for avoiding it or handling it positively.

Education and Training are not activities normally identified as part of the armoury of O.D. but both may be necessary as a concomitant of the introduction of organisational changes which require behavioural change on the part of the organisation's members. Training is unlikely in itself to bring about significant organisational change but where roles have changed or are changing, new attitudes and new behaviours may well need the aid of formal training programmes. As we argued in Chapter 8, there are close links between Management Development and O.D.

292

Conclusion

O.D. has shown that it can be an effective means of improving an organisation's effectiveness but not all attempts at the implementation of a programme have been successful. We may usefully end this chapter by sounding a few warnings.

It may by now be clear to the reader that O.D. practitioners tend to subscribe to a common set of values. They are behavioural scientists by training, by experience and by inclination and their approach to organisations is broadly humanistic. That is to say, they tend to judge organisations by the quality of working life of the employees, by the extent to which human needs and human dignity are accorded priority, by the honesty and the integrity with which relationships are conducted and by the opportunities for initiative and personal development. Their stance, therefore, tends to be anti-bureaucratic yet it is almost certainly true that more organisations would benefit from more detailed and clearly defined structures and procedures than would benefit from fewer. The O.D. consultant turned loose in such organisations might well do more harm than good. The humanistic preoccupation may also result in inadequate attention being paid to technical deficiencies even though their correction might be a necessary precondition for the building of constructive interdepartmental and interpersonal relationships.

Disappointment may be experienced by the failure to achieve quick results. We have emphasised that an O.D. programme may well take several years and set-backs must be considered inevitable, yet managers are results oriented and can quickly become discouraged. One of the roles of the consultant is to help the client group to handle failure and to learn from it. There will not be uniformly enthusiastic support in the organisation for the changes which are in process. Autocratic behaviour which has served a manager well for many years will not be abandoned overnight. Not only will the need for change be unrecognised and the attitudes relevant to a participatory style rejected, but the skills to behave differently will not have been learnt. Managements must not underestimate the enormity of their expectations when launching an O.D. programme. A highly bureaucratic structure provides security for its members; their roles and the limits of their responsibilities are clear. To take away, or at least to weaken, that structure is threatening and the pressure to cling to old behaviours and habits is strong. It is no wonder that the time span for an O.D. programme should be measured in years and not months.

Finally, provision must be made to check any tendency for the organisation gradually to slip back once the impetus of the change effort has diminished. The organisation needs to have developed the capacity to engage in a continuous process of self-analysis and to retain the willingness to modify its structures and processes as circumstances may require. All too easily, crisis conditions can induce a revision to centralised autocracy.

Suggested Reading

For an excellent general coverage see:

W L French and C H Bell, *Organisation Development: Behavioural Science Interventions for Organisation Improvement*. Prentice-Hall, 2nd edition, 1978.

The managerial grid was introduced by:

R R Blake and J S Mouton, *The Managerial Grid: Key Orientations for Achieving Production Through People*. Gulf Publishing Company, 1964.

Later books by Blake and Mouton develop the concept of the grid and show its wider applications.

A deeper analysis of the work of the O.D. consultant is offered by:

C Argyris, *Intervention Theory and Method: A Behavioural Science View*. Addison Wesley, 1970.

Questions

1 What do you consider to be the main advantages and disadvantages of a bureaucratic organisation?

2 How does the role of the O.D. consultant differ from the role of the traditional consultant? How do you explain these differences?

3 What problems would you expect an organisation to encounter when its management decide to embark on an O.D. programme?

Author Index

295

296

Subject Index

Ability, 97, 102, 103, 120, 121, 129, 130, 134, 136
Absenteeism, 96, 111, 114
Action Learning, 189-190
Action Research, 286
Advisory, Conciliation and Arbitration Service (ACAS), 220-221, 223, 227, 229, 230
Application Forms, 45, 51, 55, 56-57
Assertiveness, 188
Assessment Centres, 65-66, 205
Attendance Motivation, 114-115
Authority, 12, 13

Behaviourally Anchored Rating Scales, 208
Bevin, E., 4
Biases in Perception and Judgement, 134
Biographical Data, 51, 56, 57
Bonus Schemes, 86
British Leyland, 248
Bureaucracy, 278-280

Cafeteria Payment Systems, 112
Central Arbitration Committee (CAC), 221, 230
Certification Officer, 221
Citizenship Behaviours, 115-116
Civil Service, 212
Closed Shop, 219, 220, 222
Coaching, 188-189
Collective Bargaining, 237-241, 248
    Company Level at, 240
    Establishment Level at, 240, 241
    Industry Wide, 238, 239
    Multi-Employer, 238
Collectivism, 7
Commission for Racial Equality, 228, 229

Commission for the Rights of Trade Union Members, 223, 225
Commitment, 96, 100
Communication, 249
Conflict Resolution, 290-292
Consultation, 249
Contingency Approach, 213
Contracts of Employment, 226
Contracts of Employment Act (1963), 218
Corporate Strategy, 6, 8
Corporatism, 245
Cost Centres, 7
Cost of Living Allowance, 78
Counselling, 133, 188
Critical Incident Technique, 48
Culture, 281

Decentralisation, 257, 263, 274
Decision Making, 259-260, 263, 274
    Centralised, 273
    Decentralised, 269, 274
    Operational, 257
    Strategic, 257, 269, 275
Decisions, 267, 269
Delegation, 188
Demographic Time Bomb, 7
Department of Employment, 37
Deregulation, 222, 224
Disciplined Subjectivity, 204
Disputes Procedures, 238
Distance Learning, 190-191
Distributive Industry, 26
Division of Labour, 258, 261, 262
Divisional Structure, 268-270
Donovan Report (see also Royal Commission on Trade Unions and Employers' Associations), 5, 239
Dotted-Line Relationship, 270
Dualism, 18

Education and Training, 292

Managing Face to Face Communication: Survival tactics for people and products in the 1990s,
by Allen E Ivey

Much of the manager's day is spend communicating with others. A recent study found over 500 separate interactions during a single working day. Face to face communication is too important to be left to chance.

Communication can be managed to substantially improve your company's product and service lines as well as to enhance morale and discipline in the workplace. The book shows how to communicate for concrete results- how to pace and understand the point of view of others and how to lead and influence.

It aims to optimise your ability to question proficiently, listen intelligently, diagnose complex situations and obtain the results you want in meetings and brief interpersonal encounters. The final chapter covers the use of face to face communication skills in product development and marketing.

Communication skills and management problems can be broken down into their component parts and then arranged into a system to provide more efficient communication flow for the workplace for both people and products. Effective face to face communication can be achieved by breaking down a complex process into specific steps. Each of these steps requires practice to achieve mastery. Skilled and controlled performance does not come easily.

90 pages, 1988, ISBN 0-86238-160-6

Inside Data Processing
Computers and their Effective Use in Business
by Alastair de Watteville

Companies rely increasingly on the effective use of computers to stay competitive. This book will help you to evaluate existing arrangements and identify, assess and control new tasks for computers.

It is divided into three parts - each well illustrated, clearly written and enjoyable to read.

Part one identifies and explains the principles on which modern computers and data communications networks operate, and the equipment and software used. Major DP application areas are discussed. Part two covers DP projects, beginning with their nature, benefits, risks, and structure. The processes and issues involved in Project Planning and Appraisal, and evaluation and selection of software, hardware, contractors and consultants are then clearly explained. Part three focuses on the DP management and organisation issues that are important to users, with chapters on manning, data privacy, installation security, and trends in information technology. Appendices include a full glossary of terms. The author is Director of Highwood Management Consultants.

173 pages, ISBN 0-86238-181-9 ACCESS/VISA HOTLINE 01-467 1956

Management Development:
KEY CONCEPTS FOR MANAGERS & TRAINERS
by Christopher Molander

In a concise and straightforward way, this excellent book gives practical techniques for a more efficient and systematic approach to Management Development.

Molander points the way to achieving cost effectiveness and job competence , and shows the vital role that the line manager should play in exercising responsibility for staff development.

Written with the practical manager and training professional in mind, the book is a distillation of courses held at the University of Bradford Management Centre.

ISBN 0-86238-083-9, 166 pages, 1986.

Available from good booksellers or direct from Chartwell-Bratt

Qualitative Methods in Management Research

by E Gummesson

This book is an analysis of the roles and methods used by management consultants and academic researchers when working with change processes in companies and other organisations. It deals with case studies as a research method and advocates more involvement by the researcher and consultant through increased application of participant observation as used in anthropology, and through action research/action science (which is a method to combine the roles of researcher and the consultant) and other qualitative methods. In particular, the book stresses the problems of access, preunderstanding and awareness of one's own paradigm.

The book is a contribution to the theory of science and methodology for those involved in management studies and research: management consultants and their clients, academic researchers, and students at business schools.

202 pages, 1988, ISBN 0-86238-197-5